Beyond All Evil

Beyond All Evil

June Thomson & Giselle Ross

with Marion Scott and Jim McBeth

HarperElement
An Imprint of HarperCollins*Publishers*
77–85 Fulham Palace Road,
Hammersmith, London W6 8JB

www.harpercollins.co.uk

and HarperElement are trademarks of
HarperCollins*Publishers* Ltd

First published by HarperElement 2011

1 3 5 7 9 10 8 6 4 2

A catalogue record of this book is
available from the British Library

ISBN 978-0-00-743851-8

Printed and bound in Great Britain by
Clays Ltd, St Ives plc

MIX
Paper from
responsible sources
FSC™ C007454

FSC is a non-profit international organisation established to promote
the responsible management of the world's forests. Products carrying the
FSC label are independently certified to assure consumers that they come
from forests that are managed to meet the social, economic and
ecological needs of present or future generations,
and other controlled sources.

Find out more about HarperCollins and the environment at
www.harpercollins.co.uk/green

To little Jay-Jay, Paul, Ryan and Michelle –
forever innocent, forever loved

Contents

Acknowledgements

To writers Jim McBeth and Marion Scott, who had the commitment and understanding to empower us, in the hope that we can save one life and prevent just one more tragedy.

June: To my father, Jim Martin, who is everything a parent should be. To my brothers Jim, Gordon and Roger and sister Linda, for unfailing support. To my sons, Shaun and Ross. To Doreen, who is more than a friend.

Giselle: To my parents, John and Jean Ross, who shaped my world with love. To my brothers Tam, Alex, William and Johnny and sisters Katie and Janie. To my niece Giselle, the daughter I would wish for. To Alastair Douglas, who stands on the hill. To Paul Martin MSP, for actions and not words. To my dear friend Lynn Manners.

To criminal psychologist Ian Stephen, who has looked so often into the eyes of evil and recognises the monsters in our midst.

To lawyer Cameron Fyfe, a warrior on behalf of the isolated and the abused.

To Paul McBride QC, for his insight into the criminal justice system.

To Frank Pilkington, for guiding us towards the light.

To our literary agent Clare Hulton, for believing that a dark and difficult story for our times demanded to be told. To our editor Vicky McGeown at HarperCollins, for having the courage to make it happen.

To everyone living in fear … You are no longer alone.

Foreword

What follows is a conversation between two mothers who are leading each other from the darkness to the light.

Before they were united by two unspeakable acts of evil, June Thomson and Giselle Ross did not know each other. Today they are the closest of friends. In their hearts they wish they had not been brought together by incomparable loss, but now that they have found each other they are able to walk together towards a future neither of them believed was possible.

Only Giselle can appreciate how June has suffered; only June can understand the monumental effort it takes for her friend to rise and face each new day. This bond has already saved their lives, dragging them back from the edge of madness and giving them the courage to endure unimaginable pain.

On the same day, a few miles apart, June and Giselle's estranged husbands, Rab Thomson and Ashok Kalyanjee, murdered their children. The men were not driven by rage. The killings were planned and carried out with precision, and designed to crush the women they had once dominated.

The names of the lost innocents are Ryan and Michelle Thomson, and Paul and Jay Ross, whom you will come to know and love as little 'Jay-Jay'. Ryan was seven. His sister, Michelle, was 25, a wonderfully innocent woman-child, who had an intellectual age equivalent to that of her brother. Paul was six and lived for Spiderman. Jay-Jay was two, he loved Bob the Builder, and was still wrestling with the mysterious joys of a world in which he would not grow up.

Their fathers were the worst of all predators, perfect examples of what has become known as the 'family annihilator' – parents who kill their own children in an unfathomable act of revenge.

It is a psychological syndrome that is becoming disturbingly prevalent, but which no mother's intuition or father's sixth sense can predict.

According to the eminent clinical and forensic psychologist Ian Stephen, such killers are now responsible for more than one-third of all child murders. Throughout the pages of this book – and after the mothers' story has been told – Stephen will offer his professional insight into the minds of the murderers and the women who once loved them.

It may seem a bitter irony that, while their crimes have united their wives, Thomson and Kalyanjee have also been brought together. They languish in the same jail, where they have yet to offer any explanation or display remorse. Their silence continues to devastate both June and Giselle, for no power on earth can erase the misguided guilt they have assumed – the belief that somehow they should have *known*.

The mothers have lived with that erroneous belief since their children were killed. At least they are now insulated by sisterhood and the memories of the happy times with their children.

They have been empowered, each giving the other the strength to tell their unique story – the first true account of family annihilators by women who lived with them and survived.

It is a warning and a cautionary tale, but above all it is a story of love and a testament to the human spirit.

Both women endured dreadfully unhappy marriages. June's life with Thomson was a dark, turbulent and miserable existence, characterised by mental torture, physical violence and even rape. Giselle's relationship with Kalyanjee had been a strange and remote affair, of lives spent apart before, during and after their marriage.

In spite of this, their relationships produced treasured children. But on one terrible Saturday in May, the last normal day of their lives, the misery of their marriages swiftly receded into the past.

Both women were on the threshold of a new future. They no longer wanted or needed the men who had ruled their lives but they believed it was important for their children to maintain a relationship with their fathers.

If only they hadn't. The consequences of their trust were unutterably appalling.

This is the story of the parallel journeys that took them to that terrible day when they and their children became the prey of two monsters in our midst.

Marion Scott and Jim McBeth

PROLOGUE

Fairy Shoes and Toy Soldiers

June: Shoes for Michelle. I had to have them.

Fairy shoes. They glistened with a life of their own, as if they could dance from the shelf. The shop lights, bright and harsh, caused their red, glittering surface to shimmer. Shoes for a princess. Shoes for my Michelle. I could picture my daughter, laughing with delight, her dark-blonde curls streaming behind her as she flew to the wardrobe to pick a party dress to match these beautiful *Wizard of Oz* shoes.

Christmas music flowed from hidden speakers. Garlands and decorations hung from every wall. I was in a crowded place but, until a few moments ago, I had never felt so alone. Excited voices overwhelmed me, the sounds of mothers, fathers, grandparents and children making plans for the big day. So much excitement to contain, so much to look forward to. I could almost smell cinnamon and spiced apple, the memories of Christmases past.

The room was alive but I had felt dead for so long now. Yet somehow these shoes had brought me to life. I had to have them. They were in my hand. In my bag. Michelle would be so pleased. So pleased.

The part of my brain that knew my Michelle was gone had shut down. A voice spoke to me from very far away. A woman's voice.

'Who are the shoes for, June?'

The use of my name suggests familiarity, but I don't think I know her. It's become a common occurrence. Since it happened, everyone knows me.

'Michelle,' I answer, still under the spell of the shoes.

'You've put them in your bag, love.'

'I know. I have to have them,' I said, walking to the door of the shop. I could hear Michelle's laugh, see her face and imagine her pulling on the shoes. Running to the mirror. My beautiful, damaged daughter with the body of a woman and the mind of a child.

Outside the shop. Assailed by the winter cold. Then a new voice, harsh, authoritative.

'Madam! I have reason to believe you have goods you have not paid for. Would you open your bag?'

I do what he asks. He fingers the shoes.

'You can't have them! They're for Michelle!' I tell him.

'You'll have to come with me!'

I follow. Everyone is looking, shocked expressions, judging faces. They don't understand. Tears prick my eyes. The spell of the shoes is broken. I can see the man's face clearly now.

'I'm sorry,' I say. 'I deserve to be punished. I took the shoes. I had to have them. Can I pay for them, now?'

His face tells me what I already know.

'I have money,' I add, showing him my purse containing £160.

In my mind, I try to tell him I couldn't go to the cash desk. They would have recognised me. They know my daughter is dead. They would have told me Michelle was gone. I was suddenly cold. I wanted to go home.

A policeman and policewoman had arrived. I recognised the woman from the days following the murder of my son and daughter. She spoke quietly to her colleague, who then had a hushed conversation with the store detective.

'Come with us, June,' said the policeman.

His voice was not unkind. The fairy shoes were gone. They had taken them from me.

It was cold on the car journey to the police station. We passed beneath blurred neon signs that gave only the appearance of warmth. The police station was as brightly lit as the store had been but it was stark, devoid of decoration. I stood before the imposing figure of the desk officer.

How did I get here? How did I get to this?

The big man looked at me. He was conflicted. I was ostensibly a thief, but a very different kind of thief from those he usually dealt with.

'Time you went home, Mrs Thomson,' he said.

I walked away, my face burning with shame.

Now I was at home, sitting in the dark, the illumination of the street lights washing the mantelpiece and the framed photographs of Ryan and my Michelle. I cried.

What on earth had I wanted with fairy shoes?

———————————

Giselle: I know why! The same reason I buy toys for my babies.

They lie before me on the cold, hard ground, frozen to the earth in their packaging, these gifts that I have chosen so carefully for my sons. Spiderman for Paul; Bob the Builder for little Jay-Jay. Toys that will never be played with by boys who will never grow up.

As the seasons come and go, the colour of the packaging fades, the boxes disintegrate. My babies know they are there. Michelle would have known, too, about the glittery new shoes.

I never miss a Christmas, or a birthday. Wherever they are, they all know – Paul and Jay-Jay, Michelle and Ryan. They know. That knowledge keeps us going.

There were days when I prayed for death to take me to them. I hated the winter nights and the coming of darkness when they locked the gates of the cemetery and I had to leave my boys. I would go home and ask God to allow me to be with them. But morning inevitably came and I was still here. Part of me was glad. It allowed me to resume my vigil.

So I sit here on the hill, where my sons rest, embraced in each other's arms beneath two marble teddy bears. And so it will go on, as long as I have breath. On a clear day, I can see in the distance the prison where their killer was taken – their father.

On the day they were laid to rest, I knew he was there – but there was no communication, no word of remorse, no flowers for his dead sons. I still do not know if, to this day, he knows where they lie. It is of no consequence to me. As long as I know, as long as I am close to them, keeping them safe in death as I could not do in life.

I am the sentinel.

I have only been absent on a few days. Those were the days when I tried to end it all. Now I will never miss a day. I have stopped trying to kill myself with cuts to my wrist, pills swallowed by the handful. I have come to realise that suicide should not be my destiny.

People know where to find me. I am surrounded by the thousands who passed away long before my babies. I embrace myself against the cold. I bake in the sunshine. I lower my head against the rain. The doctors tell me I torture myself, perpetuate my anguish. They don't understand.

I watch for signs from my sons – the wind that drives the windmills on their grave speaks to me in their voices. The marble teddy bears watch me with unblinking eyes. Gold-leaf inscriptions on their bodies record the names of my sons. Spring, summer, autumn and winter, flowers decorate the resting place.

When my babies were first placed there, I wanted to climb in beside them. Now this graveside is my sanctuary. When I arrive each morning I tell them my news, such as it is. They know I am here and what I bring – the small, bright pebbles, the toys, the gifts to place beside them.

Before I leave I repeat the words I had inscribed on the teddy bears. To Paul: 'Goodnight my little angel, love Mummy xx.' To Jay-Jay: 'Goodnight my precious baby, love Mummy xx.'

I want them to know that Mummy is with them and that she loves them. When they had needed me most, on the day the monster took them from me, I had not been there.

My babies, if only I had known, I would have thrown myself in front of his knife, offering my life for yours. I promise I would have saved you. But I didn't know, my babies, I didn't know.

If only I had, if only …

Beyond All Evil

I

Beginnings

'They would become the perfect prey for the perfect predators'

Ian Stephen, MA, Dip Ed, Dip Ed Psych,

clinical and forensic psychologist

June: Did you ever doubt if you were loved? I did. I remember that cold feeling, as if it were yesterday …

Dad was in the kitchen. He was at the cooker. Something was wrong. Why was *he* making the dinner? Where was mum?

'Dad?' I asked.

He didn't respond.

Something definitely wasn't right. This tall, strong man at the heart of my life lit up whenever he saw any of his five children. No matter what drama was being enacted in our household, Dad could always be relied on to comfort us with his strong arms and soothe away our troubles in a gentle voice.

But he was silent and I was suddenly afraid. I couldn't see his face, couldn't read his eyes, but I knew even by the set of his shoulders that he was burdened by an ineffable sadness.

I had barged in through the door, trailing early evening air and winter cold into the warm kitchen. I was elated. Teenage hormones and the adrenalin rush created by sprinting from school had made me feel quite giddy.

All the way home, my thoughts had danced with the delights of lipstick, boys and David Cassidy. I was madly in love with the American teen heartthrob – heaven forbid, it was the Seventies after all – and all I wanted to do was play my one and only record on the precious stereo Dad had given me for my birthday.

I had sung the words of 'How Can I Be Sure' in my head on the journey. I longed to reach home, to rush to my room, to languish on my bed and let David's velvet voice wash over me while I gazed adoringly at his poster on the wall. He was the most beautiful thing I had ever seen.

But David and my girlish crush on him were driven from my mind in an instant. I felt a chill that had nothing to do with the weather.

I laid down my schoolbooks on the table and slipped into one of the chairs clustered around it. I traced confusion and concern with my finger tips on the Formica surface. I took a deep breath.

'Dad?' I said again. 'What's wrong? Something's happened.'

He still wouldn't turn round, still wouldn't look at me. He had a spatula in his hand and he was using it to flick over meat in a frying pan.

'Your mother's gone,' he replied in a voice that was weighed down by his obvious sadness.

'Where?' I said, rallying for an instant, believing that she must have left early for her beloved bingo hall.

'She's just gone,' he said in the same voice: 'And she won't be coming back. Not this time.'

He turned to me now and the pain was etched in his face. I felt anger.

'I hate her!' I said.

'Don't!' he said: 'Don't say that about your mum ... ever!'

'But Dad!'

'Dad nothing. She's your mum. She always will be.'

Those would be the last words Dad would ever speak to me, or any of us, about Mum. He never uttered a bad word about the woman. I was about to reply but my rancour was stilled by faces at the door – my brothers and sister.

'June,' Dad went on: 'You're a big girl now, the oldest, and I'm relying on you to help me with the others. We're a family, we'll get through this together, you wait and see.'

Dad's words had the same effect as always. I was soothed. I extended my arms to Roger, Jim, Linda and Gordon, who was little more than a tot. They filed into the kitchen, a deserted, sheepish little bunch seeking comfort and reassurance.

I tousled Gordon's hair, lifting him onto the chair as the others took their places around the table. Dad hoisted the pan from the cooker and said: 'The tea's ready.'

I had grown up in an instant. My childhood had become as much of a dream as my love affair with David Cassidy. I didn't know it then but I was taking my first steps on a journey into a future in which my personal sense of unworthiness would convince me that I did not deserve to be happy. I was, in a sense, being trained to put up with less, to accept rejection as the norm.

Giselle: I never doubted for a second that I was loved.

'Giselle!'

My mother's disembodied voice. Trying her best to sound angry and failing. My dinner must be ready.

'I'm coming, Ma!' I shouted from the bedroom.

I turned back to the mirror. For the thousandth time I was appraising my looks, and I hated what I saw. Who could love me? I stood out like a sore thumb in my class at school. All of the other girls were tall, pretty or blonde, or all three. Here I was, aged 13; short, gap-toothed, red-haired and covered in freckles. Not a pretty sight, I thought, especially when accompanied by a crippling shyness that could make me blush to the roots of my hair if someone so much as spoke my name.

'Gi-selle!'

This time there was an edge in Ma's voice, which suggested she was running out of patience. I wasn't unduly worried. Ma's bark was far more ferocious than her bite. In fact, she didn't have a bite. She was a softie, a sweetheart, who was loved by all. That's not to say she was a pushover, because she wasn't. But to this day, when I conjure her up in my mind's eye, I picture a woman with a smile on her face. When my mother Jean was alive, it took a lot to switch off that smile.

'Gi-se-lllle!'

I realised suddenly that the voice was closer than it should be.

'Ma?' I said, as she appeared at the bedroom door.

She wore an expression of mock anger, her brow furrowed in a feeble attempt to look stern. I almost laughed, but I didn't. This was a game we played. The rules were simple. She would look angry. I would look penitent. Anger wasn't in Mum's nature and I had never known a reason to fear her or my big, bluff father, who, when it came to his family – and his youngest daughter – had an awesome bark but even less of a bite.

'You looking in that mirror, again? You'll wear it out!' she said.

'Look at me, Ma! Red hair and freckles! God hates me!'

'But I love you, darlin'. C'mon, you're beautiful,' she said, enfolding me in her arms.

'I'm not! I'm not! I'm not like the other lassies. They're pretty and tall, not a wee carrot-head like me!' I cried.

'I've seen the lassies in your class,' she said. 'They all look the same. You're special. None of them can hold a candle to you. You're a lot prettier than they are. You wait and see. When they grow up they'll all wish they looked like you.'

All lies, of course, but beautiful lies, spoken by a kind woman who for all of her life would live in the confines of a small, safe world, the boundaries of which extended no further than her home and her family.

'You get in there and get your tea,' Mum said, guiding me out of the bedroom. *I was momentarily buoyed by her support.*

Perhaps my red hair and freckles weren't so bad after all. Somehow, though, I wasn't convinced. But my mother – and my father – had a knack of arming me against the world. My mother held my hand as she led me to the kitchen. For as long as she lived, my mother would hold the hand of her 'baby'.

The kitchen was pandemonium, loud with the sound of my brothers and sisters – William, Alex, Johnny, Tam, Janie and Katie. It was a typical Glasgow household. Some of them had already left home, but they always found their way back to Ma's for tea.

'Giselle Ross,' said Da. 'At last! We can eat now.'

Da never called me or my sister Katie simply by our Christian names. He always appended our surname. Don't ask me why. It was just a tradition and it always sounded as if he were about to give us a telling off. Nothing could have been further from the truth. Da was like Ma, a sweetheart. You wouldn't think it, if you met him. John Ross is a pre-war model, a long-distance lorry driver, and a bit of a man's man. Ma was always hugging and kissing us, but it has to be admitted that the modern expression 'touchy-feely' was not coined on behalf of my father. He loves us all fiercely, but we don't demand big public shows of affection. Christmas and New Year in his home are marked by a firm handshake for his sons and a peck on the cheek for his daughters.

When I was a child and being bullied at school, Dad would tell me, 'If someone hits you, Giselle Ross, you hit them back. If you don't, lady, I'll come and hit you.'

Of course, he would do no such thing. It was his clumsy psychology lesson on how to stand up for yourself. I looked around me. I was safe. I was secure. What did it matter if I had red hair and freckles? I had all the love I needed. I never wanted to leave this place and I wouldn't for the next two decades. I didn't know that then, of course, but my brothers and sisters would fly the nest, one after the other, and I, the youngest, would stay. I would live a cloistered existence of my own making and not for a single second regret it by worrying whether I was missing out.

What had the world to offer me that I could not find at home?

6

June: You were so fortunate. If my mum couldn't love me, how could anyone else?

Mum had cleared at arguably the most vulnerable time in the life of a teenage girl.

I was sad, deeply sad, but I tried to hide it behind a mask of indifference and bravado. A mother's love should be the rock upon which each of our lives is built, but in my case it wasn't to be the case.

Did my mother not love me enough to stay? If she had loved me why would she leave me? Perhaps I'm being too harsh, but I could not help how I felt then, and I can't help how I feel now.

I'm certain she must have loved me in her own way – or is that just something I comfort myself with? I still don't know. What I do know is that from that moment I knew I couldn't rely on her.

Her leaving had dredged up many emotions which I now realised had been experienced subconsciously. Even when she was in my life, I did not feel the closeness with her that I had with my father.

I had been able to identify with my pals' closeness to their own fathers because that was my experience. I never doubted for a single second that Dad loved me. Our closeness was a living thing and it remains so. I have no idea what the catalyst was for Mum leaving us for good. I wouldn't see her for many years and then I would learn that she had eventually met someone else.

Mum and Dad had very different personalities and it was a period when ordinary couples were not expected to be openly affectionate towards each other. So there had been no real tell-tale signs indicating her impending departure. One day she was there, the next she was gone.

To this day, Dad will still not say a bad word about her, but I have always had the impression that he was secretly relieved when she left.

It must have been very difficult for him but he was armoured by his reputation for being a good and decent man. He was held in such high esteem and so well liked in the community that no one dared gossip about the breakdown of his marriage.

Dad was a foreman at the local dye works and he continued to work in the factory and function as father and mother to us all. In those days, in those circumstances, no one would have raised an eyebrow if Jim Martin had decided to deliver his children into the care of social workers. In fact, this was commonplace when a working man was deserted by his wife.

He was, however, made of sterner stuff. It must have been hard for him in a town such as Kilbirnie, in Ayrshire, a grim, grey industrial place that produced a similar breed of people.

Dad did not whine. He just did the best he could and his best was very good.

Ironically, I would repay him by going off the rails.

_____

Giselle: Wherever I turned, wherever I looked, Ma and Da were always there ...

The words written in my final school report card declared that Giselle Ross had grown into an amenable young woman who might do well in the world if she would just 'push herself forward a bit more'.

Fat chance. I had no wish to push myself forward, or to trek too far into the world beyond the confines of my home and family. The word 'confine' conjures up a sense of being restricted. I wasn't. I embraced the safety of home life. I harboured no ambition for a high-powered executive career. Was that wrong of me? Maybe. But I was being true to myself. One must never confuse contentment with a lack of ambition.

Teenage love affairs were mysteries to be experienced by others. I had never had a boyfriend. I was – and I remained for a long time – an innocent. My days revolved around the home, like a wheel that turned contentedly through one day to the next. Ma and Da were the hub, my brothers and sisters the spokes of the wheel. I had no notion of becoming a mother, but Ma demanded that her house be 'filled with babies', and in time it would. I would then become a brilliant auntie to the children in this ever-extending family.

When Katie had her two children, Paul and little Giselle, I drew them into my loving world. I saw them every day. I was like a second mother to them, as Katie would become a second mother to my Paul and little Jay-Jay when they came along.

From time to time, Ma and Da would, to coin a phrase, make efforts to persuade me to get a life. I had a life, a wonderful life, and one that satisfied all of my needs. I felt no jealousy of others who lived a different kind of life.

And so it would go on.

———————

June: You were the perfect daughter; I was acting like a brat ...

I wasn't so much bad as wilful, an attention-seeker. These days psychologists would have a name for it and I'm sure they could come up with any number of reasons to explain why I began acting out. It doesn't take a degree in psychology to recognise that the change in my behaviour coincided with abandonment and a flood of teenage hormones. I may have been secretly relieved that Mum was out of our lives but it did leave a huge void.

Afterwards, I felt as if I were searching, always searching, for something or someone to fill the emptiness. I pushed back the boundaries – pinching and drinking vodka from Dad's cupboard; staying out late; running away from home. All stupid stuff, really. I just yearned to be noticed, to be valued; for someone to put their arms around me and assure me that I was safe. In the aftermath of my misdemeanours, my granny was drafted in to bring me back to my senses. She was a lovely old woman with a particularly simplistic view of the universe, which, as far as she was concerned, was painted in black and white.

She would declare, 'Just remember, June, once you've made your bed you have to lie on it – think of what you're doing to yourself and your dad.'

Poor Dad. He was so busy with work and looking after the home that the only way – in my confused mind – that I could get his full attention was by getting into bother. I can still remember the weary conversations, the pained expressions on his face.

'Why are you doing this, June?' he would say in an exasperated tone of voice, in reference to my latest escapade.

'Why can't you just behave like everyone else?' he would go on.

Dad could not fathom why I was playing truant constantly and getting into daft scrapes. In retrospect, it is almost as if I was being 'bad' to test his love, trying to establish how far I could push him before he, too, abandoned me.

'I can't,' I would reply, without knowing why, my face set in a perpetual scowl. His hurt looks wounded me to the core, but I could not help myself.

One of the worst things I did to him was to run away from home. I decided I would hitchhike to London. I set off with two pals, not giving a second thought to the pain it would cause him. When it was discovered that we were gone, he had everyone out looking for us: friends, relatives, the police. Our big adventure was, of course, doomed to failure. We actually made it south of the border but it wasn't long before we ran out of money and were forced to throw ourselves on the mercy of the police. We were returned home in disgrace by social workers.

Dad was mortified and he lambasted me. Did I know the trouble I had caused? Did I realise how worried he had been? What kind of example was I to my brothers and sister? I stood, head bowed, stung by his words – but for some inexplicable reason a part of me was pleased to be the centre of attention.

I would never again run away from Dad, but it would take me a long time to shake off my recalcitrance. If someone said, 'Don't do that, June,' that is precisely what I would do. What I needed was to be truly loved, to find someone of my own, someone who would make me the centre of his whole world. I would find him. Desperation shines like a beacon, and so often a light in the darkness attracts a predator.

His name was Rab Thomson.

———————————

Giselle: As time passed, we were walking to the same destination – but from different starting points ...

The woman in the mirror was far less vulnerable than the girl had been. I swept the brush through my gleaming red hair. Ma had been right. The hair I had hated so much as a teenager had become my crowning glory.

It had been a long time since I had first stood in front of this looking-glass, bemoaning my perceived imperfections. I still did not care much for what I saw, but I was safe, perennially cloistered by invisible walls that had been built over so many years by my loving family. My brothers and sisters had long since gone, creating new lives of their own outwith the fortress. I remained. My 'job' was still to look after my parents.

My mother's health had deteriorated badly. She suffered from chronic asthma, which obviously affected her breathing. It was extremely debilitating. She would spend nights in the living room, sleeping in a chair, propped up by pillows. I was never far away. I delighted in being able to look after her – and Da – as they had looked after all of us. I still had no sense that I was sacrificing myself and I had long since come to terms with my detachment from the 'real' world. It was a price worth paying. I was content. I saw the good in people, rather than the bad. I had learned how to do that from Ma. She helped her neigh-

bours. She would not pass a beggar without giving him money. She bought sweets for children who had none.

When we were young, Ma and Da would take us on trips, days out in the car, walks in the countryside, strolls along seaside promenades. It was my turn now to chaperone them. I loved them. I loved their safe world. I embraced it. I never wanted to leave it. It might have remained so until one day, at the age of 32, I walked into our local post office with Ma. The man standing behind the polished wooden counter had soft brown eyes and he smiled at me.

His name was Ashok Kalyanjee.

———————————

2

Love of Our Lives

'From the beginning, they were brought together
by what I call a constellation of symptoms ...
which would have catastrophic results.'

Ian Stephen

**June: Isn't it so strange how two chance encounters brought
all of us to this place?**

They were lining the back wall of the dance hall, a posse of
young bucks with drinks in one hand and cigarettes in the
other. They wore leather and short-sleeved button-down
shirts, and affected a couldn't-care-less attitude. This languid
disdain was a smokescreen. Their eyes were watchful, scanning, taking in the 'talent'.

Saturday-night meat market in Kilbirnie. Everyone looking for something, anything to dispel the gloom and break
the Monday-to-Friday monotony. I was 17 and I shouldn't
have been at the over-18s dance, but small-town childhoods
are short; everyone grows up quickly when there is so little to
look forward to. You might as well get on with a life that is

pretty much mapped out for you from the moment you're born. Go to school, leave school, get a job, marry the first man who is nice to you, have his kids. The line of our horizon struggled to go beyond the edge of town.

I was determined to break the mould. No matter what, I was planning to go to London. I had been saving my 'tips' and whatever I could spare from my wages as a trainee hairdresser. The money would take me to the bright lights and freedom. We – the girls – were dancing with each other, waiting for the 'tap' on the shoulder. There were few niceties involved in this mating ritual – a grunt, the tap, and if you were fortunate, a mumbled 'You dancin'?' Whenever this was said to me, I always had to suppress the urge to reply, 'Of course, I'm dancin'. What do you think I'm doing, signalling to the boats at sea?' Of course, I never did. It would have been a break with protocol.

I was fighting a losing battle against the pounding music in a vain attempt to tell my friend Wilma that it was time to go. And then I saw him. He had broken away from the posse and was heading for me, walking across the crowded dance floor through a tobacco haze that transformed his friends into ghosts. I knew instinctively that I was his target. He walked with purpose, his long mane of strawberry-blond hair flowing behind him. Perhaps it wasn't time to go after all. I signalled to Wilma with my eyes, the semaphore of the dance hall. She looked behind her and turned back to me, making a face.

'Pig!' she mouthed silently.

I laughed, the sound drowned by a wall of Pink Floyd. The young man skipped between the dancers. I knew him. In this town there were no strangers. He was a well-known 'bad boy'.

He dispensed with words and I received the tap. He turned and walked to a gap on the floor. I followed. He hadn't doubted that I would.

From the moment Rab Thomson chose me, he took control.

Giselle: As innocent as I was, I knew he had chosen me ...

It was stifling hot. It always was on pension day. The majority of people in Royston, a district in the north of Glasgow, are not well off, least of all the elderly. In the tiny post office section of the corner shop, the old folk had gathered to gossip, catch up with friends and pick up their meagre benefits entitlement. Strong summer sunshine flooded through the window behind me, transforming the security glass on the post office counter into a white, impenetrable wall.

'Hot!' I said to my mother. We were in a snaking queue.

'Not half,' Ma replied, adding, 'Won't be long, though.'

I took Ma shopping every day. They were outings rather than spending sprees. Ma loved looking at things she would never own. She rarely bought anything for herself, but she delighted in choosing 'mindings' for her grandchildren. When we got out of here we were going to Ma's favourite shopping centre at the Parkhead Forge. There she would make her slow and stately progress along the shop fronts, halting every few steps to allow friends and old neighbours to pay their respects. If my identity was not apparent, Ma would introduce me by saying, 'This is my baby, Giselle!'

I was 32 years old.

I say that without rancour. Never for one minute did I fall into the trap of believing that I was somehow missing out. How could I, with so much love around me? I had always been content and happy, and I could not conceive of any other way of life.

'Not long now,' said Ma, dragging me back from my reverie.

The queue in front of us had been reduced to three people. The glare on the glass had dissipated and I saw a stranger behind the counter. Dark, handsome, a gentle face, a shock of luxuriant hair. Must be a new guy, I thought, feeling self-conscious for no reason I could explain. It was such an odd feeling. He looked up from what he was doing, caught my eye and smiled. My hand flew instinctively to my hair and I pushed wisps behind my ears. Did I look nice? I thought. Thank God, I had on lip gloss and mascara.

I was suddenly taken aback. Such thoughts? Where were they coming from? What the hell did I care what I looked like? What was happening? This was new territory. I was bothering about my looks for the first time in years. I had long since come to terms with the mirror in my bedroom. I was still searching for an answer when I realised the queue had cleared and we were at the counter.

The handsome man spoke. 'Next, please,' he said to my mother, who handed him her pension book. He was looking at me. The old and familiar crimson flush reached from my breast-bone to my forehead.

'Hello,' he said.

'Hi,' I stuttered, turning away quickly.

A rack of newspapers to my right had become utterly fascinating. I stole a glance at him and he was still looking, his smile full of the knowledge of the effect that he was having. I was *discomfited. I had never had a boyfriend and I had given up the notion that I ever would. But there was just something about this man that touched me in a way I had not experienced – something in the way he looked at me. I knew instinctively that he was 'interested'. He was good looking. Why would he be attracted to me? I must be misreading the signs, I thought.*

I tried to shrug off the feeling that secret signals were passing between us. But when I looked at him again, I could still feel the tension. I wasn't mistaken. If I had been required to speak at that moment, I don't think I could have. I would have babbled like an idiot. I was torn between emotions. One half of me wanted to tell my mother to hurry up and get out of here; the other wanted this moment to last. The spell was broken by the thump of his stamp validating her pension book. She was, as usual, chattering away as if she had known him all of her life.

'You're new, son, aren't you? What's your name?'

'Ash,' he said, to me as much as to her.

'Ashley,' she replied.

'Close enough,' he said, laughing.

'See you next week, son,' Ma said, gathering up the cash and pushing it into her purse.

'See you,' he said. He was talking to me.

I managed somehow to utter a strangulated 'cheerio' and fled. As we left the shop, Ma took my hand. My sense of regressing into a love-struck schoolgirl was complete.

'Seems nice, that boy,' said Ma, adding, 'Ashley's such a lovely name.'

There was a moment's silence, no more than a heartbeat, and then she said, 'You liked him, didn't you?'

Nothing much gets by you, Ma, I thought. Is it possible to keep a secret from your mother? I went an even deeper shade of

crimson. Was I really so transparent? I looked over my shoulder.
Ash's eyes were still on me. He smiled.

As innocent and naïve as I was in the rules of courtship and
love, I knew that he had chosen me.

June: This wasn't going to be any Mills & Boon romance.

'I'm Rab!' he said.

Pink Floyd was silent now, replaced by Tavares. 'Heaven Must Be Missing an Angel' flowed sweetly from the speakers.

'I know who you are,' I said.

'Hate this disco shite,' he bawled.

'Me, too.'

I didn't know why I had automatically agreed. I didn't 'hate this disco shite', but he had spoken the words with such confidence that they defied disagreement. For some reason, which I had yet to fathom, I so wanted to please this young man. With his long hair, he might have looked like all of the others, but, unlike them, there was about him an alluring air of menace that set him apart from the crowd. I did not fear him – not yet – but I sensed that the anger in him simmered close to the surface.

Wilma had retreated to the wall opposite where Rab's friends were congregated. She was scowling. She did not like Rab. That was clear. I shrugged in her direction and she stomped off towards the cloakroom. I didn't need to tell her that I would be leaving with him. It had been a foregone conclusion from the moment he tapped me on the shoulder.

'Let's go,' he ordered.

I obeyed. He strode off, giving a thumbs-up to his mates. They smirked, acknowledging the signal that Rab had 'clicked'. I tottered behind him on my Saturday-night heels. The peremptory nature of this encounter might surprise some women, but where I came from there were no hearts and flowers, no softly spoken words of romance. You were chosen and you were taken. That was the way it was. No Mills & Boon novel has ever been set in Kilbirnie.

'See you outside,' he said, walking to the dance-hall door. I was left to retrieve my coat. Wilma was in the cloakroom, waiting for me.

'What are you doing with him? You know he's a pig.'

'He's lovely,' I said.

'He's trouble!'

The truth was that everyone knew Rab was trouble, but Wilma realised that the more she protested, the more I would dig in my heels. In those days I rarely listened to anyone, an attitude that had got me into more than a few scrapes. I always knew best. I didn't, of course, but such are the follies of youth. And anyway, I reasoned, what did I have to lose? London beckoned. The more bad things said about Rab, the more I was determined to have him, if only for a short time. He had a reputation for fighting, stretching back to his schooldays. He was fearless, a hard case who wore his aggression like a badge of honour. Scrapping was a rite of passage where we grew up and it had won him the 'respect' of his peers.

Wilma was of course right, but I couldn't countenance that anyone could know better than I did. I was contrary. I hate to admit it now, but the fact that my best friend disliked him was precisely what made Rab even more attractive.

'Everyone hates him. They think he's a thug,' Wilma said.

'I don't care what everyone thinks,' I told her.

'They've got good reason,' she warned.

'Well, I don't care. I like him, and what does it matter anyway? I'm going to London.'

I terminated the conversation by turning on my heel and walking away. I would defy them all. I'd show them. In the years to come I would be haunted by that conversation – and by my recalcitrance. If only I had listened. But I didn't. I left her that evening, determined to prove everyone wrong.

Rab was waiting for me on the pavement, his blond hair shining in the light of a street lamp. I walked into his arms.

'Chips!' he said. No Mills & Boon hero.

'Okay,' I replied, as if he had just said suggested that we fly to Paris for the weekend.

'I hate salt and vinegar on chips.'

Another unequivocal statement that brooked no argument. I liked salt and vinegar, but I said, 'Me, too!'

Once again, I had fallen into step behind him. I couldn't analyse why. I just had.

'The car's over there,' he said.

I was impressed. I didn't know any other teenager who had a car. Rab jumped into the driver's seat of the Ford Cortina. I still remember the registration number – TAG 350J. The things you remember. It didn't occur to him to open the passenger door for me, but it didn't matter. I slid in beside him as the engine roared into life, breaking the stillness of the night.

My friends, who were either walking home from the dance or waiting for the late-night bus, turned in the direction of the noise. As we drove past them, I could see envy in their eyes. I knew then that this was what I had been missing, what

I had longed for. I felt different, important … special. I stole a glance at Rab's profile. He was looking straight ahead. His face was set, free of doubt or uncertainty.

Even if I did go to London, I was his.

Giselle: It was as if I were under siege. They call it love-bombing these days.

'Giselle!' Ash beamed.

He knew my name now. It had been weeks since that first excruciatingly embarrassing encounter. Now, when I saw him, I only flushed pink instead of deep crimson. I was a grown woman, but the emotions that crowded in on me made me feel as if I had returned to childhood.

'Hi,' I said, with a great deal more confidence than I had shown on the day I first set eyes on him.

We had not progressed beyond the relationship of shopkeeper and customer, but in recent weeks he had grown bolder, making little jokes, complimenting me on the way I looked. It was an innocent intimacy. I was conscious that he treated me differently from the other customers. I learned that he had a reputation for brusqueness, and few of the people from the neighbourhood had a good word for this new and 'superior' sub-postmaster. Ash's manner was a talking point. One of our neighbours was having tea with Ma when my dear old mother revealed that 'Ashley had a fancy' for me.

'Ma! I said in a tone of voice my mother was no stranger to.

'He's a bit snooty,' said our neighbour, between mouthfuls of biscuit.

'He's always nice to the baby,' replied Ma, looking at me.

She was incorrigible.

'I get the impression he doesn't think much of the folk around here,' our neighbour went on. 'He can be a bit sharp, as if he can't get you away from the counter quickly enough.'

'He's not like that with our Giselle,' Ma told her.

'Ma!' I said again.

'It's true,' she said. 'He's got a fancy for the baby. He's not sharp with her.'

'Well, I don't know about that,' said our neighbour. 'But he's a bit of a cold fish with the rest of us.'

I had been replaying that conversation in my head when I was brought back to the present by Ash speaking again.

'What can I do for you today, Giselle?' he asked.

Ash had escaped from behind the glass screen of the post office and was serving in the main shop.

'A loaf, thanks,' I replied, my heart beating hard against my chest.

'You must like your bread; you buy enough of it,' he said, smiling, and reaching behind to a shelf packed with baker's goods.

Looking back, it is astounding how many loaves were in Ma's bread bin during that period. I had been finding more and more reasons to go into the shop. Everyone needs bread, after all. I took the loaf and stuffed it into my shopping bag. Ash came around the counter and escorted me to the door. He held it open, and I was exhilarated by a combination of cold air and his presence. I looked up at him shyly and muttered a sheepish 'Thank you'.

He said, 'Well, when are you going to come out with me, then?'

I laughed, as I always did. It was not the first time he had asked me out. It had become something of a ritual. Part of me regarded it as polite banter. A secret side of me hoped that he meant it. I lacked the courage to take it seriously. I was in so many ways still that little schoolgirl standing in front of the mirror. I was walking out of the shop when he said, 'Oh, well, maybe next time.'

'Maybe,' I said, playing the game.

'One of these days you'll say "Yes",' he replied.

I floated off, back to my secure and safe little home, where Ma and Da were waiting. I had just closed the door of the flat when I heard Ma asking, 'Is that you, darlin'?'

Da was in the kitchen and I found Ma in the living room.

'Did you see Ashley?' she asked, her eyes twinkling.

'Ma-aa!' I said.

'He ask you out again?'

'Maa-aaa!'

'One of these days, you're going to have to say "Yes",' said Ma.

'Say "Yes" to what?' asked Da, returning from the kitchen.

'Our baby ...' began Ma.

'Maaaaa!' I said, interrupting her before she could say any more. 'Nothing, Da. She's pulling your leg.'

My angry eyes ordered Ma to be silent. Her serene eyes danced. She loved this.

'I'll get the tea,' I said.

'Is there enough bread?' Ma asked.

I glared at her.

———————————

3

Moths to a Flame

'Rab the brute sensed June's neediness; Ash the clever charmer savoured Giselle's innocence ... they are two sides of the same coin.'

Ian Stephen

June: I was drawn back like a moth to a flame ...

'That's you back, then?' Rab said.

Another night, the same dance hall. Kilbirnie on a wet weekend. He was unchanged, still with the long blond hair, the attitude, and the knowledge in his voice that sooner or later I was bound to return, drawn irresistibly back into his orbit. It was as if he had known it was inevitable from the moment I stepped off the bus from London. In my heart, I did too.

London had failed to excise Kilbirnie. In spite of all my childlike dreams and the desperation to get away, the city lights had paled. It was good to be home, where familiarity, however banal, offered a sense of comfort and safety. I know it will sound crazy to Londoners – and to all those who have deserted their little home towns to make their life in the capital – but I couldn't settle. I had arrived with such high hopes, but very quickly – and like so many before me – I had made three salient discoveries. The first was that the streets were not paved with gold. The second was that glamorous destinations may be wonderful to visit, but when you have to make a living the daily grind wears you down. The third discovery was perhaps the most telling and curious of the three. I was homesick.

Don't ask me why, but I couldn't get back to Ayrshire quickly enough. My sojourn had been a great adventure, but it's difficult to overcome small-town bones.

For the first few months I had worked in a hotel alongside a great bunch of girls, most of them from places other than London. We decided we would share a flat. We had really great times, four young women not yet grown up, finding their feet far from home. I soon moved on from the hotel and got another job with a clothing manufacturer. My job was to make the clothes, but after a while the boss approached me.

'You're tall and slim, June,' he said. 'How would you like to show off the clothes to the buyers?'

I was taken from the assembly line and sent on to the catwalk – 'showing off' the new designs at trade shows. I had stumbled into modelling, of all things. To a girl like me, it was glamorous – but with a small 'g'. However, there are only so many parties you can throw; only so many places you can go. When most of your time is spent trying to pay the bills, it doesn't matter where you are: the most exciting city in the world or a windswept corner of north Ayrshire.

It was time to go home.

And here I was, peering through the half-light of the dance hall, with Whitesnake blasting my eardrums, and Rab trying his best to look 'cool' and indifferent. I realised again that he had played a big part in my decision to return home. I knew it hadn't been a conscious element in my thinking, but while I was absent I had replayed in my mind our first encounter in this dance hall.

We were back where we began. I looked at Rab.

'Love Whitesnake!' he shouted.

'Me, too,' I lied.

A moth to a flame …

Giselle: I thought … so this is what they mean by fate.

The wipers beat away incessant rain. The world, as seen through the windscreen of my car, was drenched, the wet streets illuminated by large rectangles of light from the display windows of shops that would soon be closing. Passers-by, reduced to the evanescent substance of shadows, flitted across my path and disappeared into the gloom. If I hadn't been slowing down I wouldn't have seen the figure at the bus stop. I was on my way to a late-night pharmacy to pick up a prescription for Ma.

The figure was indistinct but familiar.

'Ash?' I said to myself.

I leaned closer to the windscreen and dropped down into second gear.

'Ash,' I said again, certain now that it was him, huddled against the downpour.

I came to a halt at the bus stop. I slid down the passenger window, and the noise of the rain and the street rushed into the car.

'Ash!' I said loudly to the figure with its back pressed against the Perspex wall of a shelter that was offering scant protection from the rain.

He heard me and ducked down to look into the car, his face wet and wearing a look of puzzlement. He had only ever seen me in the shop. I was a familiar face in unfamiliar surroundings. Then he recognised me.

'Giselle?' he said, a question mark in his voice.

'Get in!' I ordered.

He pulled open the door and slid into the passenger seat, shaking his head and spattering me with droplets. He brought with him the fresh smell of the outside.

'Thanks, Giselle,' he said, drying his face with the palms of his hands.

He turned to me and smiled, and his eyes were shining.

Like June said, both of us were drawn like moths to a flame. It was as if we couldn't help ourselves.

———————————

June: As far as Rab was concerned, it was as if I had never been away.

'Not interested!' Rab said. 'Don't care what you did when you were away. You're back and that's that.'

We were sitting on an ancient, overstuffed sofa in the living room of Rab's flat. The television was muted and I was trying for the umpteenth time to share with him the stories of my adventures in London. It had been six weeks since I had returned to the crushing ordinariness of life in Kilbirnie. London was a memory, one that I was now painting with a veneer of glamour it probably didn't deserve. I had become something of a heroine to my circle of friends because I had escaped small-town life, albeit for only a relatively short period. They demanded that I regale them with tales of London life, which I was happy to do, and bask in the reflected glow of their admiration.

Rab, on the other hand, seemed determined to obliterate my brief bid for freedom, ordering me to 'shut up' whenever I broached the subject. As far as he was concerned it was as if it had never happened, as if I had never been away. Any lingering sense I had of being special for having escaped the monotony was quickly stifled.

I was here, we were together, and that was an end to it. Nothing and everything had changed since I had been away. Rab had also left Kilbirnie for a little while, travelling to the Highlands, where he worked briefly for the Forestry Commission. He, too, had come home, and with enough money to rent a one-bedroom flat. He had quickly got another job.

Rab was a workhorse; he never shied away from labour, but he was too much of an outdoorsman to be dragged into an office or succeed in business. He had grown up on a farm on the outskirts of Kilbirnic. Like me, he came from a big family. He had four brothers and two sisters. His father, Alexander, was a successful businessman, with many interests locally.

Compared with my upbringing, Rab's early years appeared to me to have been privileged. While my father walked to work, Rab's dad drove large, flashy cars. There did not seem to be any lack of money in the family, but, according to Rab, love was in short supply in his home and he claimed his childhood was miserable. His father, he said, had been tough and often brutal, thrashing him regularly with a horsewhip for any and all small acts of disobedience. I could never equate Rab's description of his father with the jovial man whom I came to know. But as my granny – a woman who loved her homilies – was wont to say, 'Who knows what goes on behind closed doors?'

Rab also insisted that his mother, Helen, was a cold and unemotional woman. When I met her, I certainly found her to be undemonstrative and not the type to encourage a kiss or a hug. She was by nature reserved, a woman seemingly overly concerned with what 'outsiders' thought of her and her family.

I could never be certain if Rab was telling the truth about his early years or whether they were the lies of the 'black sheep' of the family. That was certainly Rab's place in the scheme of things. While his brothers and sisters did well for themselves, Rab was the one who never quite made the grade. His reputation, such as it was, was for being a very hard worker in a series of undemanding outdoor jobs. He had another, less respectable reputation for an explosive temper and a volatile nature. He fought with everyone: his brothers, his so-called friends, strangers in the street, in fact anyone who penetrated his thin emotional defences.

I was now part of Rab's world, for good or ill. I was sitting in his flat. It was inevitable that I, too, would soon be calling it home. Rab raised the volume on the television, signalling an end to our conversation.

'Forget this London shite … what about my tea?'

———————————

Giselle: Ash was swamping me with his kind of 'love'.

He asked if I liked the perfume.

'I'm sure it's lovely,' I said, unscrewing the silver top from the clear glass bottle and holding it to my nose. Lemon, orange, mandarin and grapefruit exploded in a citrus burst.

'It's lovely,' I murmured, inhaling the fragrance.

'It's Happy,' said Ash.

'Happy?'

'It's called *Happy*,' he said. 'By Clinique! I saw the name and I thought of you. You make me happy.'

I laughed, caught between pleasure and self-consciousness. To my untrained ear, Ash's compliments still sounded contrived, but what did I know? This was all new to me, being fussed over by a man. It was the fifth bottle of perfume Ash had bought for me in as many weeks since that night in the rain. The others were in the drawer of my dressing table. Ash and I were still a 'secret', even from my mother. Especially from my mother. She would go to town and her teasing would reach epidemic proportions. If she had anything to do with it, my burgeoning relationship would be the talk of the town.

'I want you to wear it!' Ash said, taking the bottle out of my hand and spraying perfume in the direction of my neck.

I recoiled instinctively.

'Don't you like it?' he said.

There was urgency in his voice, an edge that hadn't been there a moment before.

'Of course I like it,' I said, pushing away a sudden sense of unease.

He smiled and seemed relieved.

'You're sure?' he said.

'I'm sure,' I replied, taking the bottle from him and spraying perfume onto my wrists.

I didn't particularly like the fragrance. I preferred floral perfumes.

He was looking at me intently. I sprayed more perfume, this time on my neck.

'See,' I said. 'It's lovely!'

It just seemed easier to please him. He relaxed. I replaced the top on the bottle and slid it into my bag.

'That smells nice,' said a new voice. A waiter had materialised at the side of the table.

We were in the dining room of a small hotel on the outskirts of the city. Our relationship had thus far been a series of such assignations. When Ash finished work in the evening, I would be waiting for him in the car, somewhere nearby where we couldn't be spotted from the high flats. We had just slipped into this way of doing things. On the night I had rescued him from the rain we had gone for a drink in a bar near where he lived. With our coats sheltering our heads, we had sprinted from the car to the welcoming warmth of the little pub. Every eye looked up as we swept in through the doors, breathless with laughter.

For the first time in my life, I had been devoid of self-consciousness. I was happy. Free. Giselle Ross, aged 32-and-a-half, was on a date. It may have come about by default, but it was nonetheless a proper, grown-up date.

If I had bumped into Ash on the street, on a sunny summer's day, I would have offered him a timid 'Hi!' and walked on. On that rainy night, my natural inclination to help had emboldened me to offer him a lift. We were together now. How could I believe that this was anything other than meant to be?

Within an hour, the handsome man from behind the glass partition of the post office had emerged as a real person. He was no longer just the joker who teased me, no longer the aloof shopkeeper so disliked by many of my neighbours. I learned about his life, how he lived with and cared for his mother. He told me of his dreams and aspirations, and of how he was going to be 'somebody' some day. By the time I had dropped him off at his home later that evening, I felt exhilarated. Was this what it felt like to fall in love?

In the weeks following, I would learn the answer to that question. He overwhelmed me with flowers and tokens of his affection, the latest of which had just disappeared into my handbag. I placed the bag under the table and looked up at the waiter.

'Would you like to order now? Madam?'

'She'll have a medium steak, with salad,' Ash said, adding, 'Bring me the same.'

He closed the burgundy-red leather menu and handed it to the waiter, without looking at the man.

'To drink … Madam?' the waiter asked, looking at me.

'Diet Coke,' said Ash. 'And can you bring a jug of water? I'll have a large vodka and lemonade.'

The waiter was still looking at me. He smiled, closed his order book and walked away. Ash's eyes followed him.

'Do you know him?' he asked.

I looked in the direction of the retreating waiter and said, 'No. I've never seen in my life before. Why?'

'It was just that he was looking at you,' Ash said.

June: I should have walked away the moment it happened.

The back of Rab's left hand, enlarged to the size of a dinner plate, smashed into my face, his knuckles connecting with my nose.

My head snapped back and I heard rather than felt the sound of the blow. I was momentarily plunged into darkness. When the fog cleared, my hand was on my face, blood pouring through my fingers. I could taste metal and for a few seconds I could not fully comprehend what had just happened. His lips were close enough to my face to spray spittle on the back of the hand that was pressing on my nose.

'Fuck do you think you're doing?' he growled.

'Wha ...'

I couldn't even finish the word.

'You fucking ever look at another man, you'll wish you'd never been born.'

He was furious. Tears were running down my face, mingling with the blood. We were in Rab's car. It was raining outside and the windscreen was smeared. I couldn't tell if it was the effect of the rain or if I was still disoriented. Voices from outside wafted into the car and I saw five of my workmates walking through the gates of the factory where we worked.

And then I remembered. Rab had come to pick me up and I had just got into the car when my colleagues appeared. All of them were men. I rolled down the window and shouted to them, telling them to have a good weekend. I waved as they returned the greeting. I had just rolled up the window and was turning towards Rab when he hit me.

No one else had seen what he had done. I slumped down in the seat as Rab drove through the gates, passing my work-mates, who waved in the direction of the car. I was frozen with shock. I could see the puzzlement on the men's faces because I hadn't responded. The rest of the journey passed in a silence pregnant with menace. I didn't dare utter a sound.

Rab seethed. I had retrieved a handkerchief from my pocket and dabbed my nose. I pulled down the sun visor, and looked in the small vanity mirror. My reflection revealed a blood-stained face. The blood was caked around my nostrils and mouth. My blouse was splotched with dark stains. I didn't think my nose was broken, but an angry weal stretched across the bridge. My teeth ached.

Rab glared at me, silently daring me to say a word.

I said nothing. I was terrified. This was the first time he had struck me. I had witnessed his rages, seen his fists flying, but they had never been directed at me. My mind raced. Shock, anger, and a sense of betrayal and fear competed with each other. Every instinct told me to remain silent. We came to a halt outside Rab's flat, where we were now living together.

'Get up the fucking stairs,' he said.

I pushed open the car door, trying to keep my head still. I felt that if I moved too quickly it would fall off. I walked pain-fully, slowly, pausing at the door of the flat to allow Rab to unlock it. He loomed over me. I was intimidated.

The only other time I had felt like was when Rab tore to shreds a brand-new black cat-suit I had bought. In the few months we had been together I had learned that Rab had very specific ideas about how he liked me to be dressed. A slinky, figure-hugging one-piece suit was not acceptable. Whores dressed like that, he insisted. When I had first seen the cat-suit in the shop I had fallen in love with it. I couldn't wait to wear it for him, to show it off. I had spent hours doing my hair and make-up.

When he saw me, he said, 'Take it off!'

'What's wrong?' I asked.

'Take that thing off.'

'Why?' I pleaded.

'Take off that fucking whore's outfit or I'll take it off,' he shouted into my face.

He followed me into the bedroom, and I was still struggling to get out of the suit when he grabbed it and began tearing it apart. He was utterly furious, enraged, for no reason I could understand.

Now, as I sat on the bed, nursing my battered face, I wept silently for fear that my tears would provoke more anger. My best friend's words came back into my mind. Wilma had warned me, 'Stay away from him, he's a pig!'

I remembered my defiant response.

'No, he's not. He's lovely. I'll show you all. I'll change him.'

How could I go crawling back now and admit that they were right – and I was wrong? I could hear their words of comfort and see their told-you-so expressions. Granny had warned me often of lying on beds of my own making. I lay back now – on Rab's bed – closed my eyes against the light and tried to shut down the turmoil in my head. I heard a sound at the bedroom door. Rab had come into the room. He looked down on me and I felt my stomach lurch.

'We should get engaged,' he said.

Giselle: His mother knew we were getting married – before I did.

'We should get married,' Ash said.

We were sitting in my car, looking out at Kelvingrove Park, the most beautiful of Glasgow's many open spaces. The red sandstone of the magnificent Victorian museum and art gallery was darkening with the setting sun. I was overwhelmed.

I didn't reply right away. We had known each other for only a matter of months and he had yet to meet my family. He knew Ma and my sister, Katie, and Katie's daughter, Giselle. He knew of my father, but only through the post office. Ash hadn't 'officially' met any of them, and now he was asking me to be his wife.

'We'll have a large house, a lovely garden, big cars in the drive, and I'll be an important lawyer,' he said.

By now I was beginning to wonder what it was that Ash actually wanted to do with his life. He was forever dreaming of grandiose schemes. In the short time I had known him he had wanted to be a businessman, a bank manager or, it seemed, any profession which had status and attracted 'respect'. He was nearly 40, and he had a perfectly good job as the post office manager in the local shop.

I had certainly not put any pressure on him to be anything other than what he was. Ash drove his own extraordinary ambitions. He talked incessantly about how his father had left his mother years earlier and how it had become his duty to care for her. It was an attitude I found admirable. After all, I had spent most of my life doing the same thing for my own parents. Apart from the revelation about his father, I knew little about his background, other than that he had been born in India and had *spent part of his early life in London. He also had a sister who lived in Oxford. He said she was a businesswoman and I always got the impression that Ash was jealous of her success. It was as if he craved something that always seemed to be just out of his reach.*

He had become the perpetual 'student', combining his day job with one educational course after another, none of which seemed to be leading to any career destination. Ash had already told me that he had gone to Oxford University and claimed to have a 'number of degrees' and 'letters after his name'. I didn't care one way or another. I loved him and, if it made him happy to strive for something more than he had, then so be it.

'Mum's given me money so we can get married,' he said.

I felt as if cold water had been thrown on my face.

'What?' I said sharply.

'I told her we were going to get married. She gave me money,' he went on.

'Why would you tell your mother you wanted to marry me – before you had even asked me?' I said.

'I knew you would want to marry me.'

I did love him, but the length of our relationship could be counted in weeks.

'I've seen a dress for you,' he said.

'What? You're choosing my wedding dress?'

'It's beautiful. White, long, with a lengthy train. It's in a shop in Glassford Street. You'll look beautiful.'

I was dumbstruck.

'It's awful soon,' I said, trying to buy time. 'I'm still living at home. There's my mum and dad to think of. And I've only just met your mother. You haven't even officially met mine, or my father, or my brothers and sisters.'

Ash took my hands. He looked into my eyes and said: 'You love me?'

'Yes,' I said quietly.

'Well then, why don't we just get married and have a long and happy life together?'

'Ash ...'

He silenced me by placing a finger on my lips.

'Just think, Giselle ... We'll have such beautiful babies.'

4

Rings on Our Fingers

'If they were ever to break away, it would have
to be now – it would soon be too late.'

Ian Stephen

June: I was so desperate to be loved.

I slipped the ring onto my finger and held it up to the light.
The blue sapphires gleamed. They were surrounded by a
circle of glittering, ice-white diamonds that appeared to have
been planted in black velvet. I was mesmerised. I had never
seen anything so beautiful.

'Is that the one you want, then?' Rab said. His voice was
weary.

The well-dressed young jeweller, with his beautifully
manicured hands, was making Rab feel uncomfortable. Rab
probably assumed the man was gay because of his appearance and the manner in which he had been fussing around
me since we entered H. Samuel in Glasgow's Argyle Arcade.

The Victorian arcade of jewellery shops is a mecca for
courting couples. Rab had planted his big workman's hands

on the gleaming glass counter but he withdrew them quickly when the young man rested his own delicate fingers next to his. I could read Rab like a book. He was fed up. We had traipsed the length of the arcade, lingering at every brightly lit casement window as I searched for the ring. I had now found it.

'It is lovely, isn't it?' the jeweller said. 'And it fits perfectly.'

'Is that the one you want, then?' Rab repeated.

I wanted to savour the moment. Rab was behind me but I could feel the heat of his simmering irritation. He'd had enough.

'Yes,' I said.

'Give her it, then,' Rab said brusquely, pulling a wad of notes from his trouser pocket.

'Do you want to keep it on your finger?' the jeweller asked.

'Oh, yes,' I told him. 'I don't want to take it off.'

I could hear the child in my voice.

'I'll get you the box,' the jeweller said, delving into a cabinet behind him and locating a navy-blue leather box decorated with gilt scroll.

Rab laid down £98 on the glass counter. The price of happiness. I looked at my ring and pledged no one would ever take it from me. For some reason, I remembered the stereo record player from my teens, the most special gift my father had ever given me. I now felt the same about the ring. Like that stereo, this was something just for me. I would never take it off. It was Valentine's Day, 1981, and £98 was a lot of money. Rab had worked many 12-hour shifts to pay for it.

He must really love me to give me something so special, I thought.

I leaned towards Rab and kissed him lightly on the cheek. He recoiled, embarrassed by my public show of affection. The tip of my nose brushed his jaw line and I felt a twinge. The swelling on the bridge of my nose had gone down in the last few days, but vestiges of pain remained.

I know this is the moment when everyone asks the same question. Why, in the name of God, would any woman in her right mind pledge herself to a man who had struck her just two weeks earlier?

How can I explain?

The truth is that I can't. I cannot offer any rational explanation. From where I stand today it was, of course, monstrously crazy. But who among us can look back over the course of our lives and not find episodes that provoke the question 'What in the hell was I thinking?' ?

I should have walked away when I had the chance. In fact, I should have fled. But I did not. Why? It may seem trite and too easy to blame our childhoods, to look for excuses in our past. But ...

What we become is governed by who we were. When I sat on Rab's bed, nursing my bruised face, I had been incapable of rational thought. Don't ask me why, but the pain of Rab's assault dissipated the moment he said, 'Let's get engaged!'

It would be many years before I recognised that the reason I hadn't fled was because I was so desperate to belong, so in need of being loved and so desirous of being wanted. I didn't flee. I stayed. I made the mistake so many abused women have made before me, and no doubt there are – and will continue to be – many more caught in the same trap.

However, on that day, in that shop, the engagement ring was so much more than a piece of fancy jewellery. It was a symbol of all of the things I craved. I had convinced myself that Rab hitting me was a sign of his love. His violent outburst was born of jealousy. He couldn't be jealous if he didn't love me, could he? And, of course, was it not my fault? I had provoked him by waving at the men. But that was obviously all a load of nonsense. His jealousy was a manifestation of controlling behaviour, just as tearing up my cat-suit had been. How could waving innocently to your workmates deserve a punch in the face? So, to everyone who has ever said to me, 'You should have left him,' I say to them, 'You're absolutely right.' But I didn't and I would pay a dreadful price.

Wisdom in hindsight is, after all, our only exact science.

Giselle: And I was blinded by love.

The butterfly had spread her wings but she hadn't flown far, at least not physically.

Within a few months I had moved into a new flat in a multi-storey block close to the one in which my parents lived. The blocks were crammed with families and had a population equivalent to a small town. Glasgow was dotted with such 'multis', a legacy of the 1950s and 1960s when the city fathers tore down the tenements and replaced them with what became known as 'high living'. It was only a euphemism.

I looked around my shiny new flat, with its cream walls and the peach curtains that I had made by hand. I was so pleased with my new independence. I had at last grown up. I was a woman rather than a girl, the perennial baby of the family.

So much had changed in three months since that evening in Kelvingrove Park when Ash asked me to marry him. In the interim I had stood by my decision that we should wait a bit longer. I loved Ash, and I wanted to marry him, but there was just 'something' that held me back. He was still loving and attentive, and he continued to shower me with gifts, flowers and tokens of affection. I told him not to, and yet he persisted. He made me happy but – to use that famous expression – there was a third person in our relationship: his mother.

All of Ash's grand schemes for our idyllic future behind an imaginary white picket fence seemed to involve 'Mum'. Mum would live with us; Mum would look after the babies; Mum would keep the house and cook; Mum would choose my clothes. Ash's mother was a lovely, welcoming woman, but I had a mother of my own and no one could take her place. I wanted Ash and me to be a couple, and not have his mother standing between us.

Since the evening in the park, Ash had asked me on an almost daily basis to marry him. His proposals were accompanied by elaborate word pictures of large homes, big cars, success, wealth and this mysterious term 'respect'. More than anything, he valued respect. It was a word he often used and I never quite understood what he meant by it. Men who sweep the streets inspire respect. Respect is not defined by wealth or status, but Ash seemed to believe that it was.

Even in the rosy glow of early love, I recognised that Ash's dreams were divorced from reality. How could we achieve all of the things he wanted? More importantly, why wasn't what he already had enough for him? He had a good and secure job, and I had provided a place for us to live.

When I moved out of my parents' home it had really pleased Ash. It was an obvious sign that I was trying to create what could become a world of our own. In reality, however, it seemed to have remained a world of my own. I got the flat, believing it was inevitable that Ash would move in.

He didn't. I saw him every day, but every night there would be the phone call to his mobile. It was always his mother. They would speak for several moments and then he would find excuses to leave. Strange as it may seem, this was a pattern that would be maintained throughout our relationship, even after we married and had those beautiful babies he so wanted.

In the course of our entire time together, I can count on the fingers of one hand the number of nights we spent in the same house. Looking back, I can't fathom why I put up with it, but somehow we just fell into that way of doing things. Before we were married there always seemed to be a reasonable explanation for his nightly departure. His mother was unwell; he had forgotten to tell her he would not be home; she had made his dinner and he did not want to disappoint her.

I should have put my foot down and forced him to make a choice, but I was reluctant to do so. I still lacked confidence and perhaps feared that, if I demanded he choose between us, I would lose him. I did not worry that he was being unfaithful to me as I knew that the only 'other woman' in Ash's life was his mother.

I also appreciated what it meant to feel a duty of care to your mother. I had looked after my own parents for so long and I was, in many ways, still doing so. Ash was clearly devoted to his mother and I was reluctant to make demands because a part of me believed it would be churlish to come between a parent and child. I looked around my little nest, trying to count my blessings, in the hope that everything would resolve itself in time.

The sound of a key in the lock brought me to my feet. Ash had arrived. He breezed in through the open door of the living room, one hand behind his back.

'What are you looking so pleased about?' I asked.

He was smiling broadly. By now I could recognise the expression that heralded yet another gift.

'Ash, you don't have to keep getting me stuff. I don't need presents, I just need you.'

He beamed.

'But this is special,' he said, revealing his latest offering with a flourish. 'Open it,' he said, presenting me with a tiny velvet box.

'Ash!' I said.

'Open it!' he insisted, and I identified the same tone in his voice that I had heard on the evening when he gave me the Happy perfume.

I took the box and opened it. A love-heart ring, set with a deep-red ruby surrounded by diamonds, sat in a cushion of white satin.

I slipped the ring onto my finger and held my hand up to the light …

5

Closer to the Flame

'It was too late. These men now had an almost hypnotic hold.'

Ian Stephen

June: I should have listened.

'No! No! No!' Wilma said.

'Please,' I pleaded. 'You're my best friend. I want you to be my bridesmaid. I know you don't like Rab, but look at my beautiful ring. See? He loves me, he really does.'

My words fell on deaf ears. Wilma was adamant. She wanted no part in my special day. I might have been blind but she could see all too clearly. She had no doubts that I was making a mistake but I was consumed by the dream shared by every schoolgirl, to have a fairytale white wedding. I had been so desperate to realise that dream that on the spur of the moment it was I who proposed to Rab.

My sister Linda was inadvertently responsible. Around the time we got engaged, she had married, and she and her husband were now expecting their first child. Our family

47

was carried along on a wave of happiness for her. Linda was quite rightly the centre of attention, the focus of the joy that envelops you at a time like this. I wanted it too. So badly.

I wasn't in the least jealous of Linda; I just hungered for a taste of that happiness. I couldn't get the longing out of my head. I was, I reasoned, almost married. Rab and I were engaged, and we were living together. Why wait?

We were sitting in the flat one day when I turned to him and said, 'Let's get married, soon.'

Rab didn't take his eyes off the television.

'Okay,' he said.

Giselle: I thought a wedding would solve all our problems.

'Okay! Okay!' I told Ash.

He dissolved, tears welling in his eyes.

'Giselle, you have made me so happy,' he said.

'But I don't want any big fuss,' I warned him.

'I promise. Just the two of us. We'll elope. It'll be so romantic. We'll choose a day, get married, and then we'll tell everybody. They'll be so pleased for us.'

I felt a moment of coldness. Like every woman, I wanted my parents and brothers and sisters to be there to share my wedding day, but if their absence meant that Ash would be forced to become a husband, rather than a mummy's boy, then it was a price I was willing to pay.

I held my hand up to quieten him and said, 'And we will be together, as a couple?'

I was excited yet apprehensive. The ruby ring Ash had presented to me was a turning point, I thought. It was a solid symbol of commitment. And with a wedding ring on my finger, everyone would know that we were together.

I never doubted for a moment that Ash loved me. He told me so a dozen times a day, but I was still apprehensive, still discomfited by his almost obsessive commitment to his mother. How could we be a normal couple if he was determined to run home to her each evening?

'You promise?' I repeated. 'We'll be a normal couple?'

'I promise,' he said. 'We'll be a family. I want babies. I want a daughter. Daughters have respect for their fathers. I want a son. A son would carry my name.'

I should have been carried along by his enthusiasm and, to a certain degree, I was. Perhaps marriage would change everything. A wedding would solve all our problems, wouldn't it? But still the nagging doubt persisted. I ignored it and gave myself up to his excitement.

'I'll buy a new outfit,' I said.

'No! A proper wedding dress,' he insisted. 'I've already told you – I've picked one!'

'But Ash, why go to the expense of a fancy wedding dress when there's just two of us? Who's going to see it?'

'I will,' he said. 'Our babies will. When they grow up, they'll look at photographs of Mummy and Daddy on their wedding day. I want everything to be done properly.'

'Photographs?' I said, laughing.

'Yes, official photographs,' he said pompously. 'You in your wedding dress, and me in my morning suit.'

'Tails!' I said.

'Yes, tails,' he replied.

It was difficult not be swept away by Ash's childlike exuberance. I had taken a decision that would change everything, and for the first time in my life my family were not a party to it. I had felt unable to tell my parents that Ash ran home to his mother every night. I could not reveal to them that it was she and not me who washed his clothes and cooked his dinners. It would have been incomprehensible to them. My dad was pure Glasgow East End working class, with all its traditions and boundaries. Wives made your 'tea'; wives washed your clothes. Mothers were there to be loved and visited on Sundays.

If Da had known how we lived, he would have lost respect for Ash for not putting me first. If Ma had known the truth, she too would have been mystified by my devotion to a man she would have perceived to be 'a mummy's boy'. I had solved the problem once and for all by saying 'Yes'.

Married men do not run home to mother.

June: Weren't we such fools?

I looked in the mirror, fingering the lace daisies embroidered under the tight bust-line of the white satin dress. The gown skimmed the carpet and the only visible signs of flesh were my hands, neck and face.

'Lovely, June,' said Ellen, who was standing behind me. 'You'd think it had been made for you instead of me.'

I patted my hips, smoothing down the heavy material. A veil fell on either side of my face, reaching to the hemline of the dress.

'Do you think so?' I said to Ellen's reflection.

Ellen was one of Rab's two sisters and she had offered to lend me the dress she had worn at her own wedding. Ellen had also agreed to be my bridesmaid; second choice for a bride in a second-hand dress.

It was May, and the weather was already promising summer. We were only weeks away from the wedding and yet Rab had become a stranger to me. He was working 12-hour shifts to pay for it. Since the day we, or more accurately I, decided that we were going to be married, we had been spending money like water. We soon realised that weddings were an expensive business. We were paying for everything ourselves and I was trying to keep costs down, hence my second-hand dress. I had discovered that the cost of a new one would have been astronomical. Most couples save for years to pay for a wedding. We effectively had a few weeks. Rab played no part in the preparations, but I was in my element.

When Wilma had bluntly refused to be my bridesmaid, it had not only dampened my enthusiasm – it had made me wonder whether I was doing the right thing. In spite of all the excitement, I couldn't get it out of my mind that Rab had hit me. My dad would have been horrified and enraged if he had known that Rab had lifted his hand to me. As far as he was concerned Rab was just a hard-working lad; a bit rough and ready, perhaps, but someone he believed would look after his daughter.

Somehow I convinced myself that the episode had been an aberration on Rab's part, and any lingering doubts were quickly suppressed by the planning: booking the church, renting the local community hall for the reception, hiring the band and sending out invitations. I strutted through my days in a happy haze, and now, as I looked at my reflection in the mirror, my reservations were dispelled.

I was already halfway down the aisle.

Giselle: Everything was for show.

The woman was smiling when she chided Ash.

'You know it's bad luck for the groom to see the bride in her dress before the wedding, don't you?'

Ash ignored the shop assistant, who tried to shield me by drawing the satin curtain across the changing area.

He was determined.

'I want to see her in that dress,' he told her, attempting to take the curtain from her hand.

The shop assistant's smile faded but she held firm. A faint hint of annoyance crept into her voice.

'Not until the wedding day, Sir,' she said, still trying to keep the mood light.

He was insistent.

'I want to see her,' he said.

The immaculately dressed and coiffed assistant in the salubrious wedding shop relinquished the curtain reluctantly. I could see she was embarrassed. So was I.

'Ash,' I said. 'It's bad luck.'

'Let me see you,' he said.

I stepped out from behind the curtain, my face flushing red.

'Beautiful!' he whispered, stepping back to admire the ornate, billowing gown.

The snowy-white dress was as traditional as it got. My hair was gathered beneath a pearl headdress attached to a veil that flowed down my back.

Ash began crying.

The shop assistant's eyes widened in disbelief and she retreated hastily to another part of the shop. I wilted under his intense gaze and I too had to look away.

'Beautiful,' he repeated.

'I'll take that one,' he said, in the direction of the assistant.

Her eyes flicked towards me for a microsecond.

'You do look lovely,' she said, before heading for the till.

I retreated behind the curtain and disrobed as quickly as I could. As naïve as I was, even I knew that Ash's behaviour was odd. By the time I came out the mood had changed and the assistant was all business. She was taking a sheaf of banknotes from Ash.

A new and pristine version of the gown I had just tried on was lying across the counter, sheathed in a white muslin cover.

'Thank you, Sir,' the assistant said, depositing the cash in the till.

She swung the gown high above her head, came round from behind the counter and draped it over Ash's outstretched arm.

'I hope your day goes well,' she said ... to me.

'Thank you,' I replied.

'Right,' said Ash as we headed for the door. 'Now for my top hat and tails!'

6

I Take This Man

'All June and Giselle wanted was someone to love them.'

Ian Stephen

June: Fools we might have been, but you start out with such hopes.

'June ...' Dad said. 'You look beautiful.'

My father stood in the doorway of the living room, smiling at me, pulling at the collar of his starched white shirt and black velvet bow tie. He wore a red carnation in the buttonhole of his formal suit. My dear father looked like a fish out of water.

'You don't look too bad yourself, Dad,' I replied.

I picked up my bouquet. The fussing was all over now. The car was at the front door. I was ready to go, ready to pledge myself to Rab. Dad offered me his arm. I took it.

'Ready, pet?' he said quietly.

'As I'll ever be,' I replied, in the same tone.

Dad helped negotiate my dress though the living-room door and into the hall. The front door was open, revealing a bright, warm summer's day.

10 June 1981. A lifetime ago.

Rab would be waiting at the church, a few minutes' drive away. The bells would ring, heralding my arrival, and I'd walk down the aisle to him. I had rehearsed the scene in my mind so many times. I had begun to think of the wedding as a gift. Perhaps this would be the one gift that no one could take away. There was still a part of me that was afraid. I had walked through life on heavy feet and experience had taught me that there was always a price to pay for the small patches of happiness. I felt I had been paying that price since my childhood.

However, my feet felt light today, encased in their white satin wedding shoes. I was happy. I emerged into the sunlight to a chorus of approval from the neighbours who had gathered to see me off.

'You look smashin,' one said.

'Lovely dress, darlin,' said another.

'Long life!' said a third.

I was carried to the car on a wave of good wishes and my niggling fears were dispelled. I *was* happy! Surely I had a right to be, today of all days?

'In you go,' Dad said, as I bent low to climb into the limousine.

He followed me and the driver spoke over his shoulder.

'Ready to go, June?'

'Take it away,' I said, my mood lightening by the second.

The big car slid away from the kerb and I eased back into the seat. Butterflies fluttered in my stomach. Dad recognised the signs.

'Won't be long,' he said, taking my hand.

It wasn't.

The car glided around a corner, and I saw the blond stone of the bell tower of Kilbirnie Parish Church. The entrance to the church was deserted but for a photographer and Ellen, who were awaiting my arrival.

'You look great, June. Nervous?' Rab's sister said as I emerged from the car.

'No,' I said, giggling … nervously.

I was barely conscious of the photographer fussing over my dress, ensuring it was hanging properly.

'This way, June,' he said, demanding I look in his direction.

I looked up, smiled, and he took the picture. I heard the first strains of the wedding march coming from the church organ.

'Time to go,' Dad said, as I took a tight grip of his arm.

No going back now.

Giselle: Ash didn't drop the bombshell until it was too late.

'What's wrong?' Ash asked.

'I don't know,' I told him through my tears.

I was sitting in Ash's bedroom, a room I had never shared with him.

'You'll spoil your lovely dress,' he said.

I swiped at the tears with a hankie.

'I want my mum and dad,' I said.

'Don't fret,' he said. 'Everything will be fine. The car's here. C'mon now, dry your eyes. By tonight we'll be a happy family.'

Ash was in a joyful mood that I could not share. This did not feel right. It should have been my father and not Ash standing in front of me. It should have been Da who arrived at my flat earlier, to take me to the register office. Ma and Da were at home, unaware of the momentous step I was about to take. I was sick with nerves. I'd heard of wedding day jitters but this felt altogether different. Ash soothed me with words that I now cannot remember.

25 March 2001. A day I'll regret for the rest of my life.

'C'mon, we'll be late,' Ash said.

He was dressed in a black morning suit, with a double-breasted jacket and pearl-grey waistcoat. The outfit was complemented by a silver-white cravat. He wore a white carnation on his lapel. He looked like a prince.

My beautiful dress. His elegant suit. It all just seemed too much for a wedding party of two.

'Get your bouquet,' he said.

I plucked the floral arrangement from the bed. I had spent hours making it from long-stemmed cream and peach roses. My favourite colours. They were bound by an intricate cascade of ribbon. When I was making the bouquet I had felt so happy, but now I was overwhelmed by uncertainty. I knew that I should not be feeling like this. I felt trapped. I wanted my family, but now it was too late. How could I turn up at my parents' home in a big frock and tell them to get their coats, and that they were going to a wedding?

I remembered that it was I who didn't want the fuss. I was being silly, I told myself. I loved Ash. We were about to marry and everyone would be really happy for us. I rallied, pushing away the doubts.

'Let's go,' I said.

'I love you. Do you love me?' Ash said.

'Yes,' I said.

It was the only thing I was certain of, as Ash guided me to the door and opened it. I walked into the living room.

His mother was standing there.

She was dressed exquisitely! She extended her arms to me. I felt as if I had been slapped in the face. Then I realised she was not alone; she was flanked by smiling strangers, all of whom were looking at me. I wanted to run. I looked at Ash. He was smiling. His mother was smiling. Everyone was smiling.

Except me.

———————————

June: I walked down the aisle to a 'new' Rab.

'You *cut* your hair off!' I whispered, the words partially drowned by the dying notes of the wedding march.

Rab was shorn of his mane. This was *another* Rab, stripped of his working clothes, which had been replaced by a sharp black suit. He was wearing a rare smile and looking incredibly self-conscious. I was astounded by the transformation. As Dad and I took our first steps into the church, I had seen this new Rab standing there, waiting for me. I held tight to my father's arm and processed down the aisle through the sea of happy faces.

I was in the church where I had been baptised, where I had sung in the choir and attended Sunday school. I looked shyly from left to right, offering silent greetings to our families. This was a happy place on a happy occasion. I felt that this day could change everything. This was surely indisputable.

The disappointments of the past, my emotional dislocation, and the inexplicable sense that somehow I did not deserve to be happy could all now be laid to rest.

I was five paces from Rab when he turned and smiled.

'Love the hair!' I said as my father escorted me to Rab's side.

He looked sheepish, almost vulnerable; an attitude no one would have associated with the man I knew. I was heartened. This seemed another good omen.

Would this be the Rab I would spend my life with?

Giselle: I couldn't hide; I couldn't run.

I was frozen to the spot. They came forward to greet me, these people, most of whom I had never seen in my life before. I heard Ash's voice.

'Giselle, smile!' he said.

I turned, feeling as if I were wading knee-deep through water. I wanted to throw up. I wanted to be anywhere but here. A flash blinded me. A picture had been taken, which would no doubt make me look precisely how I felt – like an animal caught in the headlights of a car. Ash was smiling broadly. He looked so smug, the man who had just sprung the big surprise. I was gutted. I had trusted his promises.

I was still in shock when he took my arm and said, 'Let's go out to the car.'

'Car?' I heard myself say.

I felt myself resisting, but then I thought, How can I do this to these people, to his mother? They didn't know we were supposed to be 'eloping'. They were here to celebrate a happy occasion. None of them knew why my mother and father were not standing alongside them. None of them realised why my brothers and sisters were absent. None of them knew that Ash had lied to me. I allowed myself to be led from the house. Ash's family and friends chattered to me. They looked proud and happy.

The 'car' was a gleaming black limousine.

'Only the best,' said Ash, in response to my blank look.

'We'll see you there,' Ash told his mother as he guided me into the vehicle.

I sank into plush leather, clutching my bouquet to my breast, as the car slid away from the kerb. I looked out of the window at familiar sights, everyday scenes I knew so well. Strangers hurried past, leaning into the wind. No one looked in our direction. I glanced at Ash, who was looking inordinately pleased with himself. The journey through the city centre passed in silence. We arrived at the beginning of a long Georgian terrace, in which one of the magnificent town houses had been converted into Glasgow's register office.

I was in a trance as I stepped from the car. Ash led me into the building to the wedding suite. Today I have little or no memory of the ceremony. All I could think about was that my mother and father were at home, sitting watching daytime television and probably wondering why their 'baby' had seemed so secretive of late.

My one clear memory is of Ash placing his hand on my wrist and guiding me as I signed the register. My fingers were stiff and cold, and I could barely hold the pen. I had never in my life felt such an overwhelming sense of being alone. It should have been the happiest of days, but I was bereft. I rose from the small table, and Ash took a firm grip on my arm and guided me from the *room. Our guests allowed us to walk past them before rising from their chairs and following.*

We led our entourage down the stairs to the main doors and out onto the steps. The photographer was on the pavement, waiting for us. He put up his hand, signalling for us to stop. Ash's mother and the others gathered around us.

The photographer raised his camera and said, 'Smile, please!' I just couldn't.

June: I went to bed wrapped in a broken dream.

'If he dis'nae look after you, darlin', I'll sort 'im out,' the tipsy man said.

He clutched a pint glass, the contents of which were sloshing onto a table that seemed to be his only visible means of support. I can't remember who my well-intentioned champion was but I didn't believe I would need his services. I didn't want to consider the possibility that Rab would ever require 'sorting out'.

The reception was in full swing in the local Labour Party hall. After all the excitement and planning I couldn't believe my special day would soon be over. The dance floor was packed. It was eleven o'clock in the evening and the band – Carnival – was still belting out old favourites.

The chair beside me was empty. Rab had strutted off a few moments earlier. Through the haze of smoke and people I could see him at the bar, standing in a line of his friends. Shades of our first meeting. That seemed a long time ago, although it was not. So much had happened. I felt that today represented a new beginning, a clean slate. I was still looking in Rab's direction when someone sat down in his chair. It was Dad.

'Had a good day?' he asked.

'A great day, Dad,' I said.

'Happy?'

'Yes,' I said, and I believed it.

'Good, darlin'. You deserve to be happy. I'll see you in a little while,' he said, rising from the chair and heading into the crowd.

I felt sad for Dad, and for myself. I had not invited my mother to the wedding. I suppose I could have but I believed she had betrayed us by walking out.

I was distracted by a shout from the dance floor.

'Juuuu-ne!' the voice cried.

It was one of my cousins. I waved.

'C'mon,' he said, beckoning me to the dance floor.

I gestured that I would stay at the table. Rab had already berated me earlier for talking 'too much' to my friends and 'dancing too much' with our guests. There was no pleasing him, even on his wedding day.

'Ladeez and gentellmmmen,' a voice cried from the stage.

The lead singer in the band.

'Please take your partners for the last dance.'

I looked over at the bar, where Rab showed no sign of making a move. I knew him well enough by now to recognise even from this distance that he had drunk more than a few pints of lager. But he wouldn't be staggering drunk. Rab liked to stay in control. I picked my way through the crowd and tapped him on the shoulder. He turned, his eyes slightly glazed.

'C'mon, let's get up. Last dance,' I said, dragging him away from his friends.

We stumbled around the dance floor, to the applause of our guests. Rab was oblivious to most of it. He was trying to make an effort, but he was never the most ebullient of personalities. As the band played the last notes of the song, the lights came on. The next 20 minutes were taken up saying hearty goodbyes to everyone.

We were soon virtually alone in the middle of the hall. I guided Rab out into the night. It was still warm and fine. Taxis were coming and going, but we had been offered a lift by one of our guests. The car drew up in front of us. We were joined by my cousin Joe and his wife, who was also called June. Joe was much older than me and he was more like a brother than a cousin. We had arranged to go to his house and spend our wedding night there.

Joe lived in Stevenson, a town not too far from Kilbirnie. We were all in good spirits on the short journey. It was, of course, too good to last. We hadn't been in Joe's house long before I was rowing with Rab – over going to bed. He insisted on staying up and having 'just a few more drinks'.

I was trying to persuade him to come upstairs, but he pushed me away, saying, 'You don't fuckin' tell me when to go to bed.'

Hot tears blinded me. The new Rab seemed to have disappeared before the honeymoon had begun. I gave up, embarrassed and angry, and disappeared to the bedroom.

I spent most of my wedding night alone, wrapped in a broken dream.

Giselle: I felt so betrayed.

'I'm your mother now,' said Ash's mum.

She wrapped her arms around me and drew me close. I was a lump of stone. I had a mother of my own. Ash's mother was trying to welcome me into her family but her words were the final straw. They deepened my guilt at having betrayed my mother and father. I had only excluded them from this day in the belief that Ash and I would be telling both our families that we had eloped. I had ended up surrounded by his family, his friends, while he laughed, joked and celebrated the big day with his loved ones. Meanwhile, my family were oblivious to it all. How could I have let this happen? They would be so hurt when they found out. They would be so insulted. How could I break it to them?

'Giselle,' Ash shouted. 'Try this!'

He held a fork in his right hand. There was food hanging from it and his left hand was cupped under it. I accepted the morsel. It tasted like lint.

After the ceremony, we had returned to the house Ash shared with his mother. A table in the middle of the living room groaned under the weight of food that one of Ash's friends had prepared. It was a lovely gesture and under any other circumstances I would have been delighted.

But there was no longer anything about this day that could make me happy. I felt isolated. Apart from Ash and his mother, I knew only one other person in the room, and then simply as a passing acquaintance. Everyone was talking, laughing and having a good time. I couldn't wait for it all to end.

Mercifully, the party eventually started to break up. Each of the guests came forward and formally thanked me for inviting them to my wedding. I tried to smile. Courtesy demanded it, but *it was a wan smile with no sincerity in it. How could it be otherwise? When the last guest had left, Ash dropped another bombshell.*

'I've prepared the room,' he said.

'What?' I demanded.

'Our room. I've prepared our room. We'll be staying here,' he replied.

I was aghast. His mother had busied herself clearing the now-empty dishes from the table. She looked happy, as if things had worked out the way she wanted.

'This is your home,' she said.

And then I realised. This was not going to be just for one night. This was, Ash believed, the way we were going to live.

'I want to go home,' I said.

'This is your home.'

'My home,' I answered. 'I want to go to my home.'

Ash realised he had gone too far and backed down.

'Tomorrow,' he said, but I knew he didn't mean it.

I went into the bedroom, shut the door separating me from Ash and his mother, and tried to gather my thoughts. I reasoned that I couldn't just walk out of the house and go home there and then, but I was determined that my stay would last no longer than one night. After a little while the door opened quietly and Ash entered.

'Time for bed,' he said with a self-conscious smile.

I undressed slowly. By the time I was changed, Ash was already in bed. I slid in beside him and he put his arms around me. I spent my wedding night with my mother-in-law in the next room. It just felt so wrong.

The following morning I was awake before daylight. Ash was still asleep as I fled from the flat, leaving my wedding dress

hanging in the wardrobe. For all I know, it may still be there.
The second I was in the safety of my own home, I pulled the
wedding ring from my finger and hid it behind the clock on the
mantelpiece.

I never wore it again.

7

The Honeymoon
Is Over

'Once they had control, there was no need of a
mask.'

Ian Stephen

June: It wasn't long before Rab was laying down the rules.

I folded the aluminium foil with care around the top tier of
my wedding cake. Tradition demanded that it be preserved
and brought out to celebrate the christening of our first born.
Generations of brides had done the same.

I could hear Rab's voice raging from the living room.

'Your cousin! Who the fuck does he think he is? Telling me
how to treat you?'

I ignored him, shutting out his anger. I was clinging to the
legacy of goodwill and happiness from yesterday, hoping that
I could carry it into today. It was a forlorn hope. It had not
taken long for the old Rab to reappear. We had been home for
only a few minutes when he exploded. I had gone to bed
alone the night before, exhausted and confused, leaving Rab
drinking into the night. I was weary. It had been such a long

day that I immediately fell into a deep sleep. It would have taken a bomb to wake me.

My first recollection of morning had been hearing Rab's snores. The curtains were drawn and the room was gloomy. My eyes were gummed with sleep. I saw him in the half light, lying next to me. He had managed to take off his wedding suit, which had been pristine the day before but now lay in a crumpled heap. He was lying on his back, his mouth gaping. Our first morning as a married couple and I was already burdened by regret. I leaned across, nudging his bicep, and he awakened with a final ear-splitting snore.

'Wha …? he said.

'Time to get up. We have to get home.'

Rab never had any trouble getting out of bed. My words had barely died when he slid from beneath the covers and padded to the bathroom. I rose and dressed quickly. I'd shower when we got home.

My cousin Joe was already up. I could hear him in the kitchen and the smell of bacon greeted me as I made my way down the stairs.

'Awright, lass?' he said as I entered.

'Fine, Joe,' I said.

'How's that man of yours?'

'On his way down.'

Rab entered the kitchen.

'Gimme some tea,' he ordered.

Joe poured it into a mug and said, 'Get that down you and I'll get you up the road.'

When we were settled at the table, Joe broke the silence.

'You know how much I love June,' he said to Rab.

Rab grunted into his tea.

'So I want you to look after her,' Joe went on.

His voice was calm but his words carried a veiled threat. Rab grunted once more. Joe rose from the table.

'I'll get the car,' he said.

Half an hour later we were on the road to Kilbirnie. When we arrived I invited Joe in for a cup of tea but he was anxious to get home. Rab had remained silent while in his company, but the moment Joe left he began ranting about my cousin's 'warning' to look after me.

'Nobody fuckin' tells me what to do!'

Before he could work himself into a fury, I retreated to the peace of the bedroom, taking the top tier of my wedding cake with me. It was now enclosed in the tin foil and secreted beneath the bed. I had made a special wish for a child not yet conceived. I returned to the living room with a heavy heart.

'You're my wife now,' shouted Rab. 'I'll fuckin' make the rules.'

His words lacked the subtly of my cousin's.

Rab's warning was all too clear.

Giselle: I hated having to lie.

'Where were you yesterday? I was trying to get a hold of you.'

Katie's question brought me out in a cold sweat. I would have to lie to her for the first time in my life. My eyes were drawn involuntarily to the mantelpiece.

'Were you away for the day?' Katie went on.

My eyes were still fixed on the mantel clock and the secret that lay behind it. I felt as if the hidden ring were glowing and that it would, at any moment, attract Katie's attention and expose me. Don't be daft, I thought. I shrugged mentally, pushing away the nonsensical thought. This wasn't an Alfred Hitchcock film.

'Ash arranged a day out,' I heard myself say. It was only half a lie. 'I didn't get back till late.'

'Anywhere nice?' Katie asked.

'Just round and about.'

A proper lie. I was ashamed but Katie was satisfied.

'I'll put the kettle on,' she said, rising from her chair.

I exhaled. How was I going to keep this up? The thought of telling lies to my family made me sick to my stomach. I was disgusted with myself. I leaned forward and buried my head in my hands. Katie's departure gave me a few moments to reflect. It was a ludicrous and unnecessary situation. Few people will recognise, let alone understand, my dilemma.

I knew in my heart that my mother and father – and brothers and sisters – would forgive me anything. All I had to do was throw myself on their mercy and tell them I had let them down. That would have been the rational thing to do. I could explain that I, too, had been duped; that I had believed it would just be me and Ash at the wedding.

But I persuaded myself that it was too late now. Ash had betrayed me. His mother had not only known about our wedding; she had been the guest of honour. I feared the effect it would have on my parents if I came clean. I would have died with shame at the thought that they believed I had deliberately excluded them.

I know it was incredibly stupid of me to think that way. They would have accepted my explanation, but I was racked by guilt. I didn't want them to think I had betrayed them. I had spent my life protecting and caring for them. I could not bring myself to disappoint them, even for a second. Silly, I know, but that was the corner I had boxed myself into.

Katie emerged from the kitchen, carrying two mugs of tea.

'There you go,' she said, handing one of them to me.

'So where did you get to yesterday?' she asked.

My head swam. I was raising the mug to my lips, trying to buy time, when I heard the key turning in the lock. Ash! My stomach somersaulted. The living-room door opened and he stood in the doorway.

'Hi Ash,' Katie said.

'Hello,' he replied.

My eyes bored into his, willing him to say nothing. How was I going to escape exposure?

Katie saved my life.

'God, is that the time?' she said, looking at the clock on the mantelpiece. 'I'm late. I'd better run.'

She leapt from the chair, grabbed her handbag and made for the hallway.

'See you later,' she shouted as she closed the front door.

My relief was immense. Ash didn't speak at first. He went to the chair opposite me and sat down with a heavy sigh. I said nothing, waiting for him to break the silence. I was still angry. I loved him but at that moment I didn't like him. He had let me down, very badly. How could I trust him again?

'Giselle,' he said.

I held up my hand. 'Don't! There's nothing you can say.'

'But Giselle, let me explain,' he pleaded.

'There's nothing to explain. You lied.'

'No! I wanted to surprise you, to make you happy.'

'I was surprised, Ash, but you didn't make me happy.'

He slumped back, bludgeoned by the truth.

I went on quickly, 'You had no intention of us living together as man and wife in our home. You decided that I would live with your mother, in her home.'

Ash interrupted. 'When my father left us, I promised I would care for her.'

'I want you to care for her,' I told him. 'I wouldn't have it any other way. I wouldn't hurt your mum for the world. But you made decisions without asking me. I won't have that. We're married now and I love you. We should have a normal life. We can look after your mum and have our own home, and our own family.'

'Mum says she will go into a home so that we can be happy.'

I was puzzled. 'How could that make me happy? I don't want her in a home. I want her in her own home with us looking after her.'

'I promise,' he said. 'It's going to work out.'

He rose from his chair and joined me on the sofa, putting his arm around me and kissing me.

'It'll be all right,' he soothed.

It was difficult to resist Ash and I felt the anger seeping out of me. I kissed him and said, 'Are you hungry?'

'Starving.'

'I'll make something to eat,' I told him.

I kissed him again, this time on the forehead, and went to the kitchen. I took a pack of meat from the fridge and laid it on the work surface. I took potatoes from the vegetable rack and piled them into a colander. I was switching on the cooker when I heard the chirrup of Ash's mobile phone. A few moments later he appeared at the kitchen door. I stared at him. He looked defeated.

'It was Mum,' he said.

As I turned back to the cooker, I heard the front door close behind him.

———————

8

The Way It Is

'Men like Rab and Ash often have difficult relationships with their mothers. Insecure to a paranoid degree, they must control at all times, at all costs.'

Ian Stephen

June: I learned to live on a knife edge, but it would soon be no longer just about me.

We had been married for only a few months and I had already learned hard lessons. The most important was not to challenge Rab when he was in what I began to call his 'black mood'. To do so was a cardinal sin, an act of defiance he would not tolerate. When he was in a fury, it was simple. I stayed out of his way if I could, if he would let me. There was no escape if I was the focus of his rage, which would detonate with the suddenness of an explosion. The distance between Rab's brutish behaviour and the deep well of anger that provoked it was veneer-thin. One minute he was almost affable; the next he was a caged beast trying to batter its way to freedom.

I was learning to judge the mood, recognise which Rab was coming through the door. Later, much later, after he had taken my children, Rab's behaviour would be tentatively diagnosed as 'morbid jealousy syndrome' by the eminent forensic psychologist Ian Stephen. But if it had been suggested to Rab that he was suffering from any form of psychological disorder he would have killed the bearer of such news with his bare hands.

Those who suffer from the condition have a complete but delusional belief that their spouse is unfaithful. I was never unfaithful to Rab but, looking back, it explains so much about his behaviour and that first 'smack' he had given me.

However, until I had his ring on my finger, I had only glimpsed the man behind the mask. Once we were married, Rab had no more need of any disguise.

'What's that filth on your fingers?' he would demand to know.

'What filth?' I replied.

'That shit!'

He was talking about the varnish on my nails.

'It's nail polish,' I said quietly.

'Get if off!'

'It's only nai—' I started to say.

'Get it *off!*' he bellowed. 'Whores paint their nails. Wives don't!'

That was an end to nail polish.

His notion of how 'whores' behaved extended to my hair and my clothes. I wasn't allowed to wear jeans and, according to Rab, only prostitutes wore high-heels. He took control of how I thought, how I looked, how I acted. The one task I was allowed to do on my own was the shopping, which Rab regarded as 'women's work'.

However, even that mundane excursion could not escape his paranoia. I would be putting the groceries into cupboards when the interrogations began. They could go on for hours. Whom had I met? What had I said? What had they said? How did they look at me? How did *I* look at them? It was as if Rab believed that a visit to the shops was my opportunity to find a new man.

'You were a bit dressed up just to go to the shops,' he would say after every trip to the supermarket.

'No, I wasn't!' I would reply.

By now I was especially careful about my appearance, but my considerations were not those of a normal young woman – or man. I did not look at my reflection in the mirror and ask, 'Do I look good?' I was establishing whether or not I was dowdy enough to placate Rab. In fact, any visit to a mirror could be construed as a sin, as far as he was concerned. One day he 'caught' me brushing my hair.

'Who are you trying to look good for?' he said.

'I'm getting ready for work.'

'Who are you meeting?' he demanded, his voice rising.

'No one. I'm going to work,' I said, turning from the mirror.

He moved so quickly that I didn't see the blow coming. I felt the impact of his fist glancing off the side of my face. Rab turned away angrily, as I stumbled and slid down the wall.

I heard the front door slam. I remained where I was for several minutes before rising and going to the bathroom. I flicked the light switch, my eyes closing in the sudden bright-ness. I shuffled to the sink and the mirror above it, dreading my reflection. I brushed my hair from my eyes and saw the tender red patch on my cheek. I must have moved my head involuntarily at the moment Rab lashed out. Thankfully, this blemish, while painful, could be hidden. I would soon become adept at hiding bruises with clever make-up and pathetic excuses.

Why put up with such a life?

I hear you scream the question. It is one I have asked myself more times than I care to remember. Millions of abused women, from every walk of life, ask themselves that same question every day. None of us has the real answer because there is no answer. Was I afraid of people telling me, 'I told you so!'? Yes, I was. Was I afraid to admit I had made a dreadful mistake? Yes, I was. Was I afraid of being left alone? Yes, I was. Desperately so. And on top of all this, there was my granny's famous bed. I had made it. I would have to lie on it. I had no choice but to get on with it. That's the way it was.

I was neither blind nor stupid. I saw other married couples who lived another kind of life, one that seemed happier and more contented. It was not my life. I had no illusions. Rab was undemonstrative, incapable of affection. That was the least of his sins. We did not make love. We had sex when he demanded it, no matter how I felt.

In time, his sexual demands would assume a more sinister and violent nature.

I would, in the meantime, have to learn how to live on a knife edge. I tried to make the best of everything and there were moments of light in the darkness. I learned to take pleasure from the small things, like when we moved into our first real home, a two-up-two-down in a terrace in Brownhill

Drive, Kilbirnie. I threw myself into making the house as nice as I could, in the hope that it might become a proper family home. This was no longer just about me and Rab.

He was going to be a father.

———————————

Giselle: I had my own special news and I prayed that, at last, it would cut the apron strings.

'Ash, I have something to tell you,' I said.

He had arrived from work moments earlier. I had watched him from the kitchen window of my flat as he left the post office and entered my building. He was barely in the front door and was still struggling out of his coat.

'What?' he said, a look of alarm creeping into his eyes.

For weeks now, I had been nagging at him about the strangeness of our life, demanding that it change, that he display a greater commitment. I had also told him that I didn't know how much longer I could put up with the situation. We had been married for two months and he was still returning to his mother each evening.

'What have you got to tell me?' Ash asked.

He was looking more worried. I think he believed I was about tell him that it was all over. I took a deep breath.

'You're going to be a daddy.'

His face froze and then dissolved into an expression of unadulterated joy. He was crying.

'A daaa-dddy,' he said, savouring the word.

He was almost dancing as I ushered him into the living room. I was happy for the first time in weeks. I had been living in this *state of tolerable unhappiness, the anger building in me because of Ash's apparent inability to cut the apron strings that bound him to his mother. In that moment my anger drained. I don't think I have ever seen another human being so happy. I couldn't help but be infected by it. I laughed with him.*

'If it's a son,' he said excitedly, 'we'll call him Matthew, after the apostle. I'll send him to a private school and, when he's 18, I'll buy him a Mercedes.'

He was almost shouting.

I put my hand on his shoulder and said, 'Whoa, I'm just two months pregnant. Give us a chance – and anyway, what if it's a girl?'

'Girls love their daddy,' he said with enthusiasm. 'Girls give their father respect.'

Ash was overjoyed. I shared his joy. I was going to be a mother and the knowledge overwhelmed all of my misgivings.

'When did you find out?' Ash asked.

'I think I've known for a while, but the tests confirmed it.'

I had realised that I had conceived on our wedding night. After all the trauma and unhappiness of that day, something wonderful had come of it.

'Wait till Mum hears,' he said. 'She'll be so happy for us.'

'I know she will,' I said.

Ash's eyes took on that faraway look. He was conjuring up new dreams.

'We'll get a shop,' he said. 'Mum can make her special dishes and you can sell them in the shop. My son – or my daughter – can help out after school. It'll be a proper family business.'

It was typical of Ash to transform the news that he was to become a father into yet another flight of fantasy.

'Let's just have the baby first,' I said, trying to bring him down to earth.

'I can't wait to see Mum's face,' he said.

The constant references to his mother rekindled my fears. Surely this would be the turning point? Surely now he would realise his place was beside me as a husband – and a father? He could not now desert me and run home to his mother. It occurred to me that, once again, she would celebrate this landmark before my own mother. The weight of secrets and lies returned to my shoulders. I couldn't keep a pregnancy secret. It changed everything. Living a double life had been draining me.

Why, oh why? It's so baffling. Even now I don't understand it. I loved Ash so much that I was prepared to put up with this sham of a life and hide it from those I loved. The longer you live a lie, the more difficult it is to tell the truth. I would have to tell my family about the baby, but I didn't know if I could bring myself to tell them about our weird living 'arrangement'. I was struck by a new fear. When they learned about the baby, they would inevitably want to know when I was getting married. I could almost hear Ma's voice: 'I'll need to buy a new frock for the wedding.' My heart sank. Another impossible situation.

I was dragged back to the present by Ash saying, 'I want to go and tell Mum now.'

He was putting on his coat, muddling up the arms in his excitement.

'No,' I said. 'Phone her later.'

'Yes, yes, okay.'

I pushed him down onto the sofa.

'I'll put the kettle on,' I said.

I returned a few moments later. Ash greeted me with a broad smile.

'Wonderful, wonderful,' he murmured. 'You've made me so happy. We'll always be together. I love you so much. I'll never let you go.'

My spirits soared. I snuggled beside Ash and allowed myself to enjoy the happiness of the moment, confident in the future. The following two hours passed in a happy blur. What did we talk about? I don't recall. I only remember the atmosphere. I felt safe, wanted, loved. Everything was going to be all right now. We lapsed into a contented silence.

'Fancy another cup of tea?' I said. Ash nodded.

I went into the kitchen. The kettle was coming to the boil when I heard the familiar ring tone of Ash's mobile. It was a sound which had always made me despondent. Not this time. This time it was different. I was pouring water into the mugs when I felt Ash's presence behind me. I turned. He was standing in the doorway. His expression told me everything I needed to know.

'No,' I said. 'Not now, Ash, not now.'

He was shamefaced, his eyes cast down at the floor.

'She's my mother,' he said quietly, without looking up.

9
Even in Darkness

'June and Giselle had seen something in these
men and they were praying it would return.
They didn't want to believe they had got it so
wrong ...'

Ian Stephen

June: Didn't the sight of your baby take away all the pain?

Elton John was crooning about a baby with blue eyes, eyes
that changed the world, held back the pain. His words seemed
to have been written for both of us.

His voice was flowing softly from a hospital radio speaker
above my head. My baby cried. The sound was a moment of
joy. Every woman who has given birth will know what I mean
when I say that the first cry of a newborn has the power to
heal. We are all familiar with the old story of how the discomfort of pregnancy and the pain of childbirth are obliterated
by that blessed noise. My Michelle wiped away more than
mere physical distress. As I held her in my arms she made me
feel whole again.

My life with Rab had been filled with torment. So I listened to that song and looked at my child, drinking in every tiny, perfect feature on my daughter's face. I knew that to find hidden meaning in a pop tune written by a superstar who did not know I existed was the result of a combination of confused hormones and sentimentality. I didn't care. It was a time to be sentimental. It was a time to surrender to emotion.

I was cradling my Michelle, the most beautiful baby in the world. She had the biggest blue eyes. They looked at me trustingly from a gentle face, framed by blonde curls. She was perfect. No one could steal this moment from me. Not Rab, not anyone. She was barely an hour old. My lovely child had arrived early, 28 weeks into my pregnancy. She weighed less than 5lbs and for the first few days of her life she would have to stay in a special unit at Paisley Maternity Hospital.

It was a miracle she was here. I had threatened to miscarry several times and I had to spend long spells in hospital, another source of irritation to Rab because his routine had been disturbed. His dinners were not on the table.

I was still lost in my daughter when a voice said, 'She's a beautiful wee thing.'

It was the nurse whom I had come to regard as my guardian. She had popped her head round the door of the room.

'Isn't she a wee cracker?' I answered.

'Yes, she is,' said the nurse. 'You've done really well.'

She left a word unspoken, hanging at the end of the sentence, but her meaning was clear. I heard the word in my mind as 'considering'. This nurse had already crossed swords with my husband and let him know in no uncertain terms what she thought about him and his selfish behaviour. Rab had acted like a pig, a chauvinist pig, according to the no-nonsense nurse.

'When the fuck are you coming home?' he demanded to know one day. 'There's fuck all wrong with you. You've got housework to do – and me to look after!'

The nurse flew at him.

'Your wife is very ill, Mr Thomson,' she told him in a voice laced with anger and disgust. 'If she doesn't rest she could lose the baby!'

Rab ignored her but he shot me one of his venomous looks.

'Tell *her* you're feeling okay!' he said.

The nurse interjected, 'We've had quite enough of you, Mr Thomson. Time you weren't here. You need to go now. June needs her rest.'

Rab seethed. He knew enough not to take on this formidable woman. This wasn't his wife he was dealing with. He stalked out of the room without another word, to the accompaniment of my silent cheers. The nurse's eyes followed him. She turned to me and said, 'Rest!' It was an order. If only I could take this woman home with me.

Sooner rather than later, however, Rab would be back in control. It was inevitable. The nurse couldn't protect me for ever. And, of course, Rab did get his way. On subsequent visits to the hospital he would wear me down to such a degree that I signed myself out.

I had only returned to the hospital when my contractions began. My special guardian had been waiting for me.

'Nearly there, June?' she said. 'Where's your husband?'

As if she cared.

'He's in the waiting room,' I told her.

'Right, let's get you ready, and you can bring him in for a little while,' she said.

I was still in a ward. They hadn't yet taken me to the delivery room.

'My contractions seem weaker,' I told the nurse.

'It happens with first births. It might be a while,' she said. 'Best thing is to rest and we'll keep an eye on you.'

Rab appeared at the end of the conversation.

'Stay with June for a few moments,' the nurse said to him in an icy voice. 'It's unlikely she is going to give birth tonight. You should go home and let her rest. If anything happens, we'll call.'

Rab didn't need to be told twice. He was out of there as fast as his legs could carry him. The nurse smiled at me, a smile that said I was better off on my own. As it happened, I would give birth that night, in fact not long after Rab left. The nurse stayed with me the whole time.

She was now looking down at me and my new child. She was the perfect nurse. You get a sense when someone has found their true vocation.

'You're lucky to have her,' she said and bustled away, no doubt to comfort some other new mother.

She had never spoken a truer word. My threatened miscarriages were only part of the story. There was that other, darker reason why I was grateful Michelle had been born safe and well.

When I had first told Rab he was going to be a father, he had been delighted and for a little while the violence ceased. Well, that's not exactly true. He was just more careful where he struck me.

But midway through the pregnancy I had the temerity to argue back when he was berating me. He pushed me down a flight of stairs. I tumbled head over heels, my face unguarded because my hands had flown to my stomach to protect my unborn child. I lay at the bottom. He made no move to help me. His face was impassive, contemptuous. I rose painfully and fled from the house, dreading that the fall had damaged the baby. The fear haunted me throughout the remainder of my pregnancy.

When I first held my Michelle, my fear was lifted. She was perfect and I had her to myself, revelling in the first precious hours of her life. Rab had yet to see his daughter. He was still at home. He hadn't made it for the birth. Oh, the promises I made to that child. I promised she would never doubt my love for one second. I promised to care, cherish and protect her. I was not being sentimental. It was the truth.

Michelle erased my troubled childhood, my life with Rab, my inability to break free of his control. She made me happy and whole. I realised for the first time that I understood the meaning of love. How could I, with all my frailties and failings, have made something so wonderful? I kissed my daughter's head and pledged that I would never allow anything bad to happen to her.

It was a promise I could not keep.

———

Giselle: I was afraid I would never hold my child.

Panic. Something was wrong. Loud electronic beeps shattered the silence. Ash's expression changed from bored resignation to concern.

'What's happening?' I demanded.

A midwife raced to the monitors.

'Get the doctor,' she told a nurse, who ran off down a corridor of Glasgow's Princess Royal Maternity Hospital.

Ash jumped to his feet but the midwife motioned for him to stay back.

'What is it?' he said.

She didn't answer. Her eyes were fixed on a monitor.

'Listen, Giselle,' she said. 'Everything's under control. I think we're going to take you to theatre, right now.'

It was my turn to panic.

'Why?' I asked, my terror rising.

'There's a bit of difficulty with the baby's heartbeat,' she said.

'Do something!' Ash begged.

'We are!' said the nurse.

It was controlled chaos. I was surrounded. The doctor arrived, said something, and the bed began to move. I closed my eyes tightly. When I opened them I was in an operating theatre. Ash was hovering on the edge of the crowd. The medical team worked at lightning speed, transferring me to a surgical table. The doctor had gowned up and looked down at me, his lips moving behind a surgical mask. From the corner of my eye I saw Ash being helped into green 'scrubs'. His body language spoke of fear and confusion. His face was ghostly white. The medics talked in clipped tones. Please God, I thought, let my baby be all right.

I had not been due to give birth until Christmas. It was 1 a.m. on 29 November. My son was arriving a month early.

A voice said, 'It's okay! Don't worry. The pain will go away!'

Numbness had already begun to creep over me. Soon it was as if I had left my body. My mind, however, remained sharp and began running over the previous eight months. It had been a difficult pregnancy right from the beginning. I had been unwell *from day one. My 'morning sickness' would last all day, every day. Within 24 hours of breaking the news to Ash that I was pregnant, I awoke to find myself covered in an angry, red rash.*

Sweet Lord, I thought. I knew German measles when I saw it. Like every other mother-to-be, I had read the horror stories about the effects it could have on an unborn child. The infection can pass through the mother's bloodstream, causing congenital rubella syndrome, the consequences of which are potentially devastating. I was terrified. The doctors were not much help. They were split over the risks. One said I should consider an abortion. Unthinkable. Another said that it was too early in the pregnancy for the risk to be significant. To his credit, Ash agreed that there was no way I could have an abortion.

'No matter what,' he said, 'we'll love the baby.'

Ironic, isn't it? That he should show compassion to an unborn child whose life he would take when it was alive. We submerged our fears while waiting for Paul to arrive. The first scan, at 20 weeks, revealed a boy.

Ash was ecstatic.

'A son,' he said. 'To carry my name.'

The pregnancy may have been dogged by illness but I cannot remember a happier time. My joy spread throughout the family. Apart from Ash, Katie had been the first to know. The news struck her dumb. She couldn't speak, she just ran to tell everyone else – and buy enough baby clothes to deplete Mothercare stocks for at least a month. My niece, little Giselle, spent her pocket money adding to my unborn son's wardrobe.

'Jeans and baseball boots!' I said to her, when she arrived with the world's smallest denims and 'sneakers'.

They looked as if they might have been stolen from a doll.

'He'll look cool,' she said.

Explanation enough.

Giselle was still at school, with an ambition to become a hairdresser – which she is now – and I had visions of my son sporting some very spectacular hairdo as soon as he had enough hair.

Gifts poured down on us. Ash's mother bought a pram. Katie arrived with a 'bouncy chair'. My mum now had a legitimate reason for haunting her favourite shops, returning each time with another 'wee something' for the baby. It was a time of undiluted joy.

I had still not told my family that I was married and I hated keeping that a secret, especially now. Looking back, I realise how crazy this must seem to an outsider. I cannot explain it, even to myself. Ash's behaviour was the reason for my reticence. He was solicitous and caring, a master of ensuring I was comfortable. He even trimmed my toenails when I was too 'big' to reach them. He was, however, still going home to his mother. I loved this man. I was having his child. And yet he denied me what I wanted most. My mind filled with forlorn hopes. I believed that when we had our baby it would change everything. We'd all live happily ever after.

'Giselle!'

The voice brought me back to the moment. A man wearing a surgical mask said, 'You have a beautiful boy ... he's perfect!'

'Let me see him!'

'Give us a moment,' the doctor said.

I watched as the tiny, bloodied baby was lifted clear of the green tent that covered the lower half of my body.

'Ohhhhhhh,' I whispered.

A sudden terror.

'Why isn't he crying?' I demanded to know.

'Give him a chance,' said the doctor, a smile in his voice.

Then I heard the loveliest sound in the world. My baby was crying, and by the sound of his voice he had a healthy pair of lungs. Paul's cry was a song sung by an angel. Ash mopped sweat from my brow. The nurse brought Paul to us. My arms were a forest of drip tubes. Ash took our son and held him up for me to see. He was crying at the sight of his son.

How could I know? How could I see the future?

I don't know how long I lay there. Time had lost meaning as we gazed at our boy.

'Let's get you back to the recovery room,' a nurse said as she whisked Paul away.

'Give him back to you in a minute,' the nurse said.

When he was returned to us in the recovery room I told Ash, 'Unwrap him. I want to see every bit of him.'

Ash unravelled the white blanket and Paul's arms reached for me. I counted his fingers and toes. I searched for any sign that he had been affected by the measles. He was beautiful. He glowed. He was barely 6lbs but he was strong and sturdy. His oval face, with its tiny, perfect features, was surmounted by a thatch of dark hair.

Ash was looking at him with a sense of wonder. 'I'm going to send him to private school,' he said.

It was still all about Ash and what he wanted.

'He can have a Mercedes for his 18th birthday,' Ash continued.

'Enough,' I said. 'Let him grow up.'

Ash turned to the nurse and said, 'I want to bring my mother to see the baby.'

'She can see him tomorrow.'

'I want to bring her now.'

'Giselle needs to rest. She's had major surgery. The baby needs to rest.'

It was half past two in the morning and she was not inclined to indulge Ash's unreasonable request.

'You get home,' she said. 'And let us look after Giselle.'

Ash kissed my forehead.

'See you later,' he said.

I was returned to the ward. I felt exhausted, but the last thing on my mind was sleep. I just wanted to look at my baby. Despite all my joy, I was sad. Ash hadn't said he loved me. Or that he was proud of me. What could I do if he didn't want to be a proper husband? All I could do was promise to be everything I could be for my baby. I repeated that promise over and over as we lay in the silence of early morning. I laid my hand on Paul's chest and felt the rhythm of life. I was drifting into sleep when the silence was shattered by the sound of a phone ringing. I knew instinctively who it was. I glanced over at the nurses' station and in the half-light I could see the hands on the clock standing at 3 a.m.

I heard the nurse say, 'Hello', and then, 'Sorry, no, you can't bring her just now.'

'No,' she repeated in a firmer voice. 'Everyone is sleeping.'

The phone was replaced and I waited. The nurse appeared. Before she could speak I said, 'I'm sorry. That was Ash?'

'It's okay,' she said. 'Sleep!'

I lay back, disappointed. It was all about Ash and his mother. I closed my eyes – until a voice whispered 'Giselle'. I awoke. The clock hands had reached 6 a.m. Ash was standing over me.

'Look who's here,' he said.

His mother was standing behind him. I was still gripped by sleep. She was cooing with delight, speaking to her son but not to me. Ash lifted Paul from the crib and handed him to her. He said something I couldn't understand, and she laughed. Ash and his mother conversed in Punjabi as she only had a basic grasp of English. She hardly left the house except to go to church and his devotion to her meant she lived a cloistered existence. I think that suited Ash. He had always kept me at a distance from her. When I tried to get close to her, the language barrier intervened. However, I did not need a translator to know that she was over-joyed by her grandson. Ash delved into his pocket and produced a camera.

'Take our picture,' he told his mother.

I felt self-conscious. Obviously, I wasn't looking my best.

'Ash,' I said. 'Give me a minute.'

He wasn't listening. He stood in front of me, excluding me from the picture with his body. He smiled broadly, presenting his new son to the camera.

When the picture was taken, he said, 'Now you!' to his mother.

He handed Paul to her and took a picture of her and the baby. He then put the camera back in his pocket.

I felt like crying.

Ash was making soothing sounds and 'mugging' faces for the baby.

'Did you phone my mum or Katie?' I asked him.

Ash didn't take his eyes off Paul.

'No,' he said.

'Who did you call?'

'Just my mother.'

———————

10

Nothing Ever Changes

'The trap closes ... Now they have an even greater emotional attachment.'

Ian Stephen

June: I thought everything would change when I brought her home, but ...

'Where's the fucking key?'

Rab was angry. We were at the front door of our house. The journey in the car from Paisley had been awkward and silent.

'It's here somewhere,' I said. 'Here, hold the baby.'

He took Michelle. She squalled.

'Where's the fucking key?' he asked again, his impatience growing.

'It's here,' I said, rummaging in my bag.

The angrier he became, the more fearful and clumsy I got.

'Oh, for fuck's sake,' he said. 'Here!'

He foisted Michelle back into my arms and reached into his own pocket, retrieving a key and unlocking the door.

'Stupid bitch!' he hissed.

He stomped into the hall, leaving me on the doorstep. Rab's delight at seeing Michelle in the hospital was but a memory. Only a few weeks had passed since her birth. The real Rab had quickly subsumed the proud father who had been a shy and uncertain creature when he was introduced to Michelle. A smile had softened his features, and when he picked up his tiny daughter he seemed almost afraid. The nurses weren't fooled. They had heard the harsh words he had spoken earlier.

'They told me you wouldn't have the baby,' he said – as if it were my fault, as if I had deliberately excluded him from the birth.

'How long are you going to be in this place?' he asked.

'A couple of days yet, but Michelle will have to stay till she's a bit stronger.'

Michelle's early birth meant she would remain in the special baby unit for two weeks. I would go home without her.

On the day I had to leave her I was dressed and ready when Rab arrived to take me home.

'About fucking time,' he said as he led me to the car.

That was two weeks ago, a period that had been hell without my child. Mothers are not meant to leave the hospital without their babies. The house, with its atmosphere of worry and uncertainty, had seemed an empty place. Rab had been uncharacteristically quiet, at times even gentle. He, too, was worried. We travelled to Paisley every day to visit Michelle. With the medical staff looking on, Rab was forced to modify his usual behaviour. Now that we had brought Michelle home, the scrutiny had ended and the pressure was off. Rab reverted to type.

'What's for tea?' he said.

'Give me a chance,' I replied wearily.

'What did you say?' he roared.

I recognised the menace in his voice and it made me even wearier.

Nothing ever changes …

———————

Giselle: *You hope … and then you realise some things never change.*

The huge blue teddy bear masked my sister. At least, I assumed it was my sister. I could only see her legs.

'Surprise!' she shouted.

It was indeed Katie, emerging from behind the biggest cuddly toy I had ever seen. Little Giselle brought up the rear, clutching a similarly sized creature, a giant snowman with a wizard's hat perched on his enormous head. Ma followed, bearing a bouquet of flowers and yet more baby clothes.

'Where's Ash?' Katie asked.

'He's away,' I said. 'I'm sorry he didn't call.'

'It's okay, I called the ward,' she said.

'Ma, I'm sorry,' I said to my mother.

'It's all right, pet,' she said.

Katie dumped the giant bear in a corner.

'Don't worry about it. Ash must have had such a lot on his mind,' she said in a voice that dripped sarcasm.

Every eye went to the crib.

'Look at him, Ma,' I said.

My mother looked at her grandchild. She laid a hand on her breast and inhaled sharply.

'Oh, my!' she said. 'Just look at you!'

'Isn't he beautiful, Ma?' I asked her.

'Better than beautiful,' she said.

Katie and little Giselle peered over her shoulder.

'You're a clever girl,' Katie said to me.

'Those jeans will look fabulous,' little Giselle said. 'And look at that hair!'

We had a fit of the giggles. My niece had been marking off the days until she could get her hands on Paul and play living dress dolls. Our laughter rang round the ward, sweeping away my disappointment at Ash's behaviour. I had my son and I was surrounded by my family.

One by one, the others came to greet their newest member. According to them, Paul was variously the handsomest, most contented, best-behaved and utterly adorable child who had ever been born. I could only agree. With each passing moment, I loved my son more. His dark eyes never wavered from me. He was as transfixed by me as I was by him. I had never felt so needed.

My family left as they had come, one by one, and Paul and I were alone.

'Won't be long before you take him home,' the nurse said.

I longed for the moment. The next three days seemed to be endless, but eventually Ash arrived to take us home. I made my way slowly to the car park. I was still in pain and my stomach felt tight and hot. Ash gently placed Paul in a baby seat. I rolled down the window and fresh air washed my face. I hadn't realised how dead the air in the hospital had been. When we arrived at my flat, I settled Paul in his cot and began unpacking.

'I have to go and get Mum,' Ash said. 'She wants to see the baby.'

'Okay,' I said. 'Hurry back. I need help.'

'Won't be long,' he said.

He returned with his mother within the hour. They crowded around Paul in his cot, talking to each other in Punjabi. I was happy for Ash's mother. She seemed so pleased. She stayed for no more than an hour before she asked Ash to take her home.

'I won't be long,' he told me.

'Okay,' I said, waving them off.

He returned to find me in tears, standing in the bedroom beside Paul's cot.

'Giselle, what's wrong?'

'I'm in pain from this scar,' I told him. 'I'm scared I won't be able to get up, to hold the baby or feed him.'

'You'll be fine,' he said dismissively.

I had placed Paul's cot in my bedroom and pushed it up against my bed. He was sleeping soundly. Ash left me and went into the living room. I heard his mobile ring. I retreated from Paul's cot and returned to the living room, where Ash was putting on his jacket.

'Where are you going now?' I asked.

'Home,' he said.

'You're at home.'

'Mum needs me.'

'What about me and the baby?'

'Mum comes first.'

'Before your wife and baby?'

'Yes,' he said. 'She always has. She always will.'

He walked to the door.

Nothing ever changes ...

11

Behind Painted Smiles

'Stripped of their own personalities, these women can express only what their husbands allow.'

Ian Stephen

June: I was walking a tightrope and I didn't dare fall.

I played the role of two very different women.

To the outside world, I was the proud new mother, accepting the good wishes of those who peered into the pram and congratulated me on my daughter. Within the walls of the prison Rab had constructed around me, I was the captive to be terrorised, humiliated and abused. I should have had friends to call on for support, but Rab had long since systematically separated me from them, a process that began the moment we married.

No one was 'good enough'. My pals were dismissed as 'sluts' or 'idiots'. If they called the house, he ranted until it became so embarrassing that I cut short the conversation. If I didn't, he'd force me to hang up. Even if it was my sister,

Linda, he'd snatch the phone from my hand and tell her, 'She hates you. You know that, don't you? And never wants to see you again.'

Linda knew I had said no such thing, and that we could speak only when he was not at home. Of everyone who was close to me, only she knew an approximation of the truth. I couldn't bear to tell her everything. I was ashamed. I had been warned, hadn't I? Wilma's words continued to haunt me. I recalled her face, dappled by the light from the circling glitter ball above our heads in the dance hall where I met Rab. *'He's a pig!'* her phantom voice told me.

How right she had been, but it was too late now. My only other friend was Carol. She and I had been at school together. She, too, was a comfort to me and she had the advantage of being acceptable to Rab because she was married to one of his friends. For that reason, if no other, I obviously couldn't tell her everything.

Rab was the least sociable of men, but when I was allowed into company – of his choosing – he demolished my self-esteem. He revelled in using social gatherings to dominate and demean me. If I dared to offer an opinion, he dismissed it as 'stupid' or 'ignorant'.

'Who asked you to speak?' he would bellow. 'I never gave you permission to talk!'

He would turn to the company and declare, 'I picked her out of the gutter. She'd be fuck all without me.'

I would cringe and those around us would fall silent. No one would speak; no voice would be raised on my behalf.

When we were alone, he would tell me, 'You're a nutter. I could get you sent to the nut house. They'd lock you up, throw away the key. All it takes is one phone call.'

I began to experience what I now know to have been panic attacks. Faced with the unpredictability of Rab's behaviour, I lived on the edge of my nerves. Which Rab was going to come through the door? The one who tortured me with taunts, or the drunk who beat me with his fists? I had nowhere to go. His family was out of bounds and my family still believed that he was a good husband. My dad would have been distraught and angered by my plight.

So, I played the happy wife. I couldn't allow Dad to believe I was anything else. If he had suspected the truth, he would have challenged Rab and it would have led to a confrontation. Rab was a brute. He would have thought nothing of hitting his father-in-law. I couldn't risk Dad getting hurt. Rab had already assumed control over every aspect of my life, and now that we had a child my job was to look after him and the baby, in that order.

He must have been delighted that I was largely confined to the role of a housewife. His jealous outbursts about my work-mates had ceased now that I was a stay-at-home mum. However, any attempt to deviate from that role provoked a fury of kicking doors, smashing furniture and punching holes in walls. The neighbours must have heard the noise and seen the marks on my face, but no one did anything. Rab's reputation preceded him. Who was going to challenge this violent, hulking brute?

When I was in the house I learned to walk softly. When I made my brief escapes to the outside world I strode with apparent confidence, wearing a painted smile. I did take delight in showing off my daughter, and in the moments we were alone I held her close to my breast, taking comfort from her. My smiles for her were real.

'I have a surprise for you, baby,' I told her. 'Mummy has a secret!'

Michelle was barely eight months old and I was pregnant again.

This time it would be a boy and I would call him Shaun.

Giselle: Playing happy families almost cost me my life.

Paul was growing.

My healthy, happy and contented son was now eight months old and I cherished every minute with him, particularly after the realisation of just how quickly I could be separated from him for ever. From the moment I had returned home from the hospital with Paul, I began to suffer complications from the birth. My legs ballooned and the caesarean scar was extremely painful. My consultant insisted that I return to the hospital each morning for injections to help reduce the swelling and control the infection, which he suspected was causing the problems.

'Don't miss an appointment, Giselle,' he warned me. 'Or we'll probably have to bring you in. It's also vital that you rest. You've been through a difficult delivery.'

I had been debilitated by pain and tiredness, but the thought of leaving my son and going back into hospital terrified me. I lived in a state of fear. Ash had revealed his priorities and I was constantly worried that ill health might prevent me from being able to care for my son. I was determined to get on with it and allow nothing to interfere – until yet another of Ash's flights of fantasy led to a 48-hour nightmare that almost robbed Paul of his mother.

I had returned from one of my morning visits to the hospital to find Ash sitting on the sofa, waiting for me.

'Ash?' I said, looking at my watch. It wasn't lunchtime. 'Is everything okay?'

'My sister's coming up from Oxford,' he said without ceremony. 'To see her nephew.'

'That's great. I'd love her to come and see us,' I said.

'She can't come here,' he replied.

'Why not?'

He didn't answer and then he stuttered, 'We have to take her out … show her the sights …'

'That's a problem, Ash. I'm ill. I need to go to hospital every day for a jab. The doctors insist on it.'

'You can miss a couple of days.'

'I can't. They've told me I can't miss a single day – and I've to take plenty of rest. But there's nothing to stop your sister coming here.'

He jumped up as if he had been scalded.

'No! No! You must bring Paul to Mum's.'

'When is she coming?' I asked.

'Today!' he said.

'Aaaa-sh!'

'You don't want to meet my sister? You want to shame me?'

'No, Ash, but I'm unwell.'

'Okay, you can go to the hospital,' Ash said. 'But you must come to Mum's.'

I was too tired to argue. I capitulated. I could see he was relieved. I didn't yet know why.

'Bring the baby's stuff,' he said.

I gathered Paul's clothes, nappies and bottles, and we left for his mother's house. When we were there, Ash and his mother seemed to be on edge. I understood why when his sister arrived. She was a strikingly good-looking woman who was obviously well off. I knew from the way Ash had spoken of her in the past that she was a success and I had the impression that he was jealous of her. My belief was reinforced when I saw them together. He was ill at ease, almost in awe of her. She had brought a bag of beautiful clothes for Paul.

I thanked her and Ash said, 'Put them in the baby's room.'

He smothered my hesitation by taking the bag and going to his bedroom. I watched as he opened the door. Beyond him, I saw an ornate and expensive cot. I rose from the chair and followed.

'This is where the baby sleeps,' he said loudly. 'Beside us!'

I looked at his mother. Her eyes were cast downwards. I was puzzled.

'Ash,' I said. His eyes warned me to 'play along'.

I looked in disbelief at the cot. It was a traditional wooden one, complete with a padded 'bumper' and matching bedding. A mobile was suspended above the headboard. The ensemble must have cost hundreds of pounds. It was certainly a lot more expensive than the cot Paul slept in at home. There was also a 'bouncy chair' – again an expensive one. Ash opened the wardrobe and laid his sister's gift beneath a hanging collection of my clothes. He had obviously taken them from my flat. I hadn't even realised they were gone. I was astonished. I knew then that he had created a charade of happy family life for his sister's benefit.

'Time for dinner,' he said, ushering me from the room, with another warning look.

I struggled through the next several hours, unable to believe the lengths to which Ash had gone to persuade his sister that we were all living together. I wondered why he had done all of this.

Dinner was a strained affair and, not long after it was over, I was able to plead tiredness and retreat to my bed. My exhaustion was not a part of the charade. I was worn out and feeling ill.

'I'll be in soon,' Ash said. 'My sister wants to go shopping tomorrow. We'll all go together.'

I was too tired to reply. I crawled beneath the covers and was asleep before Ash came to bed. I awoke next morning, feeling even more unwell than I had the day before. Ash was already up and dressed, and preparing to go out.

'We're going to Braehead,' he said, referring to the massive shopping mall near Glasgow Airport.

'What about the hospital?' I said. 'My injection?'

'Do you really have to go?' he said in a wheedling tone.

'Yessss! I have to go every day.'

Ash chatted with his mother and his sister while I bathed and fed Paul. Then I showered and dressed as quickly as I could. Each movement was torture.

When I emerged from the bedroom, Ash said, 'You're ready, then. We've been waiting.'

His voice was heavy with impatience.

As we all headed to the car, he said again, 'Do you really need to go to the hospital?'

I'd had enough of this!

'Take me there, now!'

Ash exhaled loudly, started the car, and we drove the short journey to the hospital. They waited while I went inside. When I returned Ash was drumming his fingers on the steering wheel.

'Are we finally ready to go?' he asked.

Neither of the women spoke. I felt two inches tall. The next few hours were a torturous trail around every shop in the mall.

By the time Ash's sister announced it was time for her to leave for the airport I was almost on my knees. I was wincing with pain as I said goodbye to her and watched as she disappeared through the departure gate. I turned to Ash and begged him to take me home.

'Mum, first,' he said.

I was too ill to argue. I fell into the car and held on to Paul's baby seat. The journey to the flat seemed to take forever. When we arrived, Ash didn't move. He watched me struggle with Paul and his pram.

'You might have made more of an effort for my sister,' he said over his shoulder.

'Ash, just leave me alone,' I replied wearily.

By the time I got into my flat, my clothes were soaked with sweat. I managed to undress Paul, get him into bed and strip off my wet clothes. I threw on a dressing gown and took our clothes to the washing machine. As I bent low to throw in the soiled garments, the stitches on my caesarean scar ruptured.

I screamed as gouts of blood spurted from the wound. The world went black. Before I sank into unconsciousness I heard myself pray, 'Don't let me die.' When I revived I found that I was lying on the floor. I could only have blacked out for a few seconds. I began shouting for help and I was crawling towards the front door when my neighbour burst in. Thank God for thin walls and for not locking the door after I had struggled in with Paul.

'Giselle! What's happened?' she shouted.

'Ambulance, get an ambulance!' I told her.

She ran to the phone and punched 999. She disappeared, returning with a towel.

'Hold this! Tight!' she said, thrusting it into my stomach. 'The ambulance is on its way.'

'Call Katie,' I said, struggling to stay conscious.

I drifted between consciousness and unconsciousness, hearing only parts of her hurried conversation with my sister. Katie was visiting Ma. She was in the next block. She would probably get here before the ambulance. *She'll look after Paul*, I thought, before I drifted away again.

The white towel had turned red by the time two paramedics and Katie arrived simultaneously.

Katie ran to me.

'I'm all right! See to Paul,' I told her.

I felt anything but all right, but my greatest anxiety was for my son.

'Caesarean?' one of the paramedics asked me. I nodded.

'Relax, we'll get you sorted.'

Katie reappeared, holding Paul. She was angry.

'Where've you been?' she asked.

'Ash's sister was visiting. I've been trailing round Braehead.'

'This is *his* fault!' she said.

Katie didn't know the half of it. I was too tired and too sick to explain.

'Do you want me to phone him?'

'No!' I told her. 'What's the point?'

The ambulance wailed through the city. At the hospital I was rushed into a treatment room. I was still semi-conscious, almost unaware of the doctors and nurses. Later, when the panic was over, one of the doctors arrived at my bedside.

'Just as well we got you when we did or it might have turned out very differently,' he said. 'There was a nasty infection in your wound. We've managed to bring it under control.'

'Am I going to be all right?' I croaked.

My throat was dry.

'Absolutely!' he said. 'You'll be fine, now. We just have to keep an eye on you for a while. Is there anyone we can phone? Your husband?'

'My family know where I am,' I said quietly.

'Fine,' said the doctor. 'You'll be with us until the antibiotics kick in. I'll be back in the morning.'

I couldn't sleep. Paul was safe with Katie, but I fretted. The endless night eventually passed and the doctor returned.

'I don't want to stay. Can I go home?' I begged.

'We'd really like to keep you in.'

He saw my disappointment.

'You're only going to lie there and worry, aren't you?'

My eyes answered.

The doctor looked at my chart and said, 'Tell you what. Give it a few more hours and we'll see.'

'Thank you,' I said.

'If I let you go, you must promise to rest?'

I would have promised to sell my soul to be at home.

'Okay, let's look at it later and, if there's an improvement, we'll phone your husband,' he said.

'No! My sister! Call my sister,' I told him.

'Okay,' he said.

Four hours later he returned, and I stitched a smile on my face that I hoped would persuade him that I was on the mend.

He took my pulse and checked the chart.

'Antibiotics seem to be working,' he said.

'Can I go home?' I pleaded.

'I'll make the call,' he said.

An hour later, Katie picked me up. We must have looked like a doddering old couple making their slow and painful progress to the car park. I was so relieved when I walked through my front door and I heard Ma's voice saying, 'Here she is!'

She was holding Paul.

'Hello baby, I've missed you,' I told him.

Ma and Katie were reluctant to leave, but I was feeling better already and I ushered them back to their own homes after they had elicited my assurance that I would phone them immediately if I needed help. I was on my own when Ash marched in through the door.

'Where have you been?' he demanded to know.

'Hospital,' I said. 'My stitches burst.'

He looked at me intently.

'Where have you been, really?' he said.

'The hospital,' I repeated.

'You haven't been there.'

I was aghast.

'You weren't very nice to my sister, you know.'

'I nearly *died* being nice to your sister.'

'Show me.'

'Show you what?'

'The wound!'

I opened my dressing gown, revealing the bandage covering my scar. He was placated but there was no apology for his appalling insensitivity.

'Let me see my son,' he said.

'He's in there,' I told him.

I could hear Ash talking to the baby.

Ash's 'conversation' with Paul was interrupted by that damned ringing of his mobile. He emerged from the bedroom. I made up my mind in an instant.

'Go home to your mother,' I told him.

It was the first time I had stood up to the situation. It was a turning point. I could not end our marriage, or throw him out of my life. We had a son. We were bound together and, for now, I would make the best of it.

'See you tomorrow?' he said.

_____

12

A Deeper, Darker Place

'While Rab's morbid jealousy caused him to lash out with escalating violence, Ash's character was just as black but he – mostly – kept it hidden.'

Ian Stephen

June: Rab took his dark games to an even deeper level.

'In there!' he said.

Rab had a fistful of my hair, propelling me along the hall to the bathroom.

'No Rab, please,' I pleaded.

'*Fucking get in there!*' His grip tightened.

Behind us, the door to the living room was closed. Television sounds, muffled, distant. I managed to turn my head. Rab's face. Dead eyes. Was that a smile? A grimace? What did it matter? This was now Rab's new 'game' – yet another means of torture and control.

'They'll hear!' I beseeched.

'Keep your fucking mouth shut, then.'

His voice was cold and hard. He hadn't been drinking. He battered me when he was drunk; he raped me when he was sober. The drunken Rab would at some point lapse into a stupor and there would be respite. The sober Rab was in control of himself and me, and there was no mercy. I put up my hand against the jamb of the door, a pathetic attempt to halt the inevitable. Rab booted open the bathroom door and hurled me against the sink. My hands shot upwards, grabbing at the window ledge. The door slammed shut and I heard the sharp snap of the lock.

'Stay quiet,' I told myself. 'Please God, don't let my children wake, don't let them hear this.'

Michelle, who was three years old now, was no longer my only consideration. She had only been 16 months old when I gave birth to Shaun. Since the arrival of our second child, normal sex no longer seemed to be enough for Rab. These 'episodes' came out of the blue, every few months. There was no pattern to them. He would arrive home from work, usually after I had put the children to bed. Without a word, he would grab my hair and march me to the bathroom, the only room in the house with a lock. With his children sleeping, only I could see Rab for the monster he was. Michelle and Shaun were, mercifully, sleeping now.

I had earlier lifted them from in front of the television. I allowed Michelle to be mesmerised by cartoons for half an hour before bed. Shaun was only eight months old and didn't understand what was going on, but he loved the music and his eyes delighted in the bright colours on the screen. The cartoons were still playing. The sound was a dull throb through the wall. The crazy music and wild screams of the characters were an incongruous accompaniment to what was unfolding in this confined space.

Rab knew my fears, my desperation to protect the children, and he played on it. My unease only heightened his 'pleasure'.

'Take off your clothes!' he demanded.

I hesitated.

'Take them off! Or I'll rip them off.'

He took hold of my hair, dragging my face to within inches of his own. I was trapped. In the beginning I had struggled, but I learned that resistance was futile and it only prolonged the inevitable.

'Do it!' he said, and released me.

I undressed, the shame of it burning my face. It was over quickly and he left. I slid down the wall, hunkered in the corner and gathered my clothes about me like a shield. I knew, cowed as I was, terrified, battered and devoid of confidence, that I could not put up with much more of this. I left the bathroom and tiptoed down the hall, past the closed door of the living room.

Rab was in there. I could hear him laughing at the cartoons.

Giselle: I thought I knew this man, and then the mask slipped.

'Look at me!' Ash roared.

I had never heard this voice before.

'Speak to me!'

I looked straight at him. He was furious. His features were contorted. I had never seen this face before.

'*Do … not … ignore … me!*' *he snarled, drawing back his right hand. I watched his arm arc in slow motion and then with lightning speed his hand struck my face. I fell onto the cushions of the sofa.*

'*Now, see to the baby!*' *he said, turning on his heel and heading for the door.*

Paul was lying beside me on the sofa. He was crying, a sound that would ordinarily have had me picking him up immediately. I could not move. I was stunned. I had never before in my life been struck by anyone; not by my father, my mother or even at school. I grew up in a world where violence against women was anathema. Now it had happened! The mummy's boy, the pious Christian, the obsequious Uriah Heep, who was forever in awe of authority, had done what no other human being had ever done. I was more shocked by his action than the force of his blow.

The slam of the front door brought me to my senses and I reached for Paul. I held him close and soothed him. I stood, catching sight of my reflection in the mirror over the mantel. It revealed a red weal on my cheek in the shape of Ash's hand. I paced the floor, shushing my son. He was getting heavier. He had been weighed that morning at the health centre. My routine visit to the baby clinic had begun the chain of events that had just ended with Ash assaulting me. How had it come to this?

The weather had been bright and clear when I left the flat with Paul in his pram. I was striding along towards the health centre which was in sight when I heard the toot of a car horn. I had been lost in thought and the sound made me jump. Ash had pulled up at the kerb.

'*Where are you going with the baby?*' *he asked.*

'The health centre,' I said, nodding at the building.

'Something wrong?'

'No, just to check his weight.'

'Want a lift?'

'No, I'm almost there. See you later.'

I made to walk on and he said, 'I'll give you a lift.'

I kept going. 'Ash, it's just there.'

'I'll wait.'

'It's fine. You don't have to!'

I went into the clinic. It didn't take long for the nurse to confirm that Paul was a fine, healthy boy. When I left, Ash was waiting.

'What did they say?'

I smiled.

'Your boy's blossoming.'

'Get in,' Ash said.

'For Heaven's sake, Ash. I've been stuck in the house. I want some fresh air.'

Ash drove off. I was within yards of my building when I saw his parked car. He was leaning on the driver's door.

'He's my son, too,' he said in a cold voice. 'Give him to me!'

'What's wrong with you? Of course he's your son,' I said, mystified.

Before I could say more, Ash snatched Paul from the pram.

'Ash!' I said.

He ignored me.

'Ash! Give him to me.'

I tried to take the baby but Ash was too strong. He pulled open the car door and strapped a howling Paul into the baby seat.

'What do you think you're doing?' I said.

He slammed the door shut. I stood helpless as Ash drove away. I screamed but there was no one to hear me. I made a frantic effort to stay calm. It never occurred to me to phone the police and I didn't even consider the possibility that Ash would harm Paul. The only thing I could think to do was to race home and call Ash on his mobile. It went to voicemail. I paced the floor, eventually throwing myself down onto the sofa, where I spent the longest hour of my life. Then I heard the front door open. Ash marched into the living with a screaming Paul in his arms. He laid him on the sofa.

'Take care of the baby,' he ordered me.

I experienced relief and anger in equal measure. I couldn't look at Ash, couldn't speak to him. I turned away from him in defiance.

'Look at me,' he said.

When I did, it happened. The mask of the charmer slipped away so easily.

What lay beneath it was ugly.

June: I started to believe there was only one way out.

'If you try to leave me, I'll kill you.'

I believed every syllable of Rab's threat. There was no emotion or anger in his voice. He might have been telling me the time or asking me what was for tea. It was said quietly so that Michelle and Shaun would not hear. They were playing a few feet from us, laughing and carefree. In spite of the 16-month age gap between them, Shaun was developing much faster than his sister. In fact, he was overtaking her in many ways. Michelle struggled to sit properly, and her speech and interaction with people were markedly different from her gregarious brother.

A mother knows when something is not right with her child. No matter what, she was adorable, a child possessed of a wonderful innocence. There was no point in expressing my fears to Rab. He may have been their father, but he played little part in their early lives. It was I who read to them, played with them and nurtured them. Rab was the classic good provider. He believed his role was to put food on the table. He never failed in that duty. Even monsters can be hard-working. Rab was distracted by Michelle's shrieks and, when he turned back to me, he still had the cold look in his eyes.

'Remember,' he said. 'Remember what I've said.'

I had pre-empted Rab's threat to kill me just the day before, when I tried to take my own life by swallowing pain-killers. The most recent rape episode had sent me to a dark place. I wanted to pack my bags, take the children and leave, but it was as if Rab could read my mind. He was watching me like a hawk. I was at his mercy, utterly and completely alone. I began to believe that death was my only way out. I reasoned that Linda would look after Michelle and Shaun if I wasn't there.

And so, the day before his threat, I awoke to the noise of children playing outside, a sound which, until then, had always filled me with happiness and a sense of contentment. I don't know why but on that day the sound deepened my depression. Something snapped. As the day wore on, all I could think of were Rab's taunts and the wicked things he had done to me. I accepted that there was no one to help, no escape. The only power I had was to end it.

A plan took shape. I fed Shaun and Michelle.

'Give Mummy a smile,' I told them.

Shaun shouted 'Doggie!' and waggled a toy in my face. Michelle laughed.

'C'mon,' I said.

I gathered Michelle in my arms and Shaun toddled behind me. We went next door to my neighbour. When her door opened, I made a monumental effort to smile.

'Can you watch them for me?' I asked. 'For an hour or so? There's something I need to do.'

My neighbour welcomed in the children.

'No problem,' she said cheerily.

I hugged Michelle and Shaun, kissing them for what I believed would be the last time. The door closed on them and I retraced my steps into the house, which seemed so still and quiet, but for the phantom echo of my children's laughter. I walked into the kitchen and opened a drawer. Two bottles of painkillers were hidden at the back. They had been there for weeks, out of sight of Rab and the children. I struggled with the caps on the bottles but I soon had a mound of pills on the table. I ran a glass of water and began swallowing them, one after the other.

I sat back and waited to die.

As the pills took effect, I was seized by the realisation that my children might be brought to the house and see their mother lying dead. I had to get out. The pills disorientated me but I managed to stand. I knew where to go. I stumbled out of the back door and across a field to a lonely place my children could not reach.

I would die here.

I lay on the grass, resting my head against the cool earth. Wild flowers swayed in the breeze. I closed my eyes and prayed for my pain to end.

Then the dream began.

Rab was standing over me, hurling imprecations, demanding that I come back. He must love you, a voice told me. He must love you, it repeated. He doesn't want you to go. He needs you.

'I can't come back,' I told the voice. 'It's too much, I'm so tired.'

I felt as if strong hands had taken hold of me, hoisting me to my feet and shaking me violently.

'What the fuck are you playing at?'

It was Rab's voice.

'Rab,' I slurred, as I felt my feet leave the ground.

I floated forward.

'Leave me. I want to sleep.'

The farmer's field swam into focus. I wasn't dreaming. Rab had found me. I was being dragged through a topsy-turvy landscape. The trees were enormous, the grass alive at my feet.

'Bastard!' I heard Rab say. 'What the fuck are you doing to me?'

Big hands shaking me like a rag doll. No words of sympathy. No kindnesses. Just fury.

We were at the house.

'*Gerrin' there!*'

He threw me through the door onto my hands and knees. He grabbed my hair. My head snapped back. I was propelled towards the kitchen sink. I saw his hand reach out and turn on the tap. Water rebounded from the sink onto my face. I closed my eyes.

'Stop!' I begged.

'Put your fingers down your throat!' he shouted.

I couldn't feel my arms.

'Make yourself sick!' he ordered, pulling back my head.

My arm weighed a ton but somehow I managed to obey. My stomach erupted and I choked, gasping for air.

'Stupid fuck!' he said. 'You stupid fuck! I'll kill you if you show me up.'

I laughed. Black humour. I had tried to save him the bother of killing me and still he was angry. There was no pleasing some people. I laughed again.

'Why didn't you just leave me?' I gasped.

After what seemed like an eternity, the world swam into focus. I was slumped on the kitchen floor. I could hear Rab on the phone. Respectful voice. Snatches of conversation. 'Paracetamol', 'Accident', 'Taken by mistake', 'Didn't realise she'd taken too many.'

Rab was calling a doctor.

He returned, his face black with anger, and sat at the table. I pushed myself off the floor and leant against the cabinet under the sink. Every part of me was sore. My hair was soaking, my eyes hot, my throat burning. Rab didn't speak. He was made from stone. I didn't dare say a word. He was galvanised by a knock on the door. He leapt to his feet.

'Gerrup!' he shouted over his shoulder, making no attempt to help me.

I struggled to the chair in which he had been sitting, resting my elbows on the table and dropping my head into my hands. Voices in the hall. Rab appeared, followed by a doctor I did not know. A locum?

'Mrs Thomson,' he said.

Doctor's voice. 'What's happened, then?'

Before I could speak, Rab said, 'She had a bad headache and before she realised what she'd done, she took too many painkillers.'

'Mrs Thomson?'

Concern with a question mark.

'How many did you take?'

Rab was looking over the doctor's shoulder, his eyes boring into mine.

'A few,' I said. 'I brought them up.'

Rab interjected, 'She's been sick so there's no need for hospital, or anything.'

The doctor pulled back my eyelids and then took hold of my wrist.

'You're pale,' he said quietly. 'But your pulse is normal. Are you sure everything is all right?'

Rab tensed.

'No, no, my silly fault. Didn't realise how many I'd taken.'

The pill bottles were gone. Rab must have removed them.

'We have to be careful. How many did you take?' the doctor asked.

'About half a dozen,' Rab said quickly.

'Did you lose consciousness?' asked the doctor.

'No!' Rab said. 'She just felt sick.'

'Are you sure that's all you took?' the doctor asked.

'Just a few,' I said. 'It was a mistake. Felt a bit ill. I'm feeling better now.'

'Maybe we should get you to hospital, to be on the safe side,' the doctor said.

'June hates hospitals,' Rab said.

I took his lead. 'I'm fine, honestly, don't want to be a nuisance.'

'If you're sure ...' The doctor's voice trailed off.

'I'm sure,' I said. 'There's no need for hospital.'

'Well, you might feel a bit nauseous for a while. Get yourself into bed, have a rest,' the doctor said, his hand reaching for the handle of his medical bag.

He hoisted the bag from the table and said to Rab, 'Look after her, Mr Thomson.'

'Oh, I will, doctor. Don't you worry about that,' Rab replied. He was smiling. His wolf's grin.

Giselle: I had a way out now, but could I take it?

I couldn't erase the memory of Ash's angry, snarling face.

The phone calls had begun less than an hour after he struck me. I ignored them, allowing them to go to voicemail. The phone would ring all night, the messages piling up – whining apologies, expressions of remorse and regret. I listened to them but I did not call back.

In the days that followed, the shrill ring of my mobile would become the soundtrack of my life. It was always the same number on the screen. Ash left message after contrite message. The physical sting of his blow to my face had diminished, but the psychological effect lingered. I was not inclined to forgive. In fact, if I had told my father and my brothers what Ash had done

I would have feared for his safety. But I did not tell anyone. Yet another secret kept from my family.

When I failed to respond to his calls he appeared at the flat. I had applied the deadlock. His key was useless. I stood on the other side of the door, listening to his plaintive entreaties.

'You don't understand,' he would say. 'I'm under so much pressure. I'm so, so sorry. Forgive me!'

When that did not move me, he would walk away on leaden feet. Minutes later my phone would ring. Ash would be downstairs in his car. I knew that at some point I would have to speak to him but I was not ready to offer him a way back. I held out for another week. I was putting Paul to bed when the phone rang yet again. This time I answered. There would be no peace otherwise.

'What do you want?' I said coldly.

'Giselle!' he said, surprised and grateful that I had answered.

'What do you want, Ash?' I repeated.

'Oh, Giselle, can you forgive me? I don't know what came over me. I'm under so much pressure.'

I laughed. A hollow sound.

'What kind of pressure, Ash? I don't put you under pressure. You come and go as you please. You use me. And now you've hit me. I won't have that.'

'I'll never do it again,' he whined. 'I miss you and the baby so much. Please, please, let me come back. It'll be different. Mum still says she'll go into a home, so we can be together. I promise we'll get a nice house and everything will be all right.'

The familiar litany of empty promises.

In spite of it, I felt myself weaken.

'I don't want a nice house. I – we – have a nice house. This is good enough. I don't want your mum to go into a home. I just want to be normal.'

I could hear the whine in my own voice and I hated myself for it.

'All I ever wanted was for us to be an ordinary family,' I told him.

'We will be, I promise,' Ash said. 'Give me another chance.'

And like a fool, I did.

———————————

13

If Only ... (June)

'Rab had stripped June ... of everything.'

Ian Stephen

June: If I could not kill myself, there was only one other option.

Rab lay on the couch in a drunken stupor. He was snoring, each laboured breath reeking of alcohol. He was still in his working clothes, which smelled of lime and sweat. His strong arms and grimy hands were crossed on his chest. He looked at peace, but even in repose his face was still cruel. I knew from experience that he wouldn't waken for some time, long enough for me to kill him.

I shook. From fear? No, from the weight of the shotgun that I held inches from his face. The gun swayed. It was so heavy. I prayed for the courage to pull the trigger. Icy beads of sweat trickled down my back. I looked at the man who controlled my every waking moment. The vibrant, independent girl I had once been was long gone, replaced by this broken woman. I had become an empty shell. Rab had rendered me useless and made me mortally afraid.

I had pledged in church to spend the rest of my life with this creature, but so much had happened since I stood before the altar in my borrowed wedding dress. His sneering voice and hard fists had battered my promises to death, broken me and killed my spirit. He had never once told me he loved me but I had seen much evidence of hatred. The beatings. The rapes. Not even the knowledge that he had fathered my children was going to save him.

They were in bed. I had read them their favourite stories and kissed their sleepy heads. I hoped they would not wake when I killed their father.

Now, it was just me and Rab.

The house was silent. I had taken the keys from his pocket. The smallest opened the padlock on the door of the metal gun cabinet. Rab's shotgun sat upright. A box of cartridges lay beneath it. He had once shown them to me, taunting me about what he would do with them if I left him. They were red and smooth, almost like lipstick cases, but I had witnessed the damage they could inflict on the animals Rab shot.

It was now his turn.

I had been calm when I left my children. I was still calm when I selected the gun. I walked downstairs to the living room, hearing Rab's snores before I reached the door. When he had returned from work he finished the remains of a bottle of rum. In a normal household that would have merited a tongue-lashing from any wife. I knew better. I could tell, from his footsteps and from the way he swaggered into the house, whether or not I was destined for a beating. I had learned never to meet his gaze when he was angry. A dim memory from my child-hood reading warned me that in the animal kingdom the prey must never look into the eyes of the predator.

And Rab *was* a predator.

He had trapped me. My children were hostages, too. They depended on me; my son and my innocent, trusting Michelle. I had sacrificed myself on the altar to Rab's cruelty. The sacri-fice had now become too much to bear. I was relieved he had fallen into a drunken sleep. While he slept, my face would not be slapped. I would not be punched in the kidneys. I would not be violated.

I moved as if in a trance. Closer. Closer. The barrel almost touched his head. A voice, deep within me, said that this was madness. It was shouted down by the suffering me, the one who knew only fear. His eyes were closed. Even in sleep he exerted incredible power over me. My finger hooked the trig-ger. One squeeze, and it would be over. He did not stir, unaware of how close death was.

Do it now!

I couldn't! Tears of rage flowed. I was ashamed of my weakness. I couldn't pull the trigger, and I knew I never could. How many times in the coming years would I be haunted by the memory of my weakness, when I could not find the strength to do what had to be done, to send him to hell where he belonged? If I had known that, one day, he would rob me of my children, I would have sacrificed my life that night to save them. I would have killed him in a heartbeat and gladly spent the rest of my life behind bars. But I didn't know. How could I?

As I lowered the gun, I caught sight of my reflection in the dark window. I saw a dishevelled, unhinged caricature. Rab continued to sleep. He was right. I was useless, too weak to stop him, even with a loaded gun in my hands.

If only I had known ... if only.

14

This Child of Mine

'Rab believed the family could not survive without him at its head; Ash regarded his son as a possession.'

Ian Stephen

June: I couldn't die. I couldn't kill him – and now I had three children to think about.

'She's a beautiful child,' the doctor said.

Unspoken words hung in the air. There was something he wanted to tell us. I knew that I would learn nothing that I did not already know.

Rab was another matter.

The doctor, sitting behind his desk, offered a beatific smile to Michelle. Her eyes danced with delight. She held out her hands to him. It made him laugh. She chortled in response. Michelle was always on the cusp of laughter. She wore a permanent smile. She was the happiest of children, innocent, kind, gentle and loving – a perfect human being aged five and three quarters who had yet to learn to speak properly.

She badly wanted to. In fact, the only time the smile deserted her was when she was frustrated by her inability to communicate.

I had long since accepted what the doctors had told us. She had learning difficulties. She was disabled and she always would be. There was no cure. Rab would not accept that. He would point to Shaun and our new baby son Ross, and say, 'Look, there's nothing wrong with them.'

There wasn't. The newest addition to our family was perfectly healthy and developing normally, just like his older brother. Shaun might have been 16 months younger than Michelle but he was her physical and intellectual superior. He had walked, learned to talk and was toilet-trained well within the normal parameters. Michelle could do none of these things properly. She behaved like a toddler instead of a five-year-old.

The doctor said, 'She will require specialist care for the rest of her life.'

I could feel Rab tensing. His face was dark with anger. Until that moment we – or at least Rab – had entertained the hope, however slim, that Michelle's condition was 'curable'. He had insisted that we take her to doctor after doctor, therapist after therapist. They had all concluded that she would forever be a child.

'In the simplest terms,' the doctor said, 'the messages from her brain are not being transmitted to her body.'

This was the end of the line. Rab had to accept the inevitable, no matter how unpalatable it was to him. I had no problem with facing reality.

'*I don't believe it!*' Rab said through gritted teeth.

'I beg your pardon,' the doctor said.

'Rab!' I said quietly, laying my hand on his arm.

He pushed it away.

'There has to be something that can be done,' he said angrily. 'She isn't damaged!'

The doctor stared at him. 'Your child isn't *damaged*, Mr Thomson; she has special needs.'

I had heard Rab use many horrible, unrepeatable words for people who were 'damaged'. The thought of applying them to a child he had fathered appalled him. It was as if our little girl were an affront to him.

My Michelle was a joy. She might have been trapped in childhood, but she would do no harm, commit no wrongs and she would be driven only by love. I knew Rab loved her, but the truth was he was embarrassed by her. He would feel that embarrassment more keenly as she got older, even though she would make great 'progress'.

Before too long, she would be baby-talking and her speech would continue to improve, even though anyone listening to her would recognise that she had learning difficulties. She could talk with ease to other 'children'. She was, after all, one of them. Rab could not understand or accept that his daughter's physical age had no meaning. She would always behave with the joyful abandon of an infant. My Michelle had no sense of propriety.

When she got older, she would bound up to strangers, embrace them and demand to know what they were going to have for tea. She would stroke their clothes and compliment them.

'That's a lovely jumper,' she would say to one. 'I like your hair,' she would tell another. 'I don't like your hair,' she would tell someone else.

The immediate and natural reaction of people was to look askance, but they were soon captivated by her exuberance. It was impossible to be annoyed or insulted by her.

Rab hated it, of course. If she strayed from us, he ordered me to 'get a grip' of her.

'That's no way to behave,' he would say

As she grew and the child became a young woman, Michelle would not change. She would race to play areas to join the other 'children' on the swings and roundabout. She towered head and shoulders above them.

'She's too big for that,' Rab would snarl.

'No, she's not,' I would say.

He was watchful, discomfited, always looking for the reaction of other parents.

Rab was ashamed of his precious but imperfect daughter.

Giselle: I didn't seem to matter – all Ash wanted was his perfect son.

'You are my perfect boy,' Ash said.

If there were ever a father more proud or protective of his son, then I had yet to meet him – even though I couldn't look at him in the same light since I had allowed him back into my life. I call it a life, but it was in fact a limbo that I had been unable to escape. His assault had made me wary. I convinced myself it would not be repeated, but a thin thread of uncertainty now ran through everything. The uncertainty dissipated only when I watched him with our son.

We continued to live the charade. To the onlooker, Ash was the doting father, the attentive 'husband'. On the day I allowed Ash to walk back through my door the charm offensive he launched was so effective that he had me feeling almost sorry for him. The tears that coursed down his face were real. He held me and murmured apologies in a childlike voice. Ash believed what he was saying. I am convinced of that. He was contrite, ashamed and desperate to make amends.

I had told no one that he struck me or that he had run off with Paul. I bottled it up and so I did not have the sounding board of my sisters or my mother to guide me. In spite of the incident – and the fleeting crisis it had created – everything and nothing had changed. He would be there when Paul awoke. He would visit at lunchtime. When he finished work in the evening, he would make his way from the post office to 'our' home. He probably saw as much of his son as any normal working father.

The only difference now was that each night when his mobile rang and he made to leave, I no longer pleaded with him to stay. Ash the charmer seemed to be thriving on the lack of pressure and his diffidence began to evaporate. His flights of fancy returned, as did his arrogance. One of his bugbears was that I had been claiming state benefits. I had no alternative. I had never asked Ash for money and he had never offered it. If I had given up my benefits, it would have placed me completely under his control, and I had reached the point where I would rather cut out my tongue than ask him for anything.

'Why do you take money from the Government when I am going to be a wealthy businessman or an important lawyer?' he asked.

'It's simple. I need the money to live,' I told him.

'But I get you things.'

'You don't give me money.'

When Ash visited, he would bring baby food, toys and gifts, but if Paul needed something Ash would instruct me to go to a shop, choose what I wanted and tell the shopkeeper to 'put it behind the counter'. Ash would then go in and pay, and I would return and pick up the item. It was humiliating. I hated the way the staff in the shops looked at me, as if I was a visitor from the Middle Ages. Of course, I didn't want to exist on state handouts, but what choice did I have?

'You claiming benefits could affect my career, you know,' he would say.

Dealing with Ash's double standards and snobbery was exasperating, but I tried to ignore his prejudices. I did draw the line when he began sneering at the folk of Royston.

'I don't want Paul to speak with their accent,' he told me.

'You mean my accent?' I said.

I was not ashamed of where I – or Paul – came from. Royston is a community with a heart, where you are not judged on your salary, the size of your car or the value of your house.

'We should get a big house in Bearsden,' Ash said, referring to the salubrious suburb to the north of the city.

'Ash, don't!' I said wearily.

I may have tolerated – and often disliked – the Walter Mitty Ash, but I couldn't help loving Ash, the father. He adored Paul.

'We're going to do wonderful things. You are my very special boy,' he would tell Paul, holding him so tightly that our son would squirm.

When I tried to take Paul, to soothe him, Ash would say, 'No … no … no. Daddy will sort it.'

He couldn't, of course. When a child is upset it usually wants its mother, and I had the impression that Ash was envious of that special bond. He would relinquish Paul to me reluctantly and he was displeased when the baby's mood changed almost immediately. I think Ash came to believe that he was the only one who should matter to Paul.

This strange attitude manifested itself when we went on days out and he would try to commandeer Paul's attention. He was not only jealous of me but of little Giselle, who would often accompany us. She basically regarded Paul as 'her baby'. She was little more than a child herself and Ash should have been delighted by her devotion to our boy, but he was jealous of the relationship she had with Paul. Ash's jealousy was even more intense when he witnessed the very strong bond that had developed between Paul and my mother.

Ma loved music and she would sing children's nursery rhymes to him. Paul mimicked the words in the adorable way that infants do. Ash hated it. Whenever he saw them singing together, he would take Paul away to visit his mother. He became paranoid over how often my family saw Paul, insisting that every time he visited my parents or my siblings he had to visit his mother's home to balance things out. Ash's one-upmanship exasperated me. I tried to talk to him about it, but he seemed incapable of recognising anyone else's point of view.

'This isn't a contest,' I told him. 'Paul isn't a pawn in some kind of game. It's confusing him, making him unhappy.'

'My perfect boy isn't unhappy,' Ash insisted.

'You have to let him be part of a family. His granny, his cousins, aunts and uncles – they all love him,' I said.

'But he's mine,' Ash told me.

15

So Alone

'Rab physically isolated June. Ash detached Giselle from her family psychologically. For both men, it was ultimately about control.'

Ian Stephen

June: Then Rab took me away from everything I'd ever known.

Five times I had tried to leave. Five times he had forced me to return. Three times I had tried to kill myself. Three times I had failed. The statistics of despair.

I was so ground down now that Rab's workaday cruelties had lost much of their effect. From the beginning, Rab had assumed total control. He earned the money. Everything was in 'his name' – the bank account, the insurance policies, the mortgage. Even the care package that would be set up for Michelle. There was, of course, nothing to physically prevent me from walking out the door. Rab couldn't watch me 24 hours a day, but he had already warned me that I would never be allowed to leave. I believed him. Every attempt to escape came to nothing. Rab would find me and literally drag me back. I was paralysed by fear, shackled by an invisible chain stronger than any steel.

It was not just my fear that bound me to him. I had three children who had to come first. They loved their dad; they did not know the monster – yet. I was a hostage to their needs, particularly those of Michelle. She became deeply disturbed if there was the smallest change to her daily routine. I couldn't just flee. Michelle went to a special educational facility, the James Reid School in Saltcoats, a coastal town in North Ayrshire.

She loved it there. A taxi picked her up in the morning and returned her in the evening. Michelle responded wonderfully to the care she received. With the teachers' guidance, she blossomed. Her speech improved in leaps and bounds. She was able to forge friendships and develop social skills she could not have learned without their support.

To take her away from that would have been devastating. Nature had deprived her of so much. How could I think of robbing her of even more? If I did escape, where was she to be educated? There were so few schools catering for her needs. On one of the occasions when I did flee, Rab went to Michelle's school and asked her where we had gone. My daughter was incapable of telling a lie and she told him we were in a women's refuge nearby. That evening I was called to the public phone in the shelter.

'Look out of the window!' Rab's triumphant voice said.

He was outside in his car, smiling. He had proved yet again there was no hiding place.

On another occasion, the 'system' that is meant to support battered women actually worked against me.

During one of Rab's beatings I had run from the house and taken refuge in a different women's shelter. When I tried to begin the process to get legal custody of my children it was impossible because I did not have a 'proper home'. It was catch-22. Rab held all the cards. If I wanted to be with my children, I had to go crawling back and, inevitably, I did. What mother wouldn't?

In his warped mind Rab decided that if I were to be kept at heel he would have to isolate me even further. Michelle would be the means he would use to do it. He refused to allow her to go to school, claiming the regime at James Reid was exacerbating her disabilities.

'Michelle's not nearly as bad as the others. She's copying them! She's not going to get better if she stays there,' he said.

It was nonsense, of course, but it brought us into conflict with the local authority, which threatened legal action for keeping her away from school.

'They're not telling me what to do with *my* daughter. We're going to move to another area and they won't be able to touch us,' Rab said.

'Where are we going to go?' I asked.

'I've been looking at jobs in Fife,' he said.

Fife was on the east coast, 80 miles from where we lived on the west coast – a world away.

'Fife!' I said. 'It's too far. Who do we know there?'

'It's fucking settled,' Rab said.

He was killing two birds with one stone – escaping censure from the authorities and taking me away from what family support I had.

Rab did get a job, driving heavy plant machinery for a company on the outskirts of Kirkcaldy, the main town of Fife.

He organised a council-house exchange with an Ayrshire family that wanted to return home. The miracle was that we found a special school for Michelle – the Rosslyn School, which would turn out to be a wonderful institution that she would attend until she was 19 years old.

When we left Ayrshire, Shaun was eight and Ross was a year away from starting school. They had every child's ability of being able to adapt to new surroundings and they did so with ease. Any worries I had about Michelle were dispelled when she was quickly absorbed into the life of her new school. Rab had always been a loner so he, too, had no difficulty in embracing change.

I had never felt so alone.

Giselle: Ash couldn't take me away from my family … But I was distanced from them by even more secrets and lies.

My isolation was emotional rather than physical. June was treated cruelly, displaced deliberately and dragged from one side of the country to the other, far from her family. I experienced none of those things in an overt way apart from the single occasion when Ash had struck me. No matter what Ash said or did, I was never going to be pulled away from my family. But there were barriers, invisible barriers that Ash had forced me to construct. And soon there would be something else.

'I think we should get divorced,' Ash said one day.

'Divorced?' I replied, stunned.

'Yes. Being married might harm my chances of getting a loan. I need it for my new career.'

Where had this come from? And then I knew. He was still smarting over my refusal to give up claiming benefits.

'I can't apply for a loan if you are claiming benefits,' he said.

'There's no way that should affect your chances of getting a loan,' I said. 'We've never lived together as man and wife, but if you think that way then go ahead.'

Ash's 'business plan' turned out to be driving a taxi.

The family that had owned the shop where the post office was had sold the business and Ash was out of a job. He had joined a local mini-cab business as a self-employed driver. It should have been a good job, but like everything Ash touched it was less than a success. He spent more time annoying my dad and Tam than he did driving. He would phone them at all hours, asking for directions to streets in the city. My family bent over backwards to help, as they had always done.

There was one benefit. I did not need to find so many excuses for Ash's absences from 'our' home. Taxi drivers routinely work strange hours. It was a ready-made excuse, but it was also a double-edged sword. No longer bound by his 9-to-5 existence, Ash began to turn up at all hours. And with these new hours Ash's influence over me increased. At first I thought he was merely enjoying a new-found freedom, but it quickly became apparent that he saw it as a means to drive a physical wedge between me and my family in a way he had never been able to do before, when he was trapped at the post office. Now that he was working late shifts and night duty, he began exerting more control over how I spent my days. I realise now that Ash was every bit as controlling and manipulative as Rab. He just did it differently, with charm rather than violence. I was as trapped as June. The bars of my prison were just not so evident.

He demanded to be fed information about me every minute of the day, with interminable phone calls and inquiries about where I was, whom I was seeing and where I was going. It stopped only when Paul and I were in bed.

I was still hiding this strange way of life of ours from my family, and it isolated me even further. It forced me constantly to tell small lies about the simplest of things. Why was Ash not at home in the evening when Ma or Katie called? Where was he on a Saturday morning? A Sunday? Why did he not join in with the life of our family?

Ash and I would be invited to family occasions, but he would always refuse to go and I'd be left trying to find excuses that weren't hurtful to them. I was in a real cleft stick.

I'd hidden my sham marriage from them. Now I would have to conceal the divorce.

'I'll handle all the paperwork,' he said. 'After all, I know the law. I'm going to be a lawyer one day. I'll handle everything.'

If Ash had expected me to be upset about the divorce he was wrong. In many ways it was actually a relief. If I was divorced I'd never have to mention the wedding.

'Nothing needs to change. We'll just go on as we always have,' Ash said.

June: Rab knew now that when I fell there was no one to catch me.

If I had entertained hopes of making new friends then these were soon dashed. Who was going to speak to the monster's wife?

Moving me across the country wasn't enough. Now Rab had isolated me from our neighbours. He made it his business to be as obnoxious as possible to the families in the cul-de-sac we had moved into at Oswald Court in Kirkcaldy. He began castigating our neighbours' children if they were playing in the street, shouting threats at them and ordering them away from our house. One mother tried to remonstrate. At the time Rab was working on one of his DIY projects, using a portable electric sanding machine. When the woman spoke to him Rab towered over her, his face inches from hers.

He said, 'If you don't fuck off, I'll sand your fucking face!'

The poor woman bolted.

Rab loved a scene, shouting, swearing and menacing people. If he had a row with someone, when he returned home he plotted revenge. On one occasion this involved splattering paint over a neighbour's caravan. It got so bad that even the man who drove the ice-cream van refused to enter the cul-de-sac. The driver had warned Ross that it was dangerous to hang on to the side of the vehicle. When Ross innocently told his dad that he'd had a telling off, Rab went out and rammed an ice-cream cornet in the man's face and threatened to kill him.

As his notoriety spread, I became a pariah, which suited Rab. With no family and no hope of friends, Rab had me where he wanted. He lived in a perpetual rage and, if he could find no outlet, it was then directed at me.

His violence escalated. I was standing in the kitchen one day and he was berating me. He was holding a pair of pliers and he leapt forward, grabbing me by the nose with the tool. I was dragged around the room. The pain was excruciating and I still bear the scar. Even by his own standards, Rab was descending to new depths.

On a family outing one day we were walking beside a dam. There was a treacherous drop to my right. The children were in the distance, far enough away not to hear Rab's words.

'I could kill you here and now, and nobody would know,' he said.

He was gripping my arm and his fingers dug into my skin.

'Rab,' I whimpered, feeling the emptiness of the gorge behind me.

His eyes were hard, unfathomable black pebbles. I truly believed that I could count the rest of my life in seconds. My eyes must have reflected my fear. He looked into them, laughed suddenly and released me.

'Ha … fucking … ha. Only joking.'

He walked away. I could not follow. My legs wouldn't work. Mercifully, this new level of madness did not occupy every minute of the day. There were periods of calm and what passed for normality. Rab worked incredibly hard and he was paid well. It was inordinately important to him that he was seen as the *good provider*. He had to have a bigger car and spend more money than anyone else. As a result, we wanted for nothing in a material sense, but I could be punched one day and presented with a new gold chain the next. It was like living with a cobra. Would it dance? Or strike?

Such extremes of behaviour were never more apparent than when Rab bought a caravan and decided we would go on holiday to Perthshire. We set off on a clear, bright morning, and I hoped against hope for peace and normality. I should have known better. We arrived at the campsite and settled. I put the children to bed, and Rab and I sat outside in the fading light of a summer's evening. I can't remember what I said to provoke his anger but suddenly I was being punched. I escaped, crawled into bed and rose before first light. My face was a mask of bruises, my lips burst and my eyes blackened.

Rab snarled, 'Get the fucking kids up. We're going home.'

It was quite clear that he did not want 'outsiders' seeing the state of my face. I did what I was told and I wondered yet again, for the thousandth time, how I could ever explain to anyone how or why I could put up with this.

All the way back to Fife, the children were crying, demanding to know why the holiday was over.

I turned to them with my ruined face and said, 'Mummy's fallen over.'

In a sense I was telling the truth. Mummy had fallen.

Mummy had fallen a very long way.

———————————

Giselle: And I discovered there was no escape from Ash's mind games.

We were divorced now, but if I had thought it would distance me from Ash I was mistaken. If anything it intensified the control he tried to exert over me. It was as if he were playing some secret game, the rules of which only he knew. One minute he was never away from us; the next he disappeared without warning or explanation.

His behaviour was badly upsetting Paul. He was old enough now to realise that all of a sudden his father was not there. Several times a day he would ask, 'Where's Daddy?'

'He'll be here soon,' I told him, trying to keep the concern from my voice.

I was distraught. Only Katie knew Ash had staged a disappearing act. She was the only one with whom I could share my fears.

'He's up to something,' Katie would say to me. 'Where is he?'

'I don't know,' I said.

Ash had been gone for nearly two weeks now. I was frantic. I believed something awful had happened. He didn't answer his phone or respond to my messages. I called hospitals, fearing he had been injured. After a week without news, I went to his mother's house. Ash was not there and neither was his mother. Neighbours told me she and Ash had left, carrying suitcases. I did not know whether he was gone for good.

'Phone him again,' Katie said.

I dialled. Voicemail.

How could Ash just disappear without saying a word? I was used to him calling me every hour of day, checking up on where I was, what I had been doing. And now this silence.

It would be another week before I heard anything and, when the phone rang, it was not Ash but my mother.

'Ashley is looking for you,' she said. 'Where have you been all day? He has been trying to get you on the phone. He is worried sick.'

I almost choked. I had not been over the doorstep. I somehow managed to speak.

'Everything is fine, Ma. Don't worry. I'll call him.'

I was seething. Ash had used Ma as a buffer. I dialled his mobile. There was no reply. I left a message. He called back within minutes. Instead of being shame-faced, he was annoyed.

'What's wrong?' he said.

'What's wrong?!' I said. 'Where have you been for two weeks? I didn't know if you were dead or alive.'

There was silence.

'Mum and I went to see my sister. What's wrong with you?'

I slammed down the phone. Later that evening he walked into the flat as if nothing had happened. When I remonstrated with him he shrugged, looking as if I were making an unnecessary fuss.

'It's not as if we're married any more,' he said, turning his back on me.

Paul was pathetically pleased to see his daddy.

'Daddy missed his special boy,' Ash said loudly to him. 'Daddy should have taken his special boy away with him.'

Ash hoisted Paul into the air and looked at me.

He was no longer smiling.

16

Why Didn't We Walk Away?

'By being cut off from everything they know, abused women are robbed of the strength to break away.'

Ian Stephen

June: People always want to know why we stayed, why we put up with it.

Long after my children were taken, long after my life was devastated, I was in the company of a woman who knew my story. As we spoke, I knew that she wanted to ask *the question*. Everyone who meets mothers like me and Giselle wants to ask the same question.

'*How could you stay?*'

It is a question that's rarely asked; few people have the nerve. This woman screwed up the courage. She delivered the question in the same tone of voice she would have used to ask an alcoholic how he could sacrifice his family for a drink; how a drug addict could die a little every day for a 'fix'. How could they? How could *we*? When you live without light, when you suffer abuse for so long, you become overwhelmed. It is like having a chronic illness with no hope of a cure. You endure the dull pain every day, punctuated by episodes of agony.

I did *try* to escape.

I went back because I had to. There are so many obstacles put in the way of battered women. During one of the times I tried to break free I asked a social worker if she could assist me in rearranging Michelle's care package and help me to access the benefits that would enable us to make a fresh start.

'Why bother?' she asked. 'You're only going to go back. You've gone back before.'

So you see, I was defeated before I'd even begun. And then there was the guilt every abused woman wrestles with – uprooting the children, taking them away from their school, their friends, even their toys. That is why so many of us stay. Sometimes breaking free is just too hard.

You make the best of it, rather than fleeing like refugees with the clothes you're standing in. And one of the biggest problems I faced was that my children loved their father. They did not see a cruel madman. They saw 'Dad'. It was only when Shaun got older that he witnessed things no child should see.

When they were small, I was loath to keep him from them, no matter how cruel he was to me. I knew what it was like to live in a home where one parent was absent – and I didn't want that for my children. Rab, being Rab, would use my sense of fair play as a weapon to maintain his control over me.

On one of the occasions when I fled, Rab turned up at the house I'd rented. He did not rant or rave, or demand that I return. He was perfectly reasonable.

'Look,' he said, standing at the front door, 'Mum and Dad are missing the kids. Why don't we all go to Ayrshire for the day to see them?'

I stood aside, allowing him to enter. He threw himself on my borrowed settee. I was dumbfounded, not prepared for this amenable Rab.

'Why don't you and the kids get ready?' he said.

I was about to shout up to the children when Rab added, 'When we get there, don't let on that we've been fighting. I don't want Mum upset.'

I was confused. My confusion continued throughout the journey. Why wasn't Rab dragging me back by the hair? I would soon learn why.

When we arrived at his parents' farm, we were welcomed by the family. The kids ran off to play. By now I had been totally lulled into a false sense of security.

'Come out to the car,' he said, 'I've something I want to show you.'

He walked out into the drive, opened the car door, sat down in the driver's seat and shouted out, 'Get in. I don't want the kids to hear.'

I did. I heard the 'thunk' of the central locking. Now the shouting and bawling will begin, I thought.

But he was calm.

'Why don't we just die together?' he said.

I froze.

'Then we'll be together for ever. And don't worry about the kids. My family will look after them.'

There was no way out.

Rab's left hand was gripping the steering wheel so tightly that his knuckles were white. I could still see the children playing, running carefree in the sunshine. They were shouting but I did not hear the words.

'It's the perfect solution,' Rab went on.

I forced myself to look at him. He was smiling. His right hand was down by his side, out of sight. Did he have a gun? A knife? I sucked in a deep breath and chose my words carefully. My life depended on it.

'Rab, nothing's that bad, c'mon now. We'll start again,' I said.

'But you left me, you left me,' he answered.

His tone was one of incredulity. When I looked into Rab's eyes, I was truly afraid that I would not survive the day. I stared, horribly fascinated by the half-smile on his lips. At length he broke the silence.

'Okay then, let's just go home and we'll forget all about this, eh?'

And we did.

So you see, when someone blithely tells me that I should have just walked away, I tell them, 'I did try to walk away. Your world is black and white; mine was painted in shades of grey.'

I existed among shadows.

Giselle: I'm asked the same question. My answer is always the same – I was so afraid.

My choice was simple.

Live this half-life or risk losing my son, the person I loved most in the world. It was a low-grade fear that gnawed at me

*from the day Ash snatched Paul from his pram and left me
standing in the street. That gut-wrenching hour I had spent
pacing the floor, waiting for Ash to return, was seared in my
mind. My fear had been intensified by his disappearing act to
Oxford. The memories of both incidents could bring me out in
a cold sweat. They proved to me how easy it would be for Ash to
vanish with my son.*

*There was no doubt Ash doted on Paul – and therein lay the
basis of my fear. He didn't merely love his son. He had that sense
of proprietorship. No one was good enough for his 'perfect boy'.
The Paul-sharing between our two families was only part of it.
Ash obsessed over where Paul and I were, each and every minute
of the day.*

*I would be in shops and my mobile would ring. 'Where are
you? What are you doing? When are you going home?' he would
want to know. If I had, for example, a doctor's appointment or
had to dash round the supermarket, my family was always on
hand to help out. If Ash discovered I was on my own he would
harangue me for leaving Paul in the care of my mother or Katie
for a few hours.*

*'You are his mother,' Ash would say. 'You should be looking
after him.'*

*It was a ludicrous thing to say. Paul was hardly ever out of
my sight. I revelled in my son's company. I hadn't even sent him
to nursery because I didn't want to miss one second of watching
him grow up. I was forced to tell the silliest of lies to placate Ash.
Ma and I still visited the shopping mall at Parkhead Forge. We
had been doing so for years. It was a ritual that hadn't stopped
when Paul came along. Ma loved her days out, and having her
lunch of scrambled egg and toast. She would cut up her food and
share it with Paul. I delighted in their relationship. They loved*

each other so much. When the phone rang and it was Ash demanding to know what I was doing – and whom I was with – I would fib, saying that Paul and I were on our own. It was either that, or risk fuelling his jealousy and possessiveness.

It was all incredibly wearing.

When Ash visited Paul he would put our son on his knee and spend hours with him. Ash had eyes and ears for no one else. Before the snatch incident, I had seen it only as the closeness of a father to his son. After it, this apparently innocent tableau scared me.

'Who do you love most, Paul – Mummy or Daddy?' Ash would ask.

How many times did I hear that and see the look of confusion sweeping across my son's face?

'I love Mummy and Daddy,' he would say.

Ash would look at me.

'But you must love one of us best.'

'Ash! Enough! He's only little!' I'd tell him.

This unfairness stressed Paul. He began chewing his finger-nails, a nervous tic that occurred only when his father visited. Paul was too young to understand, too young to do anything but adore his dad.

Ash had also begun to teach him a few words of Punjabi. I encouraged it. It was an important part of his heritage and I was pleased that at least one of us would be able to communicate properly with his other granny. But I would overhear snatches of conversation that set alarm bells ringing.

'I'll take you to see Granny's big, fine house. Just you and me.'

Ash had never mentioned going as a family to his homeland. My instincts screamed that any trip he was planning to take to India would not include me.

I was also becoming concerned that Ash was 'disappearing' more often. He would be posted missing for days and, when I asked him where he had been, all he would say was that he had been to London 'on business'.

Katie joked that perhaps he had a hidden life and another 'family'. I laughed it off, but when I was my own it occurred to me how very little I truly knew about Ash and his life before I met him. What if he did have another family? It might be in sprawling London or, even worse, in India. What if Ash disappeared with Paul – and his grandmother? How would I ever get my child back? How would I even know where he was?

So I decided I would wear a smile. I would play the 'wife'. I would do whatever it took. I would make any and every sacrifice. It wasn't as if my life was intolerable. Unlike June, I was not tortured or abused. Ash was a benign captor. I was as happy as I could be, given the circumstances.

I would put up with his jealousies or find ways round them. I would go for days out, take the trips to the seaside, to the funfair. I took great pains to ensure that Ash knew he could see his son any time he chose, day or night. I resolved never to do anything that Ash could perceive as a threat to his relationship with Paul. I had no choice.

I was prepared to live in the house of cards Ash had built around me.

17

These Special Gifts

'Women trapped in relationships such as these
keep going ... they need to remember the man
they first met.'

Ian Stephen

**June: As the years rolled by, I stopped trying to escape – then
the miracle happened.**

I had, amazingly, entered a period of relative calm. Rab realised I had capitulated, that I had resigned myself to incarceration behind the invisible bars he had erected around me. He
knew there would be no more escape bids. My powerlessness
appeared to have defused some of his anger. He still terrified
me and the beatings continued, but they were less frequent
and less violent.

He was my captor and, like all gaolers, he demanded a
strict regime. My days were filled with trying to fulfil the
demands of his 'lists'. They were designed to be so time
consuming that I would not be left with enough energy to
hatch any further escape plans. His lists became something of

a refuge for me. If I carried out his instructions – to the letter – I was less likely to be beaten. The lists were delivered in the form of barked orders: 'Do this! Get that! Bring this!'

His demands were precise and specific. What time tea had to be on the table; which clothes were to be ironed; which tables to be polished; which cupboards to be cleaned. He even used to dispatch me to scrap yards to locate spare parts for the car. Juggling the lists with my duties as the mother of three growing children meant I had to rise at 5.30 a.m. If it was Rab's intention to tire me out and never leave me with a moment to myself, his plan succeeded. I was a slave. I would fall into bed exhausted, but even then my duties might not be over. If Rab decided he fancied a portion of chips, I was summoned downstairs with a shout and sent to the 'chippie'.

My comfort was the children. What leisure time I had was devoted to them. I took their Sunday-school class, watched plays, attended recitals, sat in the front row for prize-giving and cheered on sports days. I cannot remember Rab being with me. I also found the time to mentor disabled children from Michelle's school. I loved doing it. I was privileged to meet so many special children and their families.

The move from Ayrshire to Fife seemed such a long time ago now and my children were getting bigger by the day. Michelle was 18 – a young woman. Ross was a bright teenager who learned quickly and my Shaun was by now a tall, solemn young man who had often cast himself in the role of my champion. When Rab's temper broke, it was Shaun who came to my defence. Poor Shaun took many a beating. Ross and Michelle were insulated, he by being the 'baby' and she by her disabilities. It was Shaun who felt his father's wrath most keenly and he would do so until 2000, when he decided to join the army.

Losing him left a gaping hole in my life but I could not stand in his way. He deserved to be free, to have his own life. I was proud of him. Later, when he was posted to Iraq, he did not let on for fear of alarming me. But he always kept in touch, phoning when his father was out of the house. He would speak to me, then to Michelle and Ross.

With Shaun gone, I lived one day at a time, throwing myself into the lives of my other children. I could envisage no other way of life. This would be the way it would always be. Or so I thought.

And then, at the age of 41, I discovered I was pregnant.

Giselle: I had given up on miracles. I never believed I'd be a mother again until blind chance intervened.

'What do you want for your birthday?' I asked Paul.

He was almost four now. Where had the time gone? He had grown so. So polite and well mannered, he always seemed older than his years. The so-called 'terrible twos and threes' had passed him by. He was a delightful child, described by all who knew him as the 'little gentleman'.

'A little baby,' he replied in his soft and serious voice.

It was as if my son could read my mind. The thought had been forming in my mind for some time. I did want a brother or sister for him, but it was a forlorn hope now that I was no longer officially married. My 'relationship' with Ash was continuing on the same path, almost as if there had been no change, but I could not conceive of Ash agreeing to have another child.

'A baaa-by?' I said. 'What would you like? A boy or a girl?'

Paul shrugged.

'A baby, Mummy ... to play with.'

The sex of the baby obviously wasn't a concern to him. My son looked at me with his shy eyes and I saw a trace of loneliness in them. There was no lack of love in his life but it was the adult love of a devoted mother, grandparents, aunts, uncles and cousins – and the father who deserted him each evening. Paul needed someone else to love. I did, too, if truth be told.

'We'll have to ask Daddy, then,' I told him.

Ash had, in the past, spoken of having another child – when he became the world's greatest defence lawyer, businessman, or whichever current daydream consumed him. I certainly did not want to conceive another child unless he wanted it.

It would, however, become a moot point. Ash took responsibility for contraceptive precautions, ostensibly because I had been so ill after having Paul. I suspect, though, that it had more to do with control than with my welfare. Little did I know the matter was about to be taken out of my hands. Soon after my birthday conversation with Paul, my mother was rushed into hospital. She had suffered from respiratory problems for years and they had now become acute.

The family took it in turns to ensure she always had someone by her bed. I had returned home from one such visit and I had barely laid down my bag when Ash appeared. He had been drinking, heavily it seemed. I was annoyed. I ushered him into the living room as I did not want Paul to see his father drunk. I asked Ash where he had been. He was his usual evasive self, mumbling something about a course he had been on – no doubt his latest path to success and riches. I pushed him down on the couch and put Paul to bed.

When he was settled, I returned to the living room to find Ash in a happy, effusive – and amorous – mood. The inevitable happened. It would be six weeks before I discovered that Ash had not been quite so 'careful' as he thought he had been.

Paul would get his birthday wish.

June: Rab had abused me but I had once loved him – could this baby restore my faith? Be our redemption?

The smile on Rab's face was a frightening, alien thing. There was no malice in it. I could detect no superciliousness, no sneer of triumph, no evil intent. He was, God help me, actually happy, ecstatically so.

'Are you sure?' he asked.

'Of course, I'm sure. I've had all the tests.'

He didn't do anything as normal or mundane as hug me, but he seemed to grow in stature, pumped up by sheer pride.

'A baby!' he said, with wonder.

I did not know how to respond to this Rab. For a few seconds there was a fleeting, tantalising glimpse of that long-haired boy in a Kilbirnie dance hall who had disappeared so long ago. For once, Rab and I were sharing a sense of wonderment, like any other couple. I had not even considered the possibility of another child. Not only was my age against me, but I suffered from endometriosis, a gynaecological condition that can cause infertility. In fact, my GP had told me years earlier that it was highly unlikely that I would ever again conceive.

I saw it as a sign. Instead of panicking, the news of my pregnancy took me to a calm, quiet place. I had grown up with faith, a belief that in times of adversity you are always sent what you need. I have to confess that there had been occasions when I thought that God had rather forgotten me. I was wrong. He was shining a ray of light into the darkness. A new life to cherish, protect and love. I was utterly delighted.

This was to be my special gift.

Giselle: After all Rab had done, you still had hope. When I heard Ash's words, any love I had for him died. I didn't care what he said; I was going to have my baby.

'Get rid of it!' Ash screamed.

His face was suffused with pure, unadulterated anger.

'You tricked me!' he shouted.

I had never seen Ash so angry. He was like a fiend.

'I want you to have an abortion!'

'I will not have an abortion!'

Ash was silenced, stunned by the fury in my voice. He had never seen this Giselle before.

'How could you even ask me to do such a thing?'

I was as angry as he was, an irresistible force meeting an immovable object.

'I will leave,' he threatened.

'Why should that worry me, Ash? You aren't here anyway.'

He was flummoxed, unsure of what to say next.

'You need me!' he said, lamely.

'No, I don't,' I shouted. 'I have Paul. I have my family and I'll have this child. If you don't want to be here, that's up to you.'

'I order you to get rid of it!' he bellowed.

'What would your mother say about that?' I said very quietly.

The mention of his mother stung Ash. He was after all the 'good Christian', forever quoting from Scripture.

'Ask your mother how she would react to you getting rid of her grandchild,' I said.

He turned on his heel and stormed out. My anger dissipated with the slam of the door and I collapsed onto the sofa, tears streaming down my face.

'Mummy! Mummy!'

It was Paul's voice, filled with concern. He had been in his bedroom. His face was drawn, his eyes luminous. He had heard the screams but did not venture into the living room until his father departed.

'It's okay, baby,' I told him. 'Mummy and Daddy have had a row.'

I picked him up and held him. He snuggled into my shoulder, wrapped his arms around my neck and began to cry.

'Shush, baby, it's not you. Everything's all right.'

Paul clung to me.

'Don't cry, Mummy, don't be sad.'

'I'm not crying,' I said, pulling myself together. 'Mummy's not sad, she's happy.'

Paul was confused.

'Sometimes,' I said, 'grown-ups cry when they're really happy.'

'Are you happy, Mummy?'

'Yes,' I replied. 'I'm really happy and, guess what, Mummy has a big surprise.'

'What?' he asked.

'Tell me again what you wanted for your birthday!'

———————————

June: Like a fool, I listened to Rab's promises. I wanted to believe that the bad times were over.

Rab's coarse hands smothered the bottle of formula as he guided the teat into the mouth of his chubby new son. Ryan was lying in his arms and Rab was cooing at him.

'You're a wee belter,' he told the baby.

Our new son was a few hours old and I was watching what would have looked to the outsider like a tender family scene. The ogre had been made gentle by innocence. I wondered, hoped, prayed that this Rab might succeed in defeating the brute within. I was weary of hearing myself say the same prayer but, who knows, perhaps this time? Time would tell.

It was 7 April 2001. Ryan had been delivered – two weeks early – in the Forth Park Maternity Hospital in Kirkcaldy. In spite of his premature arrival, he was a sturdy 8lbs 1oz. It was one of the best days of my life.

Throughout my pregnancy, Shaun and Ross had affected a bluff and wholly artificial indifference to having a new little brother. On the other hand, Michelle had lived for months in a state of euphoria. She could not wait for the baby to arrive.

When I thought of my Michelle and what this child would mean to her, I was overwhelmed by a sensation I had not felt for years. I was happy, truly happy. Because of her disabilities,

Michelle would never have a child of her own. Ryan would allow her to experience a glimpse of motherhood. Ryan would not just be my special gift.

The last nine months had been an oasis of peace. My pregnancy progressed without incident and Rab had been uncharacteristically benevolent. The prospect of having another son transformed him into what passed for a normal human being. The 'real' Rab was, however, never too far away. When it was apparent that Ryan was about to be born earlier than expected I called an ambulance. When the paramedics arrived they told Rab I was about to have the baby – on the bathroom floor. He went mad, shouting, swearing and demanding that they get me out of the house. They did. We made it to the hospital – just. I went from the ambulance straight into the delivery room, where Ryan was born within minutes. The ambulance crew was forced to stand outside, waiting to retrieve their trolley. Rab glowered at them.

His features were softened now that he was holding Ryan. I could hear him talking gently to his newborn son, telling him that he would take him fishing, shooting; promising our son that he would always look after him.

God forgive me, I believed him.

Giselle: I know why you wanted to believe, but for me there was no going back.

'I was convinced it was a girl,' I told the ultrasound operator.

'It's a boy!' she said, her hand circling the scanning device over my tummy. 'There he is!' she added, indicating my son,

who had appeared, small and fragile, on the grey, grainy screen.

'Look! That's his heart,' she went on.

A blip on the monitor showed that the tiny organ was pumping life into my unborn child.

'I've already started knitting a pink hat,' I said.

'You better rip it out and start again,' laughed the woman.

Katie joined in and we all laughed. It was my sister and not Ash who had come with me to the scan. His demand that I have an abortion had created an insurmountable barrier between us. Nothing could be the same again. Our relationship was now centred exclusively on our son. We spoke only when Ash came to collect Paul, to take him for days out or to visit his grandmother. He ignored the fact that I was pregnant and his face wore a constant frown.

I was once putting Paul into the back of Ash's car and I caught a glimpse of him, looking at me in the rear-view mirror. He did not realise I could see him. His expression was a mixture of hatred and disgust. It was utterly chilling. I tried to remain cordial. In fact, I went out of my way to ensure that Ash knew that he would always have access to Paul. I didn't do it just for Ash's sake. Paul loved his dad and I couldn't – and didn't want to – keep them apart. It was tough, however. Ash didn't make it easy. He would phone up at all hours, obviously drunk, rambling and determined to goad me. I could hear the carefully chosen maudlin music playing in the background. Elvis Presley's 'Devil in Disguise' was a particular favourite.

He would slur, 'Listen to this!' and I would hear the lyrics.

'That's you!' Ash said. 'You're a devil!'

I would tell him not to be silly and hang up. There was an eerily sinister aspect to these calls but I couldn't let Ash know he was getting to me.

I also took great pains to ensure that all of the details of the rift with Ash did not reach my family. Katie was the only one who knew the full extent of it. The rest of the family, ignorant of so much, had rallied round when they heard I was pregnant. They were ecstatic over the impending arrival of another child. I basked in the glow of it. My health, apart from a painful back and bad heartburn, had been good during the entire nine months.

On the morning that Jay was due I awoke feeling a bit off-colour. I had just got out of bed when I heard what sounded like a tremendous 'pop'. My waters had broken. I was in a panic when I phoned Katie and asked her to take care of Paul. She arrived within minutes and took him to my mother's house before joining me at the Princess Royal Maternity Hospital in Glasgow.

It would, however, be nearly 36 hours later before Jay – who was already being referred to as 'Jay-Jay' – decided to arrive by caesarean section at 4 p.m. on 7 January 2006. By then, I was in a world of my own. I could see Katie at the foot of the bed. She had assumed Ash's 'duties' in the delivery room. I watched her as her face turned from concern to wonderment. She leaned forward and accepted a tiny bundle from the doctors. It was my son. Katie raised him up, all 5lbs 9oz of him, like a winning sportsman hoisting a trophy and presented me with the most special birthday gift Paul would ever receive.

My beautiful Jay-Jay would be a day old before his father appeared at the hospital. Ash walked straight past Jay-Jay's crib without a glance at his new son and laid a bouquet of supermarket flowers on my bedside cabinet.

'When are you coming home?' he asked.

'Don't you want to look at the baby?'

'Paul is fretting, you know!'

Paul was doing nothing of the kind. He had just visited with Ma, Da and Katie. He had left ten minutes earlier, clutching the hand of little Giselle.

'Bring Jay-Jay home soon, Mummy,' he had ordered.

'Look at your new son,' I told Ash.

He walked over to where the baby lay and gave Jay-Jay a cursory glance.

'Don't you want to pick him up?'

'No, he's too small,' Ash said.

He was angry. He had kept me at arm's length for the full term of my pregnancy. But I was by now immune to his moods. Any relationship we'd had ended with his demand that I have an abortion. He still came to the flat, but it was only to see Paul.

I was frankly surprised to see him here.

'How did you know I'd had the baby?' I asked.

'One of little Giselle's pals got into my taxi. She told me,' he said, adding, 'Why didn't you phone me?'

'What would have been the point? This is the baby you wanted me to kill,' I replied.

18

The Joy
They Brought

'Abused women cling to what they can ... They
don't want to believe they have made a terrible
choice or a bad judgement.'

Ian Stephen

June: My baby brought so much joy – even when Rab
reverted to type and I thought I would lose everything.

'Ry-aaan.'

Michelle luxuriated in the sound of her brother's name.
'Ry-annn ... Ry-annn ... Ry-annn,' she would croon over and
over again, looking from the baby to me with a smile that
began in heaven. When she scooped him up in her arms, I
caught glimpses of the woman she might have become but
for her disabilities. When her face was in repose and her eyes
were quiet, she might have been any other 20-something
woman with her own child.

It was during those fleeting moments that I was assailed by
the realisation that if it had not been for Rab the scene before
me could not have come to pass. I was almost prepared to

forgive him for the years of misery. How strangely our emotions are constructed. I had not been happy for a full day in my entire adult life, but the sight of my oldest and youngest children together armoured me against the memories.

People will tell you that having babies is the most natural thing in the world. And it is. But what we cannot quantify is the magic they create in those around them. Shaun returned from the army on leave. He was a big, strong man now, a soldier who had experienced conflict and witnessed death. He was much changed from the boy who had left home, but when he held his baby brother I could see the child return to his eyes. The baby had the same effect on his other brother. With a mere gurgle and a pair of tiny arms outstretched, Ryan could in an instant rob Ross of his tiresome teenage 'cool'.

But my greatest joy was in Michelle's relationship with Ryan. My oldest daughter had never in her life been a slave to protocol or false propriety. She loved openly, fiercely and completely. Ryan became the latest recipient of that love. He was embraced, bathed, sung to, dressed up and showered with affection. In my Michelle's mind, Ryan was as much her child as he was mine. I delighted in their relationship, which would only deepen as Ryan grew older. The relationship with Ryan was different from the one she had shared with Shaun and Ross. When they were growing up, it was all rough and tumble and playing jokes on each other. It was different with Ryan. He might have been made of bone china, to watch Michelle with him. She was, of course, older now. She had left school and lived with me at home, supported by a network of carers. Because of that care system, it freed me to a great extent, and I was able to dedicate most of my time to Ryan, a luxury I had not enjoyed with my other children.

The magic of Ryan even spread to Rab. He was still working long hours, but the man who came through the door in the evening was captivated by his youngest child. He played with Ryan in a way he had not done with Shaun and Ross, and certainly not with Michelle.

For my own part, I, of course, enjoyed the unique relationship that exists between mother and child, but when I looked down at my son, I, too, had many reasons to be grateful to him.

Since his arrival, Rab's temper had been curbed to some degree. He could still explode at a moment's notice, if he chose, but the episodes were fewer now and less violent than they had been in the past.

But just when I thought I had achieved relative stability, a new threat almost robbed me of everything. I had always feared that Rab would be the one to take my life, but I had not anticipated that it would be a silent and even more deadly adversary. I awoke one morning to find one side of my body paralysed. I struggled from my bed, terrified by the numbness that reached from my shoulder down through my arm and into my leg. I looked in the mirror and one side of my face was twisted, drooping.

'Rab!' I shouted.

'What?' he said, rubbing sleep from his eyes.

'I'm not well,' I slurred.

'You're fine,' he said. 'Get the breakfast on.'

I walked to the kitchen. My arm would not work and my leg dragged.

'Rab! My face!' I said.

Rab looked at me. 'There's fuck all wrong with you … get the breakfast!'

Somehow I managed to prepare breakfast and make Rab's lunch. He walked out the door without a word and I fell into a chair in the living room.

I was half-sleeping when a voice said, 'June?' It was one of Michelle's carers.

'My face,' I managed to say.

'Can you get up?' she said. 'I should take you to hospital. I think you've had a stroke. Stay there for a second until I get help.'

The words had just died on her lips when another of Michelle's carers arrived. She was asked to look after Ryan.

'C'mon, let's get you to hospital,' the first carer said.

The journey passed in a blur and the next thing I remember was being in a bed in a ward. The doctors confirmed the carer's diagnosis. I had suffered a stroke; in fact, a series of mini-strokes that hadn't, until that morning, been strong enough to put me on my back.

The rest of the day was filled with a series of medical tests. I went to sleep that night terrified that I would die before morning and there would be no one but Rab left to look after my children. But I did survive the night and, in the morning, I found myself faced by a doctor who had come to tell me that the tests had revealed no obvious physical cause for my condition. He told me that a specialist would see me – and Rab – later that day.

Rab arrived at the hospital a few minutes before I was due to see the specialist. The numbness in my side had started to fade and I felt well enough to get out of bed. I was taken along a corridor to the consultant's office.

Rab sat by my side as the doctor perused my chart.

After a few minutes the doctor looked up and said, 'I'd like you to see a psychologist, Mrs Thomson. If you'll excuse me for a moment, I'll go and check on the availability of an appointment.'

He smiled at me and left the room.

As the door closed behind him, Rab hissed at me, 'You're seeing no fucking psychologist. You won't be discussing our lives with anyone.'

I remained silent.

'He'll take one look at you and realise what a nutter you are. They'll bang you up and take the kids.'

Long years of practice warned me not to react. Rab's eyes were blank, menacing. I knew the look.

The door opened and the doctor came back into the room.

'She's doesn't need to see a psychologist. I can sort her out myself,' Rab said.

I said nothing. The nerve endings of my emotions had long since been dulled. Rab could do no more to me than he had already done.

The doctor did not look convinced. 'I'll get a call back in a minute, Mrs Thomson, but first I'll take a few notes.'

He slipped a pen from the breast pocket of his white coat and it hovered over his clipboard.

'Now, Mrs Thomson, has there been any unusual stress in your life ...?'

God help me, I almost laughed.

Giselle: I knew I couldn't love Ash but I still wanted him to be a father to Jay-Jay.

Paul couldn't speak. He wanted to but he couldn't. His eyes were saucers of bright light. He was sitting deep in the living-room sofa, lost among the cushions and cuddly toys. Jay-Jay was draped over his lap, asleep. I hovered, preparing to leap forward, but then realised that Jay-Jay was safe. Paul was cradling him gently, looking from the baby to me.

'You love him, don't you?' I said softly.

He nodded vigorously. Words still eluded him. He was overwhelmed.

'Smile!' said a voice behind me. Katie. The camera flash exploded in a blaze of white light. I turned to see my sister examining the back of the camera.

'Nice!' she said. 'Look, Paul, there's you and Jay-Jay.'

The photo revealed my sons frozen in time, the baby sleeping, lost to the world, and Paul looking straight at me with a look of wonder on his face.

'Get in with Paul and Jay-Jay,' said Katie, telling little Giselle – their 'other' mother – to join her cousins.

Giselle didn't have to be told twice. She threw herself down beside Paul and embraced both boys in a hug that declared, 'You're mine!'

'Ah, you look bonnie,' said Ma, who was sitting opposite the children. 'They're beautiful,' she said to no one in particular.

'Da!' I shouted. He was crashing about in the kitchen, performing a very important task. He was making a pot of tea. 'Da! Come and get your picture taken with the boys.'

He, too, did not have to be told twice and he was soon ensconced in the chair with the children, his big arms thrown around them.

I sat down and surveyed my flat, which was now a shrine to childhood. There were toys everywhere – gifts of baby clothes from family, friends and neighbours were piled high on every surface. In a community like mine, the arrival of a new baby is a unifying event that encompasses everyone. There was a constant stream of people at my door, all of whom would look at my perfect son and go off to regale their family and friends with tales of his 'munchkin' face and shock of dark hair.

Everyone wanted to see Jay-Jay. Everyone, it seemed, except his father.

'Where's Ashley today?' Ma asked.

'Working,' Katie said quickly.

'Works hard, that boy,' Da said.

'Never has a minute to himself,' Katie said, giving me a knowing look.

'Where's my boys?' a voice boomed from the doorway. My brother Tam.

Paul relinquished Jay-Jay to little Giselle and leapt from the sofa to greet his uncle, who swung him high into the air to the accompaniment of Paul's whooping laughter.

Tam's arrival had, mercifully, put any more talk of Ash on the back burner. He had continued to be a frequent visitor since Jay-Jay was born but he did not share the communal joy at my younger son's arrival.

He had refused to pick us up from the hospital, and this time round there were no visits from his mother. I had asked him if he had told his mother about Jay-Jay but all he did was grunt and turn away.

I had hoped that when Ash saw the baby his heart would soften and he would acknowledge the obvious truth. But when he visited he would arrive laden with gifts for Paul and nothing for Jay-Jay. The baby was steadfastly ignored. It was as if he didn't exist. Ash's indifference wounded me but I would never let it show.

I refused to allow his mood to sour my own. Jay-Jay was fast becoming the most famous child in Royston, to be oooh'd and aaah'd over by all and sundry.

Paul adored his brother and I could see that, young as he was, he was mystified by his father's behaviour towards Jay-Jay. It was obvious that he felt uncomfortable when he received gifts from his father and Jay-Jay was ignored. Paul would immediately 'share' what he had with his little brother.

'That's for you,' his father said.

'... and for Jay-Jay,' Paul replied.

'No ... No ... For Dad's special boy.'

'... and for Jay-Jay.'

I felt such love for my kind-hearted son in those moments. His churlish father could have learned much from him. If it was Ash's intention to create a rift between his sons, it was failing.

'When will you learn?' I asked Ash.

'Learn what?' he said.

'The truth ... Look at him, he's yours!'

'How do I know?'

'Look at him!'

Jay-Jay was the spitting image of Ash.

But Ash would turn away and say, 'Night, night, Paul ... You are Daddy's only special boy.'

I was just so relieved that Jay-Jay was still too young to know that his father had rejected him.

But that would change – and I wasn't prepared for the lengths to which Ash would go to challenge the truth.

_____

19

Beginning of the End

'June kept trying to find "something", but Giselle was about to glimpse the true dark side to Ash's character, the side he hid so carefully from everyone else.'

Ian Stephen

June: I kept hoping for a new beginning ... But Muiredge was the beginning of the end.

Ryan ran through the throng of smiling, happy people. He was oblivious to them. His gaze was on me. My very special boy – my saviour in a little black jacket, kilt, white shirt and bow tie. His eyes glittered like one of the necklaces that Michelle insisted on wearing now that she was 'grown up'.

How could I know he had less than two years left to live?

Ryan collided with me, crying 'Mummy!' I held the fluted glass aloft in my hand to prevent champagne from spilling over my pale-pink two-piece suit. He had negotiated the legs of the guests who were 'celebrating' my silver wedding anniversary – a quarter of a century of less-than-wedded bliss.

The room was crowded, but until Ryan raced to me I had felt alone.

Rab was on my right, wearing a black suit, a white shirt and a white silk tie. His face glowed with bonhomie and good health. He was the centre of attention, surrounded by family and friends sharing what they believed to be a wonderful milestone in our life together. I was miserable, my painted smile only achieving true warmth when I looked down on the tousled head of my little boy.

'Watch my outfit!' I laughed as he tried to 'dance' with me.

In the five years since he had been born, Ryan had saved me with his love and his dependence on me. He had pulled me back from the edge, validating my miserable existence with Rab. The tender Rab, who had held our newborn son, had of course regressed, as I suspected he would, but he no longer held the same crushing power over me.

My eldest sons, Shaun and Ross, towered over me. They were men, no longer the boys who had relied on their mother. Michelle was 24.

She, too, would soon be taken from me.

Her days were now filled with other people, a coterie of carers who made her less dependent on me. Ryan was the only one who still truly needed his mum.

'Dance, Mummy, dance,' he shouted.

I fell in with Ryan's rhythm until I heard Rab's imperious voice.

'Have you not done enough dancing?' he said, the quiet harshness in his words audible to me alone.

He still wore his false smile. We were in a function suite of a pub, close to where we now lived on the outskirts of Buckhaven.

The house was called 'Muiredge' and I had chosen it. Rab could not have cared less where we lived, but I had been so unhappy in our previous house, living in that street of strangers. I had spent months searching for the perfect house, and Muiredge was my dream. It sat on its own, with a big garden.

A new beginning.

Rain, sleet or snow, I spent most of my time with Ryan in that garden. I would point to the tree-tops behind the house and tell him that was where the cheeky monkeys lived. I delighted in my son. We were inseparable. He loved stories and I adored making them up for him. Our days were filled with tales of fairies at the bottom of the garden, where, as far as Ryan was concerned, they coexisted happily with a witch's cat.

Muiredge was an idyllic place, where I envisaged my son growing up. As I looked down at him now, I caught a glimpse of the red ruby cluster on my finger – Rab's anniversary gift to me. He had wanted to buy me a big, flashy solitaire ring, no doubt to show off at the party. I chose the rubies. They resembled a bleeding heart.

Rab had insisted on the party. I did not want one but he would not be dissuaded. He wanted a big public show – the conquering hero, Caesar returning to Rome. Watching him take the applause filled me with an overwhelming sadness. I had wasted my life, hadn't I?

As I cut the cake, with Rab's hand laid over mine, my children smiled at me and I realised that my life had not been a waste. They were my reward. As my fingers closed around the knife, everyone shouted, 'Make a wish!'

I felt a tug on my skirt.

'What did you wish for, Mummy?' Ryan asked me.

'For you to have a long and happy life, baby!'

Giselle: I had believed humiliation was the greatest pain Ash would inflict on me. How could we know we were only two years from despair?

Jay-Jay wriggled in my arms. My body was rigid with anger. The baby was unconcerned. He laughed, as if he were being tickled.

'This is wrong,' I said to Ash and the doctor, who was swabbing Jay-Jay's mouth with an elongated Q-tip.

Ash had demanded a DNA test.

He remained silent. The doctor seemed uncomfortable, shamefaced by what he had been asked to do. He murmured to my son as he withdrew the Q-tip and secured it in a sealed tube.

'This is wrong,' I repeated. I turned to Ash. 'You know he's your son.'

Ash said nothing.

He had paid cash, counting out £300 onto a desk. As each note was laid down, my embarrassment and anger grew. I felt like one of those unfortunates who reveal their chaotic lives on car-crash television shows hosted by Jeremy Kyle or Jerry Springer.

Nothing I had said to Ash had been able to convince him he was Jay-Jay's father.

'This is your son,' I would tell him.

'How do I know?'

'You're the only man I have ever slept with!'

'I take precautions!' he said.

'*You were* drunk! *And I got pregnant.*'

'*You have to prove he's mine!*' Ash said.

'*How? How can I prove that?*'

'*I want a DNA test!*'

I refused. I was appalled, furious, but in the weeks that followed Ash was relentless, wearing me down to the point where I would have done anything to prove Jay-Jay was his son, if only to shame him.

So there I was, justifying myself to Ash and the doctor. The doctor shared my discomfort. I could sense it in his body language and, when he looked at Ash, his expression screamed disapproval.

'*You're treating me like trash,*' *I told Ash.* '*You only have to look at the two boys to see they have the same father.*'

Paul was sitting beside me. The doctor smiled at him.

He took another of the Q-tips and said in a gentle voice, '*Open up, please.*'

I opened my mouth and he swabbed.

The doctor then laid his hand on Paul's shoulder and said to Ash, '*Want me to test this little chap, too ... to see if he's yours?*'

Ash was oblivious to the doctor's sense of humour.

'*No! No!*' *he said in an obsequious tone.* '*I know he's mine!*'

When the doctor was finished, I stood up quickly and made for the door, my face burning with shame.

'*Thank you,*' *the doctor said in an apologetic voice.* '*We'll be in touch with the results.*'

I brushed past Ash and escaped.

It would be several weeks after my humiliation when Ash phoned me.

'*The results are back.*'

'*Tell me what I already know,*' *I said coldly.*

'It's 99 per cent certain that I am the father.'

I exploded. 'I told *you* that!'

'What about the one per cent?' he said.

I slammed down the phone. I felt cold. A tremendous coldness.

One per cent!

How could I have tolerated this spineless, vacillating weakling? Later, he would try to cajole me by taking an interest in Jay-Jay. He would stand by the side of our younger son's high chair and 'coo'. It was only after he became convinced that he was the boy's father that he brought his mother to see Jay-Jay. I wonder how he explained to her that she was suddenly being introduced to a grandchild she had not known existed. Too little, too late. I was immune. I could not forgive him.

'Giss-ellle!' he would whine. 'Don't look at me like that!'

'Like what?' I demanded. 'Like a liar, like a cheat, like someone who goes off and has a child with another man?'

'I didn't believe tha—' he began.

'Yes, *you* did!' I told him.

He would smile, try to embrace me, seek to persuade me I was making a 'fuss'.

'Enough!' I would shout.

And Ash would leave without saying another word.

I knew that in the weeks and months ahead it would become increasingly difficult to tolerate his presence. But I was too afraid not to keep my promise. I had two sons to lose, now.

Nothing was ever said, but I often wondered if Ash sensed my alarm, or had considered taking my boys and never allowing me to see them again. I held that thought as I went to the window to draw the curtains. Below me, in the fading light, a solitary figure was standing looking up at my window.

It was Ash.
In that second I knew he had.
I could not conceive then how he would realise my worst fear.
Two years, just two more years …

20

The Final Straw

'It's about the men ... what they need, what they want; it's all about control.'

Ian Stephen

June: Until now, it was always between me and Rab. Now he demanded that I choose ... him or Michelle.

'I'm afraid Michelle's carers won't be coming back to your house, Mrs Thomson.'

'It's Rab, isn't it?' I said. She didn't have to spell it out. I might have to put up with his obnoxious, controlling behaviour, but they didn't. They'd had enough.

We were standing in the hall. The Fife Council official spoke quietly, matter-of-factly and with utter finality.

I felt a dreadful sinking feeling. What were we going to do now? Michelle was 25, and at the centre of an elaborate and essential network. She depended on a professional, selfless and wholly committed band of carers.

'I'm so sorry,' I told the official.

She was sympathetic but adamant.

'No one blames you,' she said. 'But you appreciate our position.'

I saw her to the door, where she said, 'We'll try and work something out.'

I knew, of course, that she couldn't. I returned to the living room, where Rab was staring at the television. He looked up as I entered.

'Load of fucking shit,' he said.

'What did you do, what did you say, Rab?'

For once I wasn't afraid. My blood was boiling. I might not have been able to stand up for myself – but this was about Michelle. When it came to her well-being, I was robbed of fear.

'Fuck all!' he exclaimed.

'They don't think it's *fuck all*,' I retorted. 'You've upset them and they don't want to come back.'

He fell silent.

'Where does that leave Michelle?' I demanded.

'Fuck them! We'll put her in a home. Then they won't need to come back.'

I could have killed Rab in that moment. I thought back to the episode when I held the gun to his head.

'I should have pulled the trigger,' I whispered.

'What did you say?' he asked, mystified.

'You would put Michelle in a home?'

'What's the big fucking deal? We'll get her back when this settles down,' he said defiantly.

'*No, we won't*,' I said.

'No, we won't what?' he said.

'She will not go into any home.'

Rab looked at me intently.

'Are you prepared to break up this family for the sake of putting Michelle in a home?' he said.

'I'm not going to break up this family, Rab. I'm going to free it … from you!'

'Well, I'm not going any-fucking-where,' he said.

I stood up, looked down at him and then left the room. The phone was in the hall. I dialled the number of the woman who for years had been begging me to leave him. My sister answered.

'It's me, Linda. I'm leaving. And this time it's for good.'

Giselle: Why should we have believed any differently? It was always about them, wasn't it? It always would be …

My mother was dying. It was 16 January 2008.

We could not reach her now. We stood by her bed and we wept for her, for Da and for ourselves. The world was coming to an end. Ma had been in hospital for weeks. She had never in her life been defeated, but she was now 75 years old. Age and illness were about to claim her.

Everyone in the family was at the hospital. My two sons were at home, where Ash was looking after them. It was the only favour I had asked of him since the DNA fiasco. Paul and Jay-Jay, who had just turned two, had been to see their granny earlier in the day. The sight of her in her final hours had distressed them.

This was a woman they adored – she had sung to them and danced with them. I wanted them to carry only those memories of her.

'Ma's fading,' I had told Ash. 'I want to be with her, and the rest of the family, especially for Da.'

'How long will you be?' he had asked.

'As long as it takes,' I said.

That was several hours ago. I was looking at Ma, holding her hand, hoping she knew I was there. I'm certain she did. I stayed like that for a long time until Tam said to me, 'Pop outside, get a breath of fresh air.'

I had just gone through the doors of the hospital when my mobile rang.

'Hello,' I said.

'Where are you?' It was Ash.

'The hospital,' I said.

'When are you coming home to the boys?'

'I can't leave Ma.'

'You'll have to come.'

'I can't!'

'You must,' he said.

'What's happened? Is something wrong with the boys?'

'The boys are fine,' he said.

'What's wrong, then?'

'I've got college, you know.'

I hung up and ran back to Ma's bedside. I took her hand and said, 'Ma, please, please! Hang on until I get back.'

I drove home in a daze. Ash must have heard me coming through the door. He was pulling on his coat.

'You've been a very long time,' he said.

He didn't ask about Ma.

'Ash,' I said. 'Ma doesn't have long. Please, please, can you not miss college?'

'That's very unfair, Giselle. You know how important it is.'

'Ash, I beg you then, come back as soon as you can. Please!'

''Bye, babies!' he shouted to the boys.

I waited … and waited. For hours. I called Ash repeatedly, long after I knew that his class would be over. I left message after message on his voicemail. I had just disconnected yet another call to his phone when my own rang.

'Thank God!' I breathed.

It wasn't Ash. It was Tam.

'Ma's gone,' he said.

21

If Only ... (Giselle)

'Ash was detached now from any kind of normal emotion and he had decided what he was going to do. The planning had begun.'

Ian Stephen

Giselle: We torture ourselves with these 'if only' moments. If only I hadn't shown him where to kill my babies.

Ash did not feel Paul tugging at his jacket.

'Daddy! Daddy! Daddy!'

Ash had been lost in thought. He returned from wherever he had been and looked at our son. 'What, baby?' he whispered.

'Sheep ... sheep ...' Paul told him excitedly.

Little Jay-Jay was trying to entice the animals but he could not get his tongue around the words 'come here'. Instead he shouted: 'A'meer sheeps ... A'meer!'

I was smiling. Ash turned to me and he too was smiling. My smile faded. I found it so difficult to be in this man's company. The DNA test had humiliated me, but being separated from my mother in the last few precious moments of her life had been devastating. I despised him, but I also feared him. That was why I was keeping my promise that he would never be separated from his sons.

Ash ushered the boys away, onto the open ground where the sheep were grazing. He didn't look happy. One of his moods? I had been taken aback that morning when he phoned and insisted we all go for a day out to the spot where I had spent so many happy times as a child.

'Let's go out,' he'd said.

'Where?' I replied.

'The countryside! What about that place you used to talk about?'

'The Campsie Fells?'

I felt my skirt being tugged. 'Beenbeena,' demanded Jay-Jay. His word for Ribena. He was holding out his Bob the Builder 'sippy' cup, which he loved so much that he couldn't bear to be parted from it. I had to attach a string to the handle for him to wear it around his neck.

'Wait a minute, baby,' I told him.

I turned from Jay-Jay. 'That would be nice for the boys,' I told Ash. 'I'll get them ready.'

'Be there in an hour,' Ash said.

He arrived at the flat in his 'pride and joy' – a silver Mercedes. Of late, Ash had been moaning constantly about being in debt, which surprised me. The car must have cost a lot, but then he saw it as a symbol of a status and success he did not enjoy.

When the doorbell rang, I was tying the laces of Jay-Jay's gleaming white trainers. The boys trailed after me to the front door, where Paul greeted his father warmly.

'Ready?' Ash said.

'Don't you just want to take the boys out on your own?' I asked.

'No, no. It'll be nice for us all to go out together,' he said with a sickly smile. Trying to make up ground that could never be made up.

'Whatever,' I said.

Paul had demanded his Spiderman figure for the journey and Jay-Jay had retrieved his Bob the Builder hammer. Somehow we managed to get out of the house and into the lift that carried us down to the ground floor.

'We'll take my car,' I told Ash. 'I know where we're going.'

I belted the boys into the car. Instead of getting into the passenger seat, Ash sat in the back, sandwiched between them. I thought that was odd. We drove away and it wasn't long before we had left the city behind. The countryside was literally minutes away from where we lived and we were soon crossing the boundary, heading for Lennoxtown. I hadn't been to the Campsies for years. It was a journey I had made many times as a child, sitting in the back of my father's car. Now I was surrounded by familiar hills and memories of childhood. Ash was talking to the boys – inane chatter – but every time I glanced in the rearview mirror he was looking at me.

'All right?' I said over my shoulder.

'Yes,' he said quietly.

We reached the outskirts of Lennoxtown, which lay in a fold of the hills. I drove into a large car park, the central point for visitors who flocked to the beauty spot at weekends. We baled out of the car. Paul was dancing with excitement and Jay-Jay was mesmerised by the sheep on the hillside. The boys took off and I followed, laughing at the sight of my city boys delighting in nature. I was so caught up in their excitement that I had not *noticed Ash's air of distraction. It was only when Paul began tugging at his father's jacket that I realised he wasn't really 'with us'. I pushed aside the thought, prepared simply to enjoy the moment with my sons. I was feeling convivial, in spite of myself.*

'Look at Jay-Jay,' I said to Ash.

Ash was looking off into the distance. I looked in the same direction but I could not see what was attracting his attention. He was watchful, expressionless. And then, suddenly, he relaxed, laughed and snapped out of whatever mood he had been in. Whatever had been bothering him had been resolved, it seemed.

It was a perfect spring day, hinting at summer to come. We marched up the hill under a clear blue sky, accompanied by birdsong and a light wind riffling our hair.

'This is where you used to come, isn't it?' Ash suddenly asked me.

'When I was a girl,' I replied.

'You were happy?'

'Yes,' I said, beginning to struggle for breath. 'Ma and Da brought us here. It was our favourite place.'

Ash was looking at me so intently.

'You were really *happy here?'*

There was strangeness in his voice but I dismissed the thought. I was enjoying the sight of my boys running free in a place where I had once roamed with my brothers and sisters.

'This was our special place,' I said.

He fell silent, listening as I revisited my childhood.

'We put sausages on sticks and cooked them on little fires. Ma packed loads of stuff and Da used to throw us all into the back of the car. We'd drive here, and they'd sit and watch us running up and down the hills all day long.'

Ash had never been here before and he seemed to be trans-fixed by my story. I was surprised by his interest. He had always been aloof from my family, no matter how much they tried to include him in their lives.

I was distracted by Paul.

'Mummy, Mummy, Jay-Jay's fallen down,' he said in his proper little voice.

Paul was my angel. He was prim, reserved, always immacu-late, always mannerly. On the other hand, my delightful little Jay-Jay was a little hell's angel. He was tiny but he was a toughie.

'Get up, you,' I said to Jay-Jay, who climbed to his feet and took off again.

'This is a special place, isn't it?' Ash repeated.

'Yeah,' I said, laughing at the boys, who were now chasing each other rather than the sheep.

Ash smiled.

Seven days later, he would return to my special place and take my babies with him.

22

Saturday 3 May

'June and Giselle could not have known what
was about to happen – that's why killers such
as these are so extremely dangerous.'

Ian Stephen

**June: Our journey into the darkness was beyond knowing,
beyond understanding, beyond all evil – and it began on a
day that seemed to be filled with sunshine and promise.**

'When's Auntie Linda going to get here?'

'Soon,' I told Michelle. She was beside herself with
excitement.

'When?' she demanded.

'Soon,' I repeated.

'But when?' she pleaded.

It was impossible to be annoyed. Michelle had diamonds
in her eyes. We had been in our new home for a few days and
this morning was – to use an old cliché – the beginning of the
first day of the rest of our lives. My sister Linda, who had
lived in Liverpool for years, was on her way. She and her two

young children, Beth and Abbi, had agreed to move in with me, Michelle and Ryan. A few days earlier I had driven down south and returned with my nieces. When their mother arrived we were all going to live as one family.

'When's Mummy going to get here?' asked Abbi.

'Don't you start,' I warned her, but there was no harshness in my voice.

This was too good a day to be angry. Her sister, Beth, and Ryan picked up on the mood and came towards me.

'Soon ... soon,' I told them before the question was asked.

As I looked at the four children my sense of contentment was complete. The house was, of course, a tip, a toyshop – but it was so quiet without the pressure-cooker effect of Rab's malevolence, his anger and his demand that everything be in its place.

It was a house at peace.

When I had called Linda to tell her I was leaving Rab, she begged me to wait.

'We have to plan this,' she told me. 'Get everything organised.'

We had. I found a house for rent in Methil, a little town on the North Sea coast not too far from Muiredge. I was happy that I was no longer on my own. Linda's decision to join me would be the safety valve. If I weakened, she would be my strength.

'When's Aun—?' Michelle began.

'Soon, soon, soon, soon,' I interrupted.

I was buoyant. I couldn't remember a time when I had felt so optimistic. This was truly a new chapter. I had been away from Rab for a couple of weeks now. I had already started divorce proceedings, but I had readily agreed that he should be allowed full access to the children. I did not want to separate him from Ryan or Michelle. Shaun had returned to England and Ross had elected to remain with his father. He and Rab had always been close. He was a young man now and could make up his own mind.

I was determined that this time I would get it right. The legal agreement allowing Rab access had just been ratified at Kirkcaldy Sheriff Court. I viewed this as much more than a legal move. It was a signal to Rab that this time I would not be going back.

It was over.

As the children played around me, their squeals ringing though the house, I made a mental inventory of what I had to do that morning. Linda and her friend Jackie, who was driving the van loaded with my sister's furniture, would not arrive until the afternoon. My task for the moment was to get Michelle and Ryan ready to go out. I would deliver them to their dad at our old home for his first official access visit.

I was relieved that for a few hours at least they would be out from under my feet.

Giselle: You were planning a new life ... All I wanted to do was cuddle my boys. It felt just like any other Saturday.

'Twink-ell, twink-ell, Litt-ell Staaaarr ...'
   I didn't dare laugh. Paul was so serious as he crooned to his brother. Jay-Jay's dark eyes were bright – he was under the spell of Paul's performance of his favourite song. I was in bed, sandwiched between my babies. I shifted under the duvet, drawing

my sons closer and sending a motley crew of Spidermen and Bob the Builders clattering to the floor. The light that shone through the bedroom window was white and warm. A beautiful day. I would have to make a move soon. I was due to meet my sister, Katie, to do the big Saturday shop. I lingered, though, loath to end this magical moment.

'Twink-a, twink-a, lil' sta ...' Jay-Jay mimicked Paul.

The tune was good but the words needed work. I knew I could not contain the laughter for much longer. It was time to get up. We had a big day ahead. As well as shopping, I would visit Da. Since Ma had passed away, he so looked forward to the Saturday visits.

It was 8.30 a.m.

June: We were both consumed with such ordinary things.

'This one, Mum?' Michelle said, dragging yet another colourful pullover from the wardrobe. 'Or this one?'

'Whichever you like. They're both nice,' I told her.

My input was futile. Michelle inevitably took ages to get ready and, no matter what I said, she would try everything on at least once before deciding on something in her favourite colours of lurid purple or pale pink. I left her to it and returned to the kitchen, where Abbi had Ryan in a vice-like grip, kissing him on the cheeks. The cousins were the same age and they had become inseparable over the last few days.

'Put him down,' I told her. 'Ryan has to get dressed.'

Abbi released Ryan reluctantly.

'You, Madam, get yourself ready if you want to come with me,' I told her.

'Wanna go with Ryan and play with the trucks,' Abbi said.

My plan was to drop off Ryan and Michelle, and bring Abbi and Beth back to our new house, where we would await their mum's arrival.

'Ryan and Michelle are going to see their daddy,' I told her.

'Me, too,' she insisted.

I wasn't bothered one way or the other. Abbi loved Uncle Rab. There was no problem in leaving her with him and her cousins.

'Okay,' I said. 'Get dressed!'

Michelle emerged, wearing denims and a red T-shirt. No purple or pink? I realised suddenly how grown up she had become. She was a woman. It was sometimes hard to recognise that, given her innocence. Ryan returned wearing khaki chinos and a beige jumper, which I'd bought him a few days earlier for his seventh birthday. He, too, was growing. He looked such a little man.

I was still in my night clothes, but I showered quickly and dressed in jeans and a casual top. I glanced in the mirror, which was no longer an enemy of the 'new' me. I looked at my reflection without fear, and I did look different from the frumpy housewife that Rab had demanded I be. I now had no one to please but myself. What I wore was no longer his business. I was beyond worrying about what he expected.

I was drawn away from the mirror by the arrival of Beth and Abbi in my room. The children were soon rampaging around the house. Time to go.

'Right, you lot, in the car. Now!' I said.

We went outside and piled into the car. I drove away from the house. It would take less than 20 minutes to reach Muiredge.

It was 11.30 a.m.

Giselle: I wasn't even expecting his call.

The phone rang at 11.30 a.m. It was Ash. I felt my throat tighten.

'I want to take the boys for a game of football,' he said without preamble.

Football! At last! Something normal. Ash was finally listening to me.

'When?' I said.

'Why don't I come now? Are they ready?'

Paul and Jay-Jay were still in their pyjamas.

'I can get them dressed quickly,' I told Ash.

I said to the boys, 'Daddy wants to play football.'

'I want to stay with you, Mummy,' Paul said.

'Paul doesn't want to go,' I told Ash.

'Let me speak to him,' he said.

I handed the phone to Paul. It looked enormous in his hand. He listened.

'Okay,' he said. 'Daddy says I can have £10 for Spiderman toys,' he shouted at me.

'Well, you better get ready then,' I told him.

Paul dashed to his bedroom. He was dressed and back just as Jay-Jay was ready. I was inspecting them when the entry buzzer sounded. I packed an extra nappy for Jay-Jay and filled sippy cups with Ribena. The doorbell chimed and Paul opened the door to his father.

Ash was full of enthusiasm. 'C'mon babies, we're going to have a great time. Bring the football.'

Jay-Jay was clutching his favourite yellow ball. Paul hugged his father and asked, 'Daddy, Daddy, can I really buy Spiderman toys?'

'Of course,' Ash promised.

I wanted to see them off, so I left with them. Katie wouldn't mind me turning up a bit early. The breakfast dishes could wait.

The doors of the lift were still open. As they closed on us, Jay-Jay said, 'Stay a'Mummy, stay a'Mummy.'

I was holding his hand. 'C'mon, baby,' I said. 'Don't you want to play football with your big brother and Daddy?'

'Okaaaa-y,' he said.

I kissed the top of his head. We emerged from the lift and headed for Ash's Mercedes. He helped Paul into the car but he left Jay-Jay struggling to get in. He was so tiny and his little legs could not reach the door rim without help. I lifted him into the back seat and strapped him in. Ash started the car and as he drove off my boys craned their necks to look out of the back window. They were laughing and waving to me.

I waved until the car disappeared around the corner.

June: I thought he'd be different. But Rab couldn't change.

'Are you happy now?' Rab hissed.

I had just walked through the door at Muiredge with Ryan, Michelle, Abbi and Beth.

'What?' I said sharply, feeling my confidence draining.

His face was inches from mine.

'With all this,' he spat, waving his arms to encompass the untidy room. 'This divorce shite. You know you're going to come crawling back anyway.'

'Not this time,' I said quietly.

Rab looked at me. For the first time, I could see uncertainty in his eyes.

'You're going to end up a sad, lonely old cow, just like your fucking mother!' he growled. But it was all just bravado.

I was so weary of this. If anything reinforced my resolve to stay away, this was it. He must have known it was over. I hadn't seen him for days. The divorce papers had been lodged. The line had been drawn in the sand. What would it take to convince this man? But then, why should I have been surprised? Leopards don't change their spots.

'You've made your point,' he went on. 'It's costing a fortune on all these fucking lawyers over this shite.'

I waited for a fist to smash into my face as it had done so often in the past, but the blow never arrived. He had at last learned one lesson, it seemed. He seethed with anger, but he stepped back and looked at me from head to toe.

'And what the fuck d'ye think you're playing at, comin' out dressed like that?' he said.

I knew it. I remained silent. I had long since learned that nothing I could say or do – or wear – would deflect Rab when he was ranting. This time, however, it did not matter what he thought or said.

Beth cowered close to me, and Ryan and Abbi ran to my son's old bedroom, where all his toys were, and they began playing with his collection of trucks. Rab sat down heavily on a kitchen chair, filling the room with an air of malevolence. I looked around. There were unwashed dishes everywhere. I wasn't here any more to be his skivvy.

'Do you have any sweets for the kids? Crisps? Juice?' I asked.

'Crisps!' said Abbi. 'Want crisps.'

Rab shrugged and I turned, heading for the door.

'I'll be back in a couple of minutes,' I said.

On the journey to the shop I counted my blessings again. I had at last somewhere else to go now, a sanctuary, where I would not have to endure Rab's barracking. I returned within 20 minutes, laden with crisps, sweets and treats for the kids.

'Right, you lot,' I said. 'I've loads to do. Auntie Linda will be here soon.'

Rab drew me daggers. The very mention of Linda's name made him angry. She had always seen through the façade of our marriage. It had been my intention to take Beth with me, leaving Ryan, Michelle and Abbi behind.

As I turned to the door, Abbi grabbed my jeans and said, 'I'm coming with you, Auntie June.'

'Thought you were staying to play with Ryan?' I said.

'You better take her,' Rab said. 'I don't want her moaning once you're out that door.'

I wasn't in the mood to argue. I shrugged and said, 'C'mon, darling.' To my children I shouted, 'Michelle! Ryan! See you soon. I'll be back after teatime.'

Their disembodied voices replied 'Okay' in unison.

As I was ushering my nieces outside and into the car, I was stilled by Rab's voice.

'What are you going to do when you're left on your own, June? With nobody to love? What the fuck are you going to do then?'

I chose not to rise to the bait.

As I drove off, Michelle and Ryan were at the living-room window. Michelle was waving frantically with both hands and Ryan was holding up his favourite truck. I looked at my watch.

It was 1 p.m.

Giselle: I knew something was wrong the second I heard his voice.

I was in the supermarket, reaching up for cereal when my mobile rang. I rummaged in my bag, retrieved the phone and caught the call. Ash's number was on the screen.

It was 1 p.m.

'Hello,' I said.

Silence.

'Hello,' I repeated.

I could hear wind and outdoor noises in the background. Ash began mumbling incoherently.

'Ash? What's wrong?'

They had been gone for just under an hour and a half.

'Do the babies want to come home?' I asked.

Silence … the sound of the wind.

I was gripped by a sudden panic.

'Are the babies all right?'

Mumbling.

'Ash!' I demanded.

'Your babies are fine, your babies are fine,' he said in a monotone.

The voice of a stranger. I couldn't hear my sons. That was unusual. Something was wrong.

'Ash!' I begged.

'You will regret what you did to me in this life,' the voice said. And then the phone went dead.

'Ash!' I screamed.

I dropped my bag, bolted for the door of the store, drawing strange looks from the other shoppers. Katie ran behind me, unaware of what I had heard, but knowing instinctively that something was terribly wrong.

'What is it? What is it?' she said, breathless.

I didn't reply. I was too busy trying to call Ash's number. It was dead. I tried again and again and again. Not even voicemail.

'Please God!' I said.

'What?' Katie demanded. 'Tell me! Tell me!'

'Need to go home, need to go home, Katie.'

'It's that idiot, isn't it?' she said.

I have no memory of the journey back, no memory of what we spoke about, no recollection of dropping Katie at her gate. I just had to get home. I needed to find out if Ash had left a message on the answering machine. I barged through the entrance door and into an open lift. I stamped my feet with impatience on the excruciatingly slow ascent to my floor. I shook like a leaf, willing the lift to get there.

Eventually, after what seemed like an eternity, the doors opened. I raced to the flat, rammed the key in the lock and fell into the hall as the door flew open. Answering machine. No blinking light, no messages. I felt suddenly as if I were going to vomit. I rushed to the kitchen sink and gagged. I turned on the tap, then splashed my face with cold water.

My mobile rang.

'Ash,' I shouted. 'Thank God!'

It was Katie.

'I'm coming,' she said.

The phone died.

I paced the floor, dialling, dialling, dialling Ash's number. I must have pressed those buttons a hundred times. I heard Katie letting herself into the flat. Her face was white with worry.

'It's Ash,' I told her. 'I couldn't hear the babies. Something's wrong. I know it.'

'What did he say?' Katie demanded to know.

I broke down. 'He said I'd regret what I'd done.'

'Done what?' asked Katie.

'I don't know, I don't know. Something's wrong or he's done something. I can tell by his voice. It didn't even sound like him.'

'C'mon, we'll go and look for them. There aren't many places to play football around here,' Katie said.

It was almost 2 p.m.

June: I passed the house twice. How could I not know something was wrong?

I pulled at the bottom of the living-room curtains, making the folds uniform and even. I stepped back. Perfect, I thought. I shifted the step-ladder away from the window and turned my attention to the boxes in the middle of the room. The bedrooms had been knocked into shape. Only the living room and the kitchen needed finishing touches.

Most of the furniture that would go into the rooms was still in the back of Linda's van. She'd be here soon.

I had left my old life behind with little more than our clothes, a few duvet covers and some odds and ends. Rab wouldn't allow me to take much from Muiredge, not that I really wanted to. I needed a clean break in every sense. When our new home was complete, there would be few reminders of my past life. I had just torn the top off one of the boxes when my mobile rang. Linda.

'It's me,' she said. 'We got lost, but we're back on track and we'll be there by 5.'

'Great,' I said.

'Jackie wants a pie,' she told me.

'What?' I said, mystified.

'All the way up the road I've been telling her about Scotch pies. She won't go home without trying one.'

I laughed. 'Okay, I'll get her a pie.'

'And snowballs!' said Linda. 'She wants a snowball as well.'

Pies and snowballs, I thought. You travel all the way from England and what do you want when you get to Scotland? Whisky? Smoked salmon? Venison? No! Mutton pies and a coconut-covered sponge cake that puts two inches on your waistline just by looking at it.

'Pies and snowballs coming up,' I said and hung up.

I looked at my watch. It was just after 2 p.m. I still had a few hours before they arrived, time to unpack a few more boxes and make the trip to the local baker's shop. Time passed in a blur as I shifted books, toys and clothes into cupboards and drawers. I moved operations from the living room to the kitchen and was just drawing a wet mop over the floor when I looked up at the wall clock. Nearly 4 p.m. Pies and snow-balls, I thought. Better get a move on. I gathered up Abbi and

Beth and headed for the car. A few minutes later we were standing in the local baker's shop.

'No pies left, missus … or snowballs,' the baker told me.

Typical. I'd have to drive to Buckhaven, which meant, ironically, that I would retrace my journey earlier in the day and go past Muiredge. Sod's law, I thought, as I jumped back into the car and settled the children in their seats.

The warmth of the afternoon was gone but as I approached Muiredge it was still a blessed day. The cottage sat on a corner, surrounded by trees and green fields. I would not regret leaving Rab but I would miss the idyllic setting of the house, with its large garden. As the house came into view I felt a sudden twinge of guilt that I had taken them away from a place where we had spent so many happy hours – when Rab was at work.

I was comforted by the thought that there would be no more dark times, no more of Rab's black moods to pollute our lives. I drew level with Muiredge. Rab's car was in the drive but there was no sign of life. The curtains were drawn at the front of the house. I thought it odd, but perhaps the kids were sleeping. Michelle often needed to take a nap in the afternoon and maybe Ryan had tired himself out. As I passed the house, I glanced in the rearview mirror. I noticed the curtains were also drawn at the back of the house. They must be sleeping, I reasoned.

I kept going, reached Buckhaven, and was relieved by the sight of pies and snowballs in the window of the baker's shop on the high street. Clutching my spoils in a clutter of white paper bags, we headed back to Methil.

On the return journey I noticed the curtains were still drawn at Muiredge.

Giselle: Why didn't they help me? Why couldn't they see?

'Please help me!' I begged the woman behind the counter.

'Anything could be happening to the boys,' Katie told her.

We were in the foyer of the police station in Stewart Street, on the fringe of Glasgow city centre.

'24 hours,' said the woman, a civilian worker.

She had told me seconds earlier that a missing person's report could not be filed until 24 hours had passed.

'But these are two little boys, my babies,' I told her. 'Why can't you look for them? Can't you put Ash's registration number out there? There must be something you can do. He has my boys and something's wrong. I know it. I couldn't hear them when he phoned me.'

The woman told me to wait.

'I'll speak to the duty officer,' she said.

She disappeared, and Katie and I turned away from the counter.

'Where are they?' I asked her.

Katie had no answer for me.

The woman returned with a sheaf of papers in her hand. 'We'll fill out a report,' she said.

'Thank you,' I replied.

She shuffled papers, asking me questions I had already answered. I was terrified, unable to think straight.

I explained again and again that Ash and I didn't live together, and, no, we hadn't fallen out, and, yes, he had access to the boys whenever he wanted. It was evident that this woman had never filled out such a report before.

She was hesitant and unsure. I grew increasingly frustrated.

A uniformed officer arrived at the counter and looked over his colleague's shoulder. She kept asking him how to complete certain parts of the form. Precious minutes ticked by.

'He said I would regret what I did,' I told them. 'Does that not tell you that something is wrong?'

I was becoming hysterical, but all they were interested in was filling out this stupid form.

'Are there any court orders?' the male officer asked.

'No!' I said. 'No court orders. He sees the kids whenever he wants.'

'Have you any fears that he has taken them out of the country?' the officer went on in a tired voice.

'No!' I said. 'He only lives around the corner from here. Can't you go and look for his car?'

The woman was still fussing over the report forms.

I turned away in frustration towards a window looking out onto the street. An elderly woman was walking along the road. At first I didn't recognise her.

'God Almighty!' I said.

It was Ash's mother.

'Wait!' I shouted, and then bolted out of the police station.

'Maya! Maya!' I shouted.

Ash's mother turned in the direction of my voice.

'Giselle!' she said.

I was the last person she expected to see, running like a madwoman from a police station.

'Where are the boys?' I asked her.

She began speaking in Punjabi.

'Where's Ash?' I demanded.

She was visibly upset.

'In here!' I told her, guiding her into a newsagent's that I knew was run by an Asian family.

A man behind the counter looked up as we entered.

'Please help me,' I begged him.

'Sure, darlin',' he said in a broad Glaswegian accent.

'Tell Maya I'm looking for the babies. They're with Ash. Has she heard from him?'

The man began speaking in Punjabi and Maya replied.

'She doesn't know,' he translated.

'Has he taken them somewhere?' I asked. 'Does she know where he is? When was the last time she saw him?'

The man turned and spoke to Maya, who replied through her tears.

'He's supposed to be at work,' said the shopkeeper.

There was no point to this. It was wasting time. Maya had no answers for me. I rushed out of the shop without another word and hurried back to the police station. The officer and the civilian worker were still behind the counter.

'That was Ash's mother,' I explained. 'She doesn't know where he is.'

'Is this out of character for your husband? Are the children likely to come to harm?' the woman said, her pen poised over her forms.

It was as if she were reading from a script.

———————

June: I still couldn't see. All I was thinking was that we would all be safe now.

'Linda,' I shouted.

I had emerged from the front door in time to see her jump down from the van.

'White-van woman!' I teased.

'Did you get those pies? We're starving.'

'In the oven,' I said.

I hugged my sister as Linda's friend Jackie came round from the driver's side. She, too, was embraced.

'Muuu-mmmy!' shouted Beth and Abbi in unison, grabbing their mother around the legs.

For the next hour we trekked back and forth, carting furniture from the van.

'Empty, at last,' said Jackie, as Linda and I lifted the last of the boxes from the back of the van.

'Time for those pies,' Linda said.

The kitchen was a warm sanctuary, filled with the comforting smell of baking. The legendary snowballs sat on a plate in the middle of the table.

'They look fantastic,' Jackie said.

'They're for afters,' I chided.

It would be a makeshift banquet. Our lives were contained in boxes all around us but we sat down at the table, happy and content. A Scotch pie had never tasted so good. We polished them off and were eyeing the snowballs when I looked at my watch and realised it was just after 6 p.m.

It would soon be time to go for the kids.

Giselle: It was so bad, they couldn't bear to tell me.

It was 6 p.m. when my mobile rang.

A voice said, 'Can you come into the station?'

It was the duty sergeant at Stewart Street. Katie and I were already outside the station, sitting in the car. We had arrived minutes before after yet another tour of the area in a fruitless search for Ash and the boys.

'They must know something,' I told Katie. 'Something must have happened. They know something. What are they not telling us?'

'Let's go and ask,' said Katie. 'We'll be able to tell by their faces.'

We pushed through the doors of the police station.

The woman civilian worker and the officer had been joined at the counter by another policeman.

'What's happened? Tell me what's happened,' I demanded.

Their faces said nothing. One of them – I can't remember which one – said, 'Someone will come and speak to you.'

I was ushered towards a waiting room. Katie made to follow me but she was asked to stay in the reception area.

'I want my sister,' I told the officer.

'Better she wait here,' he said.

'What's happened?' I asked for the hundredth time.

My heart was pounding. I thought it would burst through my chest. The policeman said nothing. He guided me to the waiting room. It had a glass front and I could still see Katie. We exchanged puzzled looks.

'Why you no' speakin' tae me, darlin'?' a voice said.

I hadn't noticed there was anyone else in the room.

I looked in the direction of the voice. A drunk man, reeking of booze and sweat, was rolling on the floor.

'You no' talkin' tae me?' he repeated.

'Go away!' I said sharply.

Something in my voice penetrated his befuddled brain and he fell silent.

The police station was open-plan and I could see a flurry of activity, police officers huddled together, speaking in hushed voices and looking over their shoulders in my direction.

It was at that moment that I knew something really terrible had happened. If it had been good news they would surely have told us, wouldn't they? It had to be bad, but how bad?

The drunk rallied. 'C'mon, give us a song!' he said.

For some reason, I couldn't allow myself to let him see me cry, to see the pain I was in. I couldn't even speak to him. I looked at the group of police officers with a sinking heart. Not knowing was torture. Why couldn't they just tell me? I looked through the glass at Katie. Her anxious face mirrored my own. It was as if she had read my mind, that a silent message had passed between us. She held up her hands, imploring. I shook my head. 'I don't know,' I said with my eyes

'Give us a kiss darlin', c'mon,' the drunk persisted.

'Fuck off!' I screamed in a voice I had never heard before.

He retreated to the corner of the room, where he muttered to himself until he lapsed into sleep.

I leapt from the chair. I had been in there for almost an hour and couldn't stand any more. I went to the glass partition and stared into the foyer. Katie questioned me again with her eyes but I still had no answers. The police officers remained huddled together, but they had been joined by two new faces.

These strangers disengaged themselves from the others and walked towards me. They opened the door and one of them said, 'Will you come with us?'

'Can Katie come with me?' I asked.

They shook their heads. One of them said, 'No! We need to speak to you on your own.'

I followed them into another room, a sense of dread overwhelming me. What was going on? Had Ash absconded with my babies as I feared he would? Taken them out of the country? What?

'What's happened?' I begged.

They remained silent and ushered me into an interview room, where they laid papers down on a table. I was asked to sit at the table and they pulled up their chairs opposite me.

'Tell us everything that happened today, before you came to the police office, Giselle,' one of the officers said.

'I've already told the people at the desk. We've been here forever,' I replied.

'We just have to make sure,' said the other officer.

'What has happened to my babies? Tell me!' I shouted, my voice breaking with frustration.

'We have to verify certain things, Giselle,' said the first officer in a quiet voice. 'It's easier if you just answer our questions. What were the children wearing the last time you saw them?'

That was when I knew.

The dam burst. I sobbed uncontrollably.

My voice shrank to a whisper.

'Please, just tell me what's happened. I can't stand this. Please, just tell me,' I pleaded.

One of the officers glanced at the clock on the wall.

It was 7 p.m.

'We've found two bodies,' he said.

June: God help us! We had become pawns in their hellish game.

The house was too quiet.

No laughter. Our two dogs were outside in their kennels, still barking a welcome to me. The sound was muted now that I had entered the house. My watch said it was one minute to seven o'clock. My anger over finding the dogs tethered, the chains wrapped around their throats, was dissipating in the deafening silence.

Rab and the children had to be here. His car was still in the drive. Muiredge was too distant from anywhere for them to have ventured out on foot.

The back door had been locked, unusual in itself during daylight hours, and I had been forced to forage in my hand-bag to find the key. Why was it so quiet? I listened. Deathly quiet. Something was wrong, I could sense it. No voices. The hairs on the back of my neck sprung up.

I walked through the kitchen into the dining room, pass-ing the debris of crisps and sweets. Into the hall. All the doors leading off it were closed. Into the living room. Ryan's toys were scattered on the floor. His bedroom door was shut. I placed my hand on the handle and pushed it open, leaning into the room. My son was on the bed. Asleep.

'Ryan,' I said softly. 'It's Mum. Ryan? *Ryan?*'

He wasn't asleep. His eyes were open. Why were his eyes open? Then I saw his lips. They were blue, contrasting with the paleness of his skin. His face might have been sculpted from wax.

His little hands were arranged carefully on his chest as if in an attitude of prayer.

Blood. Blood everywhere.

A scream, long and silent, ripped through my mind. Seeing, but not believing. A nightmare. I must awaken now, but I didn't. I closed the door and opened it again. The scene had not changed.

He was dead. My baby was dead. I raced to the bed, gathering him in my arms. He was so cold. I shook uncontrollably as my hands roamed over his body looking for injuries. I could find only a single rent in his new pullover, now stained deep red.

Now I heard the deep animal howls, a dreadful guttural sound that came from deep within me. I had found my voice. I howled in anguish. Numbed, disoriented, I placed Ryan gently back on his bed.

And then I realised.

Michelle! God, no!

I sprinted to her room, opening the door onto its familiar pink and purple décor. She, too, was lying on her bed. Her lovely curls, matted with blood, were spread in a halo on the pillow. Her eyes were open, her hands arranged on the bedclothes as if she were pleading for help. There was so much blood – on the walls, the carpet, her toys – great bloody red pools.

I screamed for help.

'*No! No! Michelle! Ryan! Somebody!*'

Loud footsteps on the stairs. Ross. He had been in his bedroom in the attic.

'Mum! Mum!' he cried, his voice loud with alarm. 'What's the screaming for? What's wrong?'

I stumbled into the hall, covered in the blood of my children.

'They're dead! They're dead!'

Ross was dumbfounded.

'In there!' I screamed.

The spell was broken. Ross ran into Michelle's room, fled from there into Ryan's room and then to the back of the house, where he burst through the door.

Help, get help, I thought. Get their father. I went into the bedroom I had shared with Rab. He was lying semi-naked on the bed, motionless, his back to me.

'Rab! Rab!' I cried.

And then I saw the kitchen knife, so familiar, with its huge blade and long black handle. He's dead too! His wrists were red with blood. I was hysterical. My mind exploded.

I knew.

He had done this. *He* had done this. My instincts screamed it at me. In one sickening moment of clarity I recognised how Rab had decided to punish me.

I raced back into the hall and grabbed Ross. We held each other.

'Get help, Mum. Get help. You have to get help.'

The phone. In my confusion I called Linda and not the police. She answered.

'They're all dead. The kids and Rab. They're all dead,' I screamed.

'Call the police,' she shouted.

I managed to dial 999.

'The children. My children. They're dead,' I told the woman who answered.

Questions. So many questions. I was incoherent. I begged for help. Ross ran back to the top of the house, where his girlfriend, Kay, was still in the attic. She had been too terrified by the commotion to come down. The police operator kept me talking.

Blue lights flashing outside, the sound of a dying siren, a car skidding to a halt. The police. The first officer through the door was the local part-time bobby. I knew him.

'Sit down,' he said gently, his eyes bright with uncertainty as he prised the phone from my hand.

More officers. Crowding into the house. More sirens, heavier vehicles drawing up outside. Ambulances. Paramedics in green coveralls invading the hall, clutching large bags of equipment that would be of no use now to Ryan and my Michelle.

The police officers were looking at my bloodstained clothing, speaking to me, but I didn't understand their words.

'They're dead. Ryan and Michelle. They're dead,' I kept repeating.

They were wondering whether this hysterical madwoman was a killer. Their expressions flitted between sympathy and accusation, their mouths forming words I could not hear. All I heard was the jabber of radios and the sound of more sirens in the distance. Bedlam. The police officers were packed into such a small place, casting furtive glances towards rooms they were reluctant to enter.

'Are they really dead? Are they really dead?' I called out to the paramedics who had gone into the rooms. 'Please save them, please save my children,' I pleaded.

I knew the plea was useless. I knew they were dead but I clung to any hope, however small.

Time had ceased to have meaning. The paramedics wanted me to leave in an ambulance, but I struggled with them and the police, clinging to the chair, the curtains, anything I could grab. I could not leave my children with strangers. They needed me. I was exhausted. My body was limp and I could no longer resist the strong arms guiding me to the ambulance. I leant back against the interior wall of the vehicle and hands fussed over me, sliding a thin blanket over my shoulders.

'It's okay, it's okay,' said a soft male voice.

I looked up but I could not see his face. I was straining to see over his shoulder as the other paramedics left the house carrying a stretcher. My heart leapt. Someone was alive!

'Michelle! Ryan!' I shouted. 'Ryan! Michelle!' I shouted again.

And then I saw him. Rab. He was alive.

Now I recognised his hellish plan. Lying on the bed. Pretending to be dead. Enjoying my screams. The sick bastard! The knife on the bedside cabinet, the blade he had used to kill our children. He had left it there for me to find. He had engineered this shocking scenario, believing that, in my grief, I would stab him to death. My children would be gone – and I would be in a prison cell for his murder. It was the perfect resolution to a demonic scheme. The ultimate control.

I was suddenly filled with the strength of madness and I launched myself from the ambulance. Police and ambulance men grabbed at me, dragging me back. Somehow I still managed to get within touching distance of the stretcher that was bearing Rab to an ambulance. I wanted to tear him to pieces.

'Evil, evil bastard,' I screamed. 'I'll kill you!'

Dear Christ! The expression on his face. He was smirking. Christ help me, the bastard was smirking. I collapsed. Rab had won and we both knew it. The words he had earlier used to taunt me flooded into my mind.

'*What are you going to do when you're left on your own …*
with nobody to love?'

I watched the ambulance take him away as if through a fog. It would take him to hospital, where he would be treated for wounds that were no more than superficial. Much later, a friend, who was a nurse, would tell me that within hours he was sitting up in bed, watching the television coverage of what he had done.

He was eating his dinner.

23

Mummy Can't Fix It Now

'Ash thought of himself as superior. His superficiality covered up the evil therein.'

Ian Stephen

Giselle: You know why I had to see my babies – no matter what everyone said, I had to see them.

Antiseptic smell. The smell of sickness and death. It assailed me as I walked through the door of the dark and forbidding building.

'Giselle! Are you all right?'

I looked at the policeman called John but I did not need to answer. It had been a rhetorical question. He knew the answer. I wouldn't be all right, ever again. Three days since my babies had been taken. 72 hours that had passed in a dismal fugue induced by grief and Valium. Everyone – my family, my friends, the police – had told me I shouldn't come here. But no power on earth could have kept me away.

What had he done?

My babies, my lovely lost boys, were here, somewhere in this Victorian mortuary, waiting for me.

'Okay?' said my brothers Tam and Alex in unison.

They flanked me protectively. I did not reply. I was focused. All I could think of was being with my sons.

John the policeman and Jackie, the family liaison officer, were about to ask the same brief question but thought better of it.

We had all been arguing for days. My family and the police had done their best to dissuade me from coming here but I was adamant.

'You don't have to put yourself through it. The official identification has been done,' Tam told me.

'Why don't you want me to see them? What did he do to them?' I asked Tam.

'It's nothing to do with that, Giselle. We just think it'll be too much for you,' he replied.

'I have to ...'

My family was afraid that if I saw my babies I would be so traumatised that I would make another attempt to kill myself. I had already tried and failed, on the day my sons died. I hated God! He had taken my babies and allowed the monster who killed them to live. There would be no justice in the world ever again.

Three days earlier, when the policemen eventually told me they had found my sons, everything I loved had been taken from me. I don't remember how I got home. It must have been in a police car. I had the vaguest recollection of Katie's face being close to mine and her voice saying, 'Oh, Giselle ...'

I don't remember going into the building, only the cold, silver-steel wall of the lift against my face as it made its slow progress to my floor. I do remember Katie taking the key, which had somehow found its way into my hand, and opening the door.

'Oh God!' I moaned like a wounded animal.

My babies' breakfast plates were on the kitchen table, their clothes strewn on the settee in the living room, their toys and DVDs abandoned on the floor. I leapt forward and grabbed their pyjamas, pressing them to my face, inhaling my sons' smell. I collapsed onto the sofa. Katie gathered up the debris of my babies' lives, sheltering it from me. What, in the name of God, had happened …?

I don't know how long I sat in a dream state. The meaningless passage of time was punctuated by the phone ringing incessantly and the constant buzzing of the entry door downstairs. The media had picked up on the story. I was under siege. I didn't know then that, on the other side of the country, June's tragedy was mirroring my own. She, too, would be besieged. I wasn't the only mother whose life had ended.

No one had ever witnessed such a horror in a single day – two mothers, two monsters, four murdered children.

Katie fielded the press inquiries, telling them we had nothing to say. What could we say? Words were useless, now. How can you express devastation? I knew my babies were gone, but I still did not know why or how. All I knew for certain was that Ash had returned to a place where I had been so happy and robbed me of my sons.

There was a lull downstairs and the buzzer remained silent until a doctor arrived. A woman doctor. It may sound bizarre but I cannot to this day remember whether she was a stranger to me or from my own GP's practice. Katie buzzed her into the building and a few minutes later she came through the front door. Even in my own grief, I felt sorry for the woman. Her eyes were haunted. She couldn't have expected this type of home visit.

'Giselle,' she said in a quiet voice. Sorrow welled in her eyes. 'I can't begin ...' she began, her voice trailing off.

She knew there was nothing to say that would offer me any comfort. She rallied, wrapping herself in professionalism, and went on in a stronger voice.

'I can give you something to help you sleep.'

'Please give me a lethal injection,' I begged.

'What?'

'A jab, a jab. I know you can do that.'

She was struck dumb.

'I want to be with my babies. Please! Please!' I begged her.

'Giselle ...' she said.

'I won't tell. No one will know. Please! End this!'

Katie said, 'C'mon, Giselle, c'mon.'

The doctor foraged in her medical bag. Pills in her hand. What good were pills? Would they bring back my sons? I accepted them. Within a few minutes I felt myself slipping into a black hole from which I hoped I would never return. My drug-induced sleep was fractured by nightmares and beautiful dreams. In the nightmares, my boys were screaming for their mummy. I could see them, but I could not reach them. What was happening to them?

In the good dreams, I was playing with them, holding them in my arms, feeling their warmth, singing soft, sweet songs to my Paul and Jay-Jay.

I did not so much awake as emerge from my comatose state. The realisation that my sons were gone overwhelmed me. I howled. I was still clutching their pyjamas. Nothing had changed. My cries brought Katie to her feet. She was in a chair,

*having cried herself to exhaustion. My brothers emerged from
the kitchen, their faces white masks of pain. I tried to rise, still
befuddled by the drugs.*

'Where are you going?' Tam asked.

'Bathroom,' I said.

'You want Katie to go in with you?'

'No, need to go to the bathroom.'

*I didn't need to go to the bathroom. In that moment of awak-
ening I had decided to kill myself. I hadn't been left alone since
I heard the dreadful news. I felt suddenly crowded. They were
trying to protect me, I knew that. But no one could protect me
from the pain.*

'Hurry up, pet,' Tam said.

*I walked to the bathroom in a daze, knowing their eyes were
on me. I tried to appear in control. I didn't want anyone to know
what was in my heart. This would bring an end to it. I'd be with
my boys soon. When I closed the bathroom door behind me I
slipped the bolt and looked up at the window. So small. I felt a
moment of peace. This was what I wanted, what I needed to do.
The doctor wouldn't help me. It was up to me now. I moved
forward and released the window catch. We were so high up
there would be no doubting the outcome when I fell. A rush of
cold air hit my face. I clambered up onto the sink, brushing aside
bottles of shampoo and toothbrushes. They clattered to the floor*

*The room was crowded suddenly and hands grabbed at me,
dragging me back from the window.*

'Please, please, please, let me go,' I pleaded.

*They lifted me in their arms and carried me through the
shattered door.*

*'Right, that's it,' roared Tam in a voice laced with both anger
and concern. 'You can't stay here.'*

'*Leave me,*' I moaned.

'*No! You're coming to my house,*' he said.

I was returned to the sofa, where they stood over me like guards while Katie threw clothes into an overnight bag. In the end we could not go to Tam's house. By now all of the family's homes were besieged by the press. There was nowhere to hide for any of us, particularly me, for at long last the secrets that had held me hostage were revealed. Several of the reporters had mentioned to my family that Ash was my husband.

'*Is that true?*' Tam had asked me.

I nodded miserably. '*I'm sorry, I couldn't bear to tell you. It just got harder as time went on. I didn't want to disappoint you all.*'

'*Oh, darlin',*' he said, wrapping his arms around me.

What did any of it matter now, anyway?

When we arrived at the entrance door to the flats, police officers were on guard, denying entry to the media.

Tam spoke to the officers, explaining that he had to get me away from the place.

'*Wait inside,*' said one of the officers, who began speaking into the radio on his shoulder.

Within minutes, family liaison officers arrived to escort us from the building. The press pack parted without a word. They knew this was not a moment to blurt out insensitive questions.

The police had arranged for us to stay in a hotel in Stirling, well away from Glasgow. They believed it would offer me some respite from the pressures and give me time to come to terms with the tragedy. But how could anyone come to terms with this?

Later, I sat in the unfamiliar surroundings of an anonymous hotel room. I looked at the insipid cream walls. This could never be a home. There were no pictures of my boys, just pale prints in pastel colours.

'Let me have them,' said Katie.

'What?' I replied.

'Their jammies,' she said.

I was still clutching my boys' pyjamas. They hadn't left my hand since the moment I had arrived home. I wasn't even conscious they were there. They had become part of me. I looked down at my hands. The pyjamas were damp from my tears. I held them to my face. My babies' smell was fainter now. I was losing them.

A wave of panic.

'I have to see them,' I said.

'No, no, no,' Katie said. 'That's been taken care of. Remember them the way they were.'

'I have to see them,' I repeated.

'Don't, love,' said Tam. 'Don't torture yourself. Think of them playing, singing their wee songs. Please!'

'Tam, I must see them.'

Tam was broken-hearted. My big brother had officially identified my sons. It must have taken every ounce of his strength to look down on their broken bodies.

I knew how much that must have cost him. He loved the boys. For some reason, Jay-Jay could never get his tongue around Tam's name. When my brother appeared, Jay-Jay's eyes would light up. He'd hold out his arms and shout, 'Bam … Bam.'

It made us howl with laughter. In Glasgow, 'bam' is the vernacular for a well-meaning and jovial idiot.

'That boy may be small but he's got you sussed,' we'd tease Tam.

Tam didn't care. He was a gentle soul, but now he was playing the bluff big brother. If anyone understood my need to know what had happened, it was him. Since he had returned from identifying them, he had resolutely refused to discuss the nature of their deaths.

'Tell me, Tam,' I would demand.

'Better to remember them singin' and dancin',' Tam said, using another Glaswegian figure of speech.

However, it quickly became apparent to my family and the police that I would not be dissuaded from seeing my sons. On the Tuesday, three days after their deaths, they relented.

And now, here I was, in the place where my babies lay in death at the ages of six and two. They would never grow up, never go to university, never get jobs, never marry or bring me grandchildren. I had lost them forever.

My thoughts were interrupted by a voice that told me, 'We're here, Giselle.'

I returned to the present. We had reached a glass window that was masked by a Venetian blind.

'Let me in there,' I whispered.

'You need to stay here,' a voice said.

The blind rose slowly and, at last, I could see them, see what he had done.

My babies lay side by side on a table. Their little bodies were shrouded and only their heads were visible. They looked so helpless. I felt a moan rising from deep within me. I stifled it. The pain that took hold of me in that moment was too great to express with mere sound.

Little Jay-Jay looked serene. His face was at peace, as if he were only sleeping. But Paul's face was a mask of fear. He appeared to have aged.

'Let me in,' I said urgently.

'You have to stay here,' the voice repeated.

'I need to be with my babies,' I said, pulling away from my minders.

'Wait, wait,' said a voice.

Strong arms held me, guided me.

'Take her in,' someone said.

I weakened with each step, needful of their support.

Finally, I was able to look down at my sons. Jay-Jay was lying to the left of Paul. His hair was tousled and there was an angelic expression on his face.

Whatever terror Paul experienced had followed him beyond his life. His face was contorted. It was the face of an old man.

My little Jay-Jay's expression showed that he had passed from life to death quickly. I would learn later that Jay-Jay had been attacked first.

However, the last moments of Paul's life were there for me to see. He had witnessed his father killing his little brother. Paul was too young and too small to save Jay-Jay, but he was old enough to know what was happening. It must have been terrifying for him, this child who had experienced nothing but love in his life.

His terror will haunt me for the rest of my days. It would be some time before I was able to properly take in the full horror that lay behind the clinical words of the post-mortem report prepared by forensic pathologists Robert Ainsworth and Marjorie Black.

As well as detailing everything Ash had done to my babies, the report described what police officers found when they discovered his silver Mercedes at the Campsie Fells the previous day. It read:

The body of Jay was found lying within the footwell of the nearside rear passenger seat, with the body of his brother also lying across the back seat and his father lying unresponsive in the driver's seat. Jay was formally declared dead there at 19:10 hours.

There was a blue plastic dummy in the left side of his mouth. There was also a yellow-coloured football resting against his head. His body was warmish to the touch.

On the left side of his neck there was a single stab wound. The wound almost completely transacted the left internal jugular vein. The wound had then continued backwards to cut through the third cervical vertebral body, almost completely dividing this. The total length of the wound from the skin surface to its end point was approximately 5cm.

Jay had one other sharp cut on his right ring finger, potentially defensive in nature. It would appear that he survived for a brief period after the car fire started.

On opening the Mercedes-Benz car, there was a minor degree of fire damage within, particularly at the front. The body of Paul was found lying across the back seat of the car. He was formally declared dead at 19:10 hours.

On the front of his neck there were two deep stab wounds which appeared to pass into and through the left side of his neck.

There was a diagonal gaping through-and-through stab wound 4.2cm in length. The wound tracked almost horizontally backwards and slightly towards the midline within the neck for a distance of approximately 7cm before exiting as a diagonal wound 3cm in length. On the front of the neck, an almost vertical gaping through-and-through stab wound

7.5cm in length. The wound tracked almost horizontally backwards and to the left within the neck, passing backwards for a distance of approximately 6cm before producing an exit wound 3.3cm in length.

The following injuries were identified: transaction of the right-sided neck-strap muscles, upper trachea, oesophagus, right common carotid artery, left common carotid artery, almost complete division of the 5th cervical vertebral body.

There were temporary 'transfer' tattoos on the outer aspect of his right upper arm and on the back of the left forearm. Patchy skin blistering on the sides and back of the neck, of each ear, and beneath the chin, singeing of the hair.

It would appear that [Paul] was no longer alive at the time of the fire.

Robert Ainsworth and Marjorie Black, 'Post-mortem Report', University of Glasgow, 4 May 2008

It would be months before the true wickedness of the husband I had once loved was finally revealed. That would come when I learned of the tape message Ash had left behind.

As he sat in his car, with our babies playing in the rear seat, he had recorded, in a mixture of Punjabi and English, what he believed would be his last words:

'Death is near ...' *(Ashok Kalyanjee, speaking in Punjabi. Approximately 12.45 p.m., 3 May 2008, Crow Road, Lennoxtown, East Dunbartonshire)*

When he spoke in Punjabi it was to mask the true nature of his evil intent. Perhaps the greatest horror was that he also spoke to our sons in English, telling them what a wonderful day they were going to have.

'We're going to have a very good game today, very good fun today, babies.' *(Ashok Kalyanjee, speaking in English)*

My babies must have looked at their father with trusting eyes. It had only been a week since we had all been there together, in that very same spot, when I had laughed and played with them.

'This is a very big story. Its purpose is that I'm speaking in Punjabi because my children are with me. If I speak English, they would understand ... Today is the last day.'

How could the world have turned upside-down in just seven days? He must have been drunk by then. He had taken with him a bottle of vodka, a can of petrol and the knife. What had transformed Ash into a monster?

'We're going to live together. Nobody can separate us.' *(In English)*

It must have seemed like a game to the children, their father changing between their language and his own. How could they have known that his words were a death sentence?

'This death is near. I have become a gambler, a drunk. Nothing has become of me.' *(In Punjabi)*

His intentions would have been inconceivable to an adult, never mind two innocent little mites. Once he had completed his hell-

ish message, he would throw the tape machine out of the car window and take another swig of vodka.

And then he murdered my children.

Afterwards, he phoned me to tell me that I would regret what I had done to him in this life. He poured petrol on himself and then on the car, which he set alight.

Now, in the mortuary, as strong hands prevented me from falling, I could see the evidence of the fire on the body of my little Paul. He had burn marks to his face and his eyelashes were gone. It was no comfort to me to know that the injuries were caused after he was dead.

'Mummy can't fix it now,' I whispered. 'Mummy can't fix it.'

'Time to go, Giselle,' said a voice.

I had to leave them now. My first instinct was to struggle, but I knew I had to leave them and I allowed myself to be led away from my babies. The corridor stretched before us.

'Don't let me go,' I said.

'We won't,' a gentle voice replied.

I turned, looked through the glass partition for a final glimpse at my boys. The blind fell. For a second, I was almost convinced that the last taped words spoken by Ash were written across it.

'These children are mine and they go with me.'

24

Tranquillisers and Sympathy

'The classic family annihilator tends to wipe out the whole family. I believe Shaun would have been Rab's first victim, especially as he defended his mother. He is extremely lucky to have survived.'

Ian Stephen

June: I understand why you had to see what Ash did. I wouldn't know for a long time, and I couldn't let go of my Michelle and Ryan.

It was so cold in this garden of the dead. Even in the sunshine, even draped in its mantle of serenity with its brightly coloured flowers, its burnished brass plaques and symbols of faith, the closeness of death was overpowering and claustrophobic.

My Michelle and Ryan had been taken, but in my heart they were still so alive that I could not countenance leaving them in this place. I was alone for the moment, or as alone as one can be in the aftermath of a funeral. I had withdrawn from my family and the hundreds of mourners who had come to pay their last respects at the crematorium in Kirkcaldy.

I was, of course, grateful for their care, their kindness and their compassion, but being alone was a welcome respite from the sad expressions and words of sympathy that were incapable of assuaging my pain. In that blessed moment of peace, the smell of the sea wafted from the Firth of Forth. It was fresh, full of hope, so near but yet so far from this place of dry, grey ashes and solemn remembrance. I decided then that I would keep my children with me for the time being. Their earthly bodies were gone, but at least a part of them remained. I could, if I wished, have had their ashes interred in this garden. But I wouldn't. They would come home with me until I found a place where I believed they would be at rest. I knew I would find it, eventually.

Throughout my life, even in its darkest moments, I have always sensed a connection to *something* beyond me. A higher power? A life beyond this one? Don't ask me what it is because I don't know. But it feels somehow as if I have been guided.

A sudden flash of memory carried me back to a few weeks before the murders, when I had taken Michelle to the local health centre for one of her regular check-ups. I was standing in the car park waiting for her. I could see the interior of the centre through huge glass windows. I would have to wait a bit longer, I realised. Michelle was saying her goodbyes. This ritual involved visiting every member of staff, and offering them a kiss and a cheery farewell.

I smiled, as I always did. They say that whatever nature takes away, it leaves something else in its place. Nature had taken much from Michelle but it had been replaced with a bottomless well of love.

I was still watching when a quiet voice said, 'They are very special, aren't they?'

I had been joined by an old grey-haired lady. I do not know where she came from. She was not looking at me. The old woman was looking through the glass at Michelle.

I followed her gaze and said, 'I know exactly what you mean.'

'God only gives them to us for a very short time,' she went on.

When I turned back to look at the old woman she was gone. I shivered. I thought, 'This is weird.' I couldn't work out where she had disappeared to.

'Mum!' a voice cried, and the spell was broken. Michelle had burst through the doors of the centre and was walking towards me with her unsteady gait.

Now, weeks later, as I sat in the peace of the garden, I thought again about the old woman. What had it been? A warning? A premonition?

Today, I was dry-eyed. God knows, I had drenched the world with my tears since Michelle and Ryan had been taken from me. Could it only have been 13 days since I found them? Less than two weeks since I had run from that house of horrors? A mere hiccup in time since I had witnessed the callous, calculating smirk on Rab's face as he was carried on a stretcher from the carnage?

Only 13 days.

They had passed in a blur of tranquillisers and sympathy. I felt so tired. I closed my eyes.

I returned to Muiredge.

Flashing lights washing the walls of the house – blue, red, blue, red, blue, red. The wail of sirens in the distance drowning my screams. The minute, the hour, the day of my life I will never escape.

A strident voice in my left ear. 'June … June … Look at me!'

A policeman. I was in the rear seat of a police car. I couldn't remember how I got there from the ambulance.

'My children! Ryan! Michelle! He's won!'

'Who's won, June?' The policeman.

'Rab! He's won!'

A moment of panic. 'Where's Ross?' I demanded.

'It's all right,' the policeman said. 'He's being looked after.'

'I can't leave him on his own,' I said.

'Ross is fine,' said the soft, reassuring voice. 'Don't worry about him, June. You're safe now. We're going to the police station soon and you can tell us what happened.'

'Rab killed them. He killed my Michelle and Ryan,' I wailed.

I turned my head, looking out of the window of the vehicle. A sea of faces. Linda. My sister was on the edge of the crowd, held back by a police cordon.

'Linda,' I said. 'That's my sister over there.'

She must have raced to Muiredge after my hysterical phone call.

'You'll see Linda soon,' said the officer.

A flash of white dragged my eyes from the dark interior of the car. Ghostly hooded figures in coveralls had appeared, as if from nowhere.

'Forensic teams,' said the policeman, in reply to an unasked question.

I felt his hand on my arm. 'Don't,' said the officer gently, easing my hands away from my clothes. I had been kneading my top. I looked down.

'Blood!' I said. 'Blood!'

'We'll get you a change of clothes. Just hang on,' said the policeman.

'So much blood … But it wasn't me. I didn't kill them,' I blurted out. 'I didn't kill my Michelle and Ryan.'

'It's okay, I know,' he said.

The emergency-service vehicles made the house alternate between shadow and light. I had so wanted to live in that house. My eldest son Shaun had long since left to build his own life and Ross was at an age when he would soon follow his brother. I had realised that one day little Ryan would grow up and leave. Until Rab had made it untenable, I had hoped that Muiredge was where my dear, innocent Michelle would spend the rest of her life.

A rap on the police-car window startled me. It was another uniformed officer. He slid into the front passenger seat and said over his shoulder, 'We're going to the station now, June.'

I nodded. The first officer started the car engine. In the half-light of a summer evening, on a day that had begun with such promise, the car, with its three silent occupants, made the short journey. By the time we arrived it was the gloaming of the evening – that half-light between day and night. I was assisted from the vehicle by the first officer.

'My name is Scott,' he told me in a quiet voice, adding, 'I won't leave you.'

Inside the police station I blinked in the harsh, white light. More faces. The same looks. Was I a victim? Was I the perpetrator? The neon light revealed my blood-soaked clothing.

'My clothes,' I said.

'We'll get you a change,' Scott said. 'Come in here,' he added, escorting me to an interview room.

'Wait a second,' he said, signalling to someone I could not see.

A woman police officer materialised with a fresh set of clothes and clutching flat, empty bags. Scott retreated from the room.

'Let's get you changed,' said the woman.

I undressed slowly, discarding the bloody garments, which she placed carefully into the bags. Evidence, I thought. My clothes are evidence. When I had changed, Scott returned.

'Sit down, June. We're going to have a chat until the detectives arrive. Someone will bring us a cup of tea,' he said. Scott guided me to the chair.

'Thank you,' I said, looking at him properly for the first time.

His face was drawn, his expression strained. I knew instinctively that in the last few hours this young man had witnessed a scene that would haunt him forever.

'I know your face,' I said.

'Yeah, I live and work locally,' he replied.

What I didn't know then was that Scott was a part-time 'special' constable. He was also the local funeral director. Ironically, it would be Scott who would help me lay my children to rest.

Since I had run from the house at Muiredge, I had been swinging wildly between hysteria and an unnatural calm. I was suddenly overwhelmed and began to weep. Scott leaned towards me and offered me a hankie. As I took it from his hand, the light glinted on my wedding ring.

'God!' I said, feeling as if my finger were suddenly on fire. 'God!' I repeated, dragging the ring over my knuckle and casting it into a waste bin in the corner of the room. 'Bastard!' I hissed.

Scott made no attempt to retrieve it. It was the first time in 27 years of marriage that the ring had been off my finger. Even during the periods when I had left Rab, I continued to wear it. He would have killed me otherwise.

I felt physically sick. How could I have allowed myself to have become so unutterably ground down, so unbelievably afraid of this man to have endured such a miserable existence? I had lived in an atmosphere of fear, afraid of what he would do to me if I dared to walk away.

His threats had always been directed at me. It was always me who was punished. He had never raised his voice – or lifted a hand – to Michelle or Ryan.

How could I have foreseen that his final, terrible punishment would cost them their lives? I leaned forward, weary, resting my head on the table in the interview room.

'It's okay,' said Scott, who kept his promise and did not leave me.

Even when the detectives eventually arrived to begin their endless questioning, he did not stray far. Before their arrival, in those few short hours I spent with him, I probably told Scott more about my life and marriage than I had ever confided to any other living soul. We sat close together, almost like a priest and penitent in a confessional. But it was not my sins I was confessing. It was Rab's.

I poured it all out, a litany of all the wicked things he had done to me. I could not stop. I cannot remember now a half of what I said, but it was a cathartic experience. At one point during that long, dark night of the soul, Scott excused himself, saying he had to leave the room for a few minutes. When he returned he said, 'The detectives want to talk to you now.'

Two of them came into the room. They addressed me with quiet, sympathetic voices.

One of them said, 'June, I'm Detective ...'

'*What did he do to them?*' I interrupted.

The other detective said, 'I'm sorry, June, we can't go into the details. We have to follow protocol. You have to understand. When the case goes to court, what you say here and now could be given as evidence.'

I was determined.

'I don't care about evidence. I need you to tell me what he did.'

'We can't,' said the first detective, more firmly.

I knew that they probably thought it bizarre that I should be asking them about the murders. I had found my children. It was, however, as if the shock of it had blinded me, robbed me of my memory. Some part of my mind had shut down, as if to protect me from the horror. My only clear memories were of Michelle's bloodied curls and the single rent in Ryan's jumper.

'Tell us what happened before you arrived at the house,' said the second detective.

I looked towards Scott and he gave me a reassuring nod. I began to describe my day, painfully and slowly, telling them everything I had done, and everything that had happened.

At length one of the detectives said, 'I think you need a break, June. You should rest. We'll speak later. We'll arrange for someone to take you home.'

I was grateful to them. I was physically and mentally drained, and I so needed to be with my family. Another silent car journey, this time through the early-morning light. My sister and the others were waiting for me when I arrived at the house in Methil. It was no longer a safe haven. What a fool I had been to believe I could escape from Rab. His hellish vengeance had ensured that I would never again be free.

Thank heavens for my family. They gathered around me, attempting to sustain me, but all they could do was watch me unravel and give myself up to a grief so consuming that it drove me to the brink of madness.

We shared few words in the days that followed. What was there to be said about what Rab had done? How could we rationalise the acts of a maniac? The house was filled with family and friends who came and went, enveloping me with love. But I could find no comfort, no peace, in any of it.

At times I could not even bear to look at my little nieces, Abbi and Beth, as they played at my feet. At other times I wanted to hold them forever and never let them go. Dear little Abbi was only six years old but she knew something terrible had happened to 'her Ryan'. Abbi knew I was in pain. She was made wary by my tears, my seemingly endless anguish. One day she overcame her wariness, climbed onto my lap and gave me a cuddle. Then she took my hand.

'It's okay, Auntie June,' she said. 'Come and play with me.'

The barriers fell away. I got down on my knees and helped her dress her dollies. Tears flowed down my face. She hugged me again and gave me a kiss.

I thanked God that her uncle Rab had ordered her to leave Muiredge with me on that day. He hadn't wanted Abbi to be one of his victims. But what if she had said 'No'? The thought of it still haunts me.

I lived out those days in a haze, punctuated by interviews with detectives and visits from doctors, who decided to send me to a psychiatric hospital. They did not know what else to do with me. They thought I might commit suicide. I sat in the hospital for one day, surrounded by poor souls who were suffering from true mental illness. I felt like a fraud.

I was not mad, I was sad, I told the doctors. I insisted that they allow me to go home. They did.

I had to pull myself together, if for no other reason than to help the police build their case against Rab. It could not bring my children back to me, but I promised myself that I could at least help to ensure that the bastard would spend the remainder of his miserable, evil existence behind bars.

I found new strength. The interviews with the police were long and arduous, but I focused, talking for hours in front of a video camera. The detectives told me that they would use my testimony in court if Rab had the temerity to claim he was innocent.

'If you're incapable of facing him in court or break down in the witness box, this filmed testimony will be vital,' one of the officers told me.

By now the police were fully aware that Rab had acted alone. The officer in charge, Detective Superintendent Alistair McKeen, would say later that his officers and the paramedics had never attended such a harrowing scene. They would, however, still not tell me precisely what Rab had done.

The final hours in the life and death of my children continued to torment me. My nights, when I was able to sleep, were filled with broken dreams and nightmares, but my days were spent with the detectives. During one interview they informed me that my children would be the subject of a post-mortem examination.

I was aghast.

'Why?' I demanded to know. 'Everyone knows what happened. You all know how they died. Why do you need to violate them any more? Haven't they been through enough?'

'The pathologist has to do it,' said one of the officers. 'It's part of the judicial process. I know it's hurtful to you, June, but if it's not done it could affect the case.'

I also had to accept the situation that Rab had instructed his lawyers to demand a second, independent post-mortem. He knew it would add to my agony. He was right. I went to pieces. It was the final ignominy. I begged the police to stop it but it was his right under the law.

The pain just seemed to go on and on, a relentless living thing that reinvented itself every day, finding new ways to torture me.

It reached a zenith when the police revealed that they had recovered CCTV footage from one of the McDonald's in Kirkcaldy, which had been recorded on the day of the murders. It showed the last hours of my children's lives. Rab, Michelle and Ryan could be seen eating 'Happy Meals'. It must have been his sick idea to give them a final treat before he killed them. The people around them were lost in their own innocent little worlds, paying no attention to another family on a Saturday afternoon outing. Who can see evil, even if it's sitting at the next table?

As the days passed, the police told me Rab had been discharged from Queen Margaret Hospital in Dunfermline, where he had been taken after his abortive suicide attempt.

He was immediately taken into custody and, on 6 May, he appeared at Kirkcaldy Sheriff Court, charged with the murders of Michelle and Ryan. It was the beginning of the end for him. With Rab in jail, it would soon be time for me to reclaim my children.

I was torn between my longing to see them and the dread of the moment. They had been given into the care of the Co-operative funeral home, where Scott was put in charge of laying them to rest. I couldn't bear to go alone. Shaun, who had returned to Fife from Essex, went with me, along with one of Michelle's carers.

Scott was waiting for us when we arrived. He was kindness itself. After having unburdened myself to him at the police station, it seemed entirely natural that he should now be taking care of my Michelle and Ryan.

'Will I take you to see them?' he asked me.

I couldn't speak. I nodded.

'I'll come with you, Mum,' Shaun said.

'No,' I managed to say. 'I want to go in on my own, for a few minutes.'

This was a moment I was unable to share with anyone, not even a much-loved son.

A door in front of me opened and I stepped into the dim interior. The door closed behind me. Cool, quiet, peaceful, a room of whispers. I saw my children. They lay side by side. Michelle was serene. She might have been asleep.

But my poor boy …

He was in pain. Death had robbed his face of its softness. His expression was one of shock. Death had diminished him, made him smaller, more fragile. My lovely, sturdy, special gift was gone. I stood in the space between the two caskets, my left hand on my son, my right hand on my daughter.

'I'm sorry,' I whispered. 'I'm so sorry I wasn't there.'

I don't know how long I spent with them, but eventually the mother in me responded to the needs of my other child. Shaun was still outside. He, too, needed to say goodbye. I retreated slowly, reluctantly. I opened the door and stepped out of the room. Shaun was waiting, his eyes bright with anguish. He walked past me, laying his hand briefly on my shoulder, and entered the room. The door closed behind him. I heard him howl, this soldier who had become so familiar with death on the battlefields of Iraq, where he had served with 13 Air Assault Regiment.

I cried then, for my lost children and for the sons I still had, especially the son who had come so close to being a victim of his father's murderous rage. When Shaun had arrived from England he had revealed to me that his father had called him two days before the murders.

'He said he wanted me to help "fix the family"', Shaun told me.

At the time, Shaun was utterly mystified by his father's behaviour.

'He begged me to come home; said he'd even pay for the flight,' Shaun said, adding, 'I nearly did come home, but there was just something so strange about it all, and the insistent way Dad spoke. It made me uneasy.'

Thank God Shaun did not come home. I have no doubt that he was destined to die as part of Rab's hellish plan. I'm convinced he would have been the first victim. There would have been no way Rab could have managed to kill Michelle and Ryan if Shaun had been there, and still alive.

Shaun realised that, too. 'He *would* have tried to kill me, Mum,' he told me. Shaun was well aware of what his father was capable of. He had witnessed me being beaten, heard me being raped. Now his words confirmed the awful truth of it all. I knew now that the deaths of my children had been no moment of madness, no sudden explosion of rage. This had been planned, coldly, calculatingly, and it had been executed with chilling precision.

I wonder if Rab had decided to spare Ross. On the day of the murders, Rab sent him and his girlfriend on an errand. By the time they arrived home in the early evening, Ryan and Michelle were already dead. Ross had, like me, walked in to find the house silent. By then, Rab had showered and cleaned up, eradicating all the evidence of his dreadful deed. In fact, he had met Ross at the door, and went so far as to tell him that I had already been to the house and collected Michelle and Ryan.

Ross and his girlfriend had gone to his bedroom in the attic, where they listened to music. They were wholly unaware of what had happened.

With Ross in the attic bedroom, Rab went to his own bed, cut his wrists in a pathetic mock attempt at suicide ... and waited. For my screams.

All of these dark, dreadful thoughts were chasing each other across my mind. I was brought back to the present by the reappearance of Shaun, who had emerged from the little room where his brother and sister lay.

He looked at me with unblinking eyes and whispered, 'Evil ... pure evil!' I sensed anger rising in my son and I put my arms around him, calming him, defusing the moment.

Scott, who was standing to the one side, cast his eyes to the floor. After a few moments he said, 'Is there anything special you would like the children to wear, June?'

I let go of Shaun, cupped his face in my hands and said, 'Go to the car, son. I won't be long.'

I had known Scott would ask me that question and had spent hours going through Michelle and Ryan's clothes. It would have been so easy to choose something plain, simple and anonymous. But when you say a last goodbye to your children you are somehow compelled to surround them with the things from their lives that they have loved so much. The decisions were simple. A pair of my pyjamas with a cat motif for Michelle. Spiderman pyjamas for Ryan. They may seem strange choices to those who have not been forced to give up their children, but there was enormous comfort in the thought of having my Michelle dressed in those pink 'jammies'. She had loved them, sneaking into my room and pinching them from my drawer because she so liked to wear them. I would go into her room and find her perched on the bed.

'That's my jammies!' I would scold.

She would laugh, that adorable innocent laugh, as if she had got something over on Mum. Now she could have them forever. It was unthinkable to me that she would go to her final rest wearing anything else. I would also have her feet wrapped in fluffy socks. In life, my girl's feet were always cold. She would wear two or three pairs.

Ryan would also go to his rest surrounded by his favourite things. His world revolved around his heroes, Power Rangers and Spiderman. The small comforts we take from life become so much more important in death.

I had also gathered a collection of their toys and keepsakes to be placed with them in their coffins, including Ryan's Bob the Builder pillow, which had been his 'comfort blanket' since he was little more than a baby. It was falling apart but I knew he would want it.

'I don't want the service to be sad,' I told Scott. 'I want to celebrate their lives.'

For sentimental reasons, I chose music that included the Power Rangers' theme and Elton John's 'Baby's Got Blue Eyes', the tune that had been playing when I first held Michelle.

I told my family and friends that I did not want the mourners to wear sombre clothes. I asked for bright colours. Michelle had so loved glittery things. It would be the saddest day of our lives but I did not want it draped in black.

Scott understood. 'Go home now, June,' he said to me. 'I'll see you tomorrow.'

Tomorrow came after a night without sleep. I rose from my bed, weary beyond any physical tiredness. I dressed in my bright-red top and a trouser suit, and sat at the kitchen table, waiting.

The sound of a car arriving. Time to go. Time to say goodbye. My sons came for me. I clung to Shaun and Ross. We did not speak on the journey to the crematorium. Such a crowd had gathered. So many people. It was a beautifully warm day but I didn't care. There was no comfort to be found in the warmth of the sun.

I was helped through the throng. I tried to offer greetings to those nearest to me but I fell silent as I entered the chapel of the crematorium, passing the floral tributes that spelled the names of my children. I took my seat and a hush fell as the minister, the Reverend Wilma Cairns, took the podium.

Her voice was bright and clear.

'Ryan was a typical wee boy,' she told everyone, 'a livewire, always running about doing things at top speed. Michelle was a bright and bubbly, happy girl who loved sparkly clothes ... and chocolate.'

As she talked at length about my children I smiled in spite of myself. For days now I had been fighting to retrieve the happy memories that had been subsumed by the horror. For a few seconds I was winning them back. In the darkness one takes comfort from even a pinprick of light.

My mind flew back to just a few weeks before they died. Ryan had come home from his youth club with an elaborate chocolate egg. It was a thing of beauty and he decided he wanted to keep the egg for Easter morning.

'Put it in the fridge,' I told him. 'It will be safe there.'

He placed the egg in the fridge and closed the door. Easter Sunday must have seemed so far away to a little boy but, as it turned out, the egg would not survive until that special day.

We hadn't legislated for Michelle sneaking into the kitchen like the proverbial thief in the night – and eating it! On a bright, clear Easter morning, Ryan discovered his treasure had been plundered and he ran to me in tears.

'My egg's gone. Michelle's eaten it. I know it was her. Michelle's eaten my egg,' he howled.

Ryan hauled me to his sister's bedroom where the evidence was plain to see – the crumpled box and torn foil wrapper had been discarded on the floor. There had been no attempt to hide her nefariousness. Michelle laughed and clapped her hands.

'It was good! It tasted really good, Ryan.'

She was incapable of telling a lie. Her laughter was often an admission of guilt. Ryan forgave her, of course. He always forgave his sister.

I was still hugging that memory when the funeral service came to an end. My hand reached out involuntarily, a vain attempt to stop my children disappearing from my sight when the curtain closed around their coffins. They were gone. I walked from the chapel into the sunlight. Hands patted me, arms embraced me. Voices, soft and soothing, spoke to me. A need to be alone carried me to the garden. No one followed.

And now, here I was, sitting with the dead, in this place of remembrance.

The smell of the sea came to me again, invoking so many happy memories of the children playing on the shore; care-free days spent away from Rab. I knew then where we should say our last goodbyes. But not quite yet.

In the days that followed, I kept them close to me. I had been given their ashes, which were held in two separate urns. What was left of them in death was a paltry substitute for what they had been in life.

It was also a time of dreams. Each night my children visited me, told me they loved me. Those were the good dreams. In the others they were always beyond my reach, out of sight, trapped in a darkness I could not penetrate. I kept losing them all over again.

But then I was given the little signs: the echo of Ryan's voice from another room; the tinkle of the wind chimes above the window, which so reminded me of Michelle's laugh; the fleeting glimpses of them from the corner of my eye, which seemed to be so much more than just my imagination.

These strange goings on didn't scare me. They were crumbs of solace, a semblance of peace. I realised then that my children would always be with me. Perhaps it was time to let them go.

Early summer had replaced spring. I awoke one morning and I knew it was *the day*. I ran to Linda's room.

'We have to go on a trip, go to the beach,' I told her.

Linda was at first discomfited. I hadn't shown such purpose for weeks.

'Are you all right?' she asked in a worried voice.

'Yes, yes,' I said. 'I want to take them to the sea.'

I was almost manic.

'The sea?' Linda said.

'Michelle and Ryan! I want to take them to the sea. Phone Jim and get the girls ready.'

I knew my brother Jim would want to join us. It would be me, Shaun, Ross, Linda, Abbi, Beth, Jim, his wife and their young son.

But it was such a spur-of-the-moment thing that I couldn't get hold of Ross. I knew he would understand. I couldn't wait. I had to do it now.

Shaun was staying with me for a while, but Ross had moved into a new flat. Muiredge was out of bounds to all of us. None of us could have returned there anyway.

I ran back to my bedroom. I was swinging between agitation and exhilaration. I snatched up the urns. I removed a portion of the ashes from each one and put them in two tiny, silk bags. I placed the bags carefully in my box of memories, a collection of precious things associated with their lives.

'Jim's on his way,' said Linda, who had come into the room.

'Are the girls ready?' I asked.

'Ten minutes,' said Linda. 'But what are you doing with those?' she asked, indicating the silk bags.

'I'm keeping some back, to scatter at special places.'

Linda hugged me.

'I'm so glad,' she said.

I didn't need to ask her why she was relieved. She knew, as I did, that I had turned a corner in my grieving. Within ten minutes the living room was filled with the sound of Abbi and Beth's voices. The girls were now dressed and ready to go. Eventually I heard Jim at the door, and when he entered his face expressed puzzlement.

'What's happening?' he asked.

'We're going to let them go,' I told him.

I could see the relief on his face – and the secret look that passed between him and Linda. He, too, knew that I had made a breakthrough. Since I had lost my children, Jim and Linda had watched helplessly as my world fell apart. I had run screaming into the night. I had barricaded myself in rooms. I had wailed like a wounded animal. They were, at times, terrified I might never be pulled back from the brink of madness. Now, they could sense I was starting to heal.

'The car's outside,' Jim said, adding, 'Where are we going?'

'I want to take them to the beach at Kirkcaldy. They loved it there,' I told him.

'Let's go,' he said, and I saw him smile for the first time in weeks.

Even today I cannot fully express the emotion of those moments when I felt my burden ease, if only a little.

We ran down the path of the house and piled into the car.

Abbi and Beth chattered incessantly on the way to the seashore, the long, beautiful stretch of sand where my Michelle and Ryan had run wild so many times. It had been a place of such carefree joy.

When we arrived I felt as if they were with me. As I stepped from the car, the breeze caught my face. I was right. This was where they were meant to be. On the journey I had clutched the urns to my breast. I held my children as tightly in death as I had done in life.

I walked onto the sand, looking for the special spot where we had picnicked and played. I found it. I turned in the direction of the sea and walked towards the water.

I was about to open the urns when I felt my sister beside me. She gently took one of them from me. Linda would be by my side. I looked behind me and saw that my nieces were following us. Shaun, Jim, his wife and their son waited on the sand.

Linda and I walked out to meet the waves that lapped at our feet. On we went, up to our knees, to our thighs. Our trousers were soaked, clinging to our legs, but we didn't feel the cold. The water had no power over us. Nothing had any power over us any more. We paused, steadying ourselves against the motion of the tide. Linda and I eased the lids from the urns and slowly sprinkled the ashes onto the water. They settled for a moment in a dusty veneer. And then they gave themselves up. The pull of sea carried them away from us.

Linda and I began to walk back. When we reached Abbi and Beth we took their hands. We stood in a line, joined physically, emotionally and spiritually.

Abbi and Beth were saying, 'Bye bye, Michelle; bye bye, Ryan.'

The emotion of that moment will stay with me until I draw my dying breath. In my mind I heard again the last words Rab had spoken to me, when I left Michelle and Ryan with him at Muiredge.

'*What will you do, June, when you are alone with no one to love you? What will you do then?*'

As I said goodbye to my children I knew in my heart that Rab had been wrong. I would never be without love. My children were gone, but they were not lost.

The love I shared with them is a love that will last forever.

25

In the Arms of an Angel

'Ash wanted to ensure that Giselle had nothing left.'

Ian Stephen

Giselle: As I laid my babies to rest, I thought of you – the only other woman who could truly know how I felt.

Silence and darkness.

I was swallowed by a darkness so complete I could not conceive of how I would ever again reach the light. Faces. So many faces – beside me, around me, lining the streets, merging together. The solemn expressions of children not yet old enough to appreciate the full horror of what they were witnessing. Grannies, mothers, daughters, all crying unashamedly. Glasgow hard men who had forgotten their reputations for a moment to weep openly. A river of tears was carrying my babies to their rest.

The cortège moved at a snail's pace along Royston Road, crawling behind an escort of police cars and motorcycle outriders. The traffic lights were switched off, blank circles no longer changing from red to amber to green.

Shop fronts were shuttered. Workers and customers were crammed on the pavement, standing shoulder to shoulder. Every window of every house was open. People looked from them with expressions carved from stone. Below them, the taxis and cars were drawn in to the kerb, their drivers standing by the vehicles with their heads bowed.

Royston was a community at a standstill.

I saw everything and nothing. I sat in the car wedged between my father, my sister Katie and my brother Tam.

Thank God, I thought, that Ma had passed away before she could see this. She could not have borne such a burden. The hearse was in front of us, carrying my babies in a single white casket that looked so small. They were in each other's arms. I knew Jay-Jay was safe in the embrace of his big brother Paul, protecting him in death as he had tried to do in life.

They had been gone for nearly three weeks. The physical, emotional and spiritual pain of my loss consumed me. If anything, it was greater, more acute than it had been on the day he killed them. That pain had struck like a blow from a sledge-hammer. This pain had reached into my very heart and soul.

My arms felt empty. There was no one to hold.

I could no longer smell their hair, their skin. Their laughter was merely an echo. Now I had to give them up to the cold, hard ground. I sobbed.

My poor Da. He sat beside me. He had lost Ma and then he had been robbed of two of his grandchildren. He was inconsolable. The man had tried so hard to offer me comfort while his own heart was breaking – a bear of a man who had held little Jay-Jay with such delicacy.

'There, there,' he said to me, as if he were talking to a child.

Katie took a tighter hold of my hand. I was lost. I was a child again, as young and vulnerable as my babies had been.

'Da,' I said. It was a plea.

'There, there,' he said again.

He was weeping, this big man who had been the anchor of our lives. I had seen him cry twice – today, and the day my mother passed away. He – all of us – had been weeping since before the service, when we arrived at the funeral home to help prepare my babies. I brought the clothes I had chosen for them to wear. I also had with me toys and keepsakes. I wanted them to be dressed in their favourite outfits, for them to be surrounded with tokens from their lives.

I believed in my heart that they were bound for Heaven and that Ma was waiting for them. They needed their special things for the journey. As we pushed open the door, we were enveloped by the perfume of the flowers. Katie and Tam turned to me. They were amazed.

The flowers were a carpet, covering almost every inch of the floor, a riot of colour, from the smallest posy to the largest of wreaths. Some were traditional in shape, while others were fashioned into the most elaborate of designs. I had chosen a yellow Bob the Builder 'helmet' for Jay-Jay and a Spiderman motif for Paul. Tam had chosen the letters P and J. My oldest sister, Janie, had sent a teddy bear made from flowers.

The tributes were festooned with messages of sympathy from family, friends, neighbours, and the teachers and pupils at Paul's school. So many people wanted to let us know that they were sharing in our grief.

A pathway bisected the floral tributes. A woman came from behind a desk and took my hand. No one needed to tell her who I was.

'So many flowers, Giselle,' she said. 'I've never seen so many. People have been coming and going all day. There isn't anyone in this community who doesn't have you in their thoughts.'

I murmured my thanks.

'Giselle,' a man's voice said.

It was the funeral director who had appeared from his office. 'Come this way,' he added gently, taking my arm.

He was visibly upset. Poor man. I felt so sorry for him. He was more used to dealing with the passing of old people who had lived long and fruitful lives, not two little innocents who had been snatched away.

'Is that their clothes?' he asked.

I nodded, handing over my precious bundle. I had chosen dressing gowns and pyjamas for both boys – Bob the Builder for Jay-Jay and Spiderman for Paul.

'I'll take this,' the funeral director said.

He paused. There was clearly something else he wanted to tell me. I looked at him.

'Giselle,' he said, 'we're going to put little scarves on the boys' necks.'

I knew why. It was to hide their wounds.

'I'm sorry, Giselle. I had to tell you, so you'd be prepared.'

His voice was gentle, caring, but his words stopped my heart for a moment. The awful realisation of how their lives ended hit me all over again, but later, when I saw them in their white coffin with its silver handles, I knew their pain was over.

Paul's face still held a vestige of the fear I had seen in the mortuary, even though the funeral director had done his best to restore him to serenity. Jay-Jay still looked as if he were asleep and that he might wake up at any moment.

Of all things to think about in that second, I thought of Ash. And his Bible. I remembered how he used to want to know why I didn't read the Bible.

'I read the Bible every night, you know. I am a true Christian,' he would boast.

How could any man who believed in God have done this? To his own sons? To anyone's sons? I was suddenly revolted by his false piety. He had not only committed every sin in the book. He had committed the worst of them all.

If I could have sat him down in front of me I would have told him that he would rot in his God's hell for what he had done. I silently made a promise to myself that if I was ever given the chance to exact retribution, I would send him to that hell.

But for now, I dragged my thoughts back to what I had to do. It was time to say goodbye to my babies. I laid Jay-Jay's favourite 'dummy' by his head and stroked his hair.

I turned to the funeral director and said, 'Paul likes his hair spiky. Promise me you'll do it the way he likes it?'

'Don't worry, Giselle. It'll be lovely, I promise,' he replied.

'The family will be here to see them,' I said. 'I want the boys to be remembered the way they were.'

The family came, one after the other, silent but for their sobs. Da was devastated, his chest heaving, and he was shaking with emotion. He looked as if he had aged ten years. The sight of his grandsons made him moan.

'My little boys. My little boys,' he said in a voice so unlike his own.

Katie sobbed. Tam sobbed. Katie's son Paul looked at the coffin and fled to the other side of the room, where he wept uncontrollably.

Somehow I found the strength to look once more at my babies. I had still to give them their special toys and messages from the family. I placed my keepsakes carefully beside them. Finally, my mother's ashes were placed in the coffin with Paul and Jay-Jay.

Strong arms held me as I leaned down and kissed them for the last time. I felt the same arms easing me away from the coffin.

I had chosen a humanist ceremony. The minister, Alastair Douglas, had come to see me and we talked for hours about my boys. I told him of their devotion to each other, and of how Jay-Jay so often thought that he was the big brother. Paul was timid and gentle; Jay-Jay was a roughie-toughie.

'Night, night, mine baby,' Jay-Jay would say to Paul.

Paul would look up at me and say, 'Mummy, Mummy, I thought I was the big boy. Why is Jay-Jay calling me the baby?'

I would laugh and ruffle their hair, telling them they were both my babies. And now they were gone, and I would never say those words again.

The minister had asked me to choose a special piece of music for the funeral. I decided on a Barry Manilow song – 'Cant Smile Without You'. The song had come to mean so much to me, summing up the wonder and happiness my babies had brought me. At the end of the funeral service, the words flowed around me.

When the song ended the funeral director and his staff removed the silver-framed picture of my babies from the coffin's lid and gently lifted the coffin onto their shoulders. The family followed in procession and we watched as it was placed in the hearse.

We set off on that slow journey through Royston. I had asked the funeral director if he could ensure that the route of the cortège would take us past Royston Primary School, where Paul had been so happy.

The children were waiting for us in the playground, their little faces looking through the gaps in the railings. They blew kisses and waved their hands. Their teachers stood behind them, crying.

We came within sight of Riddrie Park Cemetery, where an even larger crowd of mourners had gathered by the gates. The cars slid past them and stopped high on a hill beside a freshly dug grave. Whatever composure I had maintained deserted me. I went to pieces and had to be almost carried to the graveside.

I could hear, sharp and clear, the words of the humanist minister as he recited the opening lines of Mary Elizabeth Frye's poem, 'Do Not Stand at My Grave and Weep'. As my babies were lowered into the ground, I heard no more, the words lost to my grief. I knew only that my babies embraced each other and my mother watched over them.

They were in the arms of an angel.

26

Tell Me Why

'Rab posed his children like angels. He thought of himself as a loving father – June was to blame.'

Ian Stephen

June: I know you felt differently but I had to see Rab. I had to have answers.

He was waiting for me.

The room was cavernous and spartan, bright lights shining down on ranks of tables. Battered plastic chairs sat on either side of each table. He was sitting at one of them, wearing what looked like a work shirt – some kind of prison uniform. I can't remember its colour.

Three warders stood by a wall to our left, their hands clasped behind their backs. They looked into the middle distance. Their faces said nothing.

It was the first time I had seen Rab since the night he had been carried from Muiredge on a stretcher. The night he killed my children. I sucked in deep breaths, trying to still my mounting hysteria. Hatred, anger, grief, sadness and bewilderment chased each other across my mind. I had to remain calm, stay focused, if I were to get answers.

Rab did not sit straight in the chair – he reclined as far as its hard back would allow. His body language said he was at ease, perhaps even bored. His face was expressionless but for the beginnings of a smirk, the same smirk I had seen that night.

His eyes never left my face as I pulled an empty chair away from the table, making a loud, harsh sound that shattered the silence of the room and caused the warders' eyes to flick towards me. I sat down and laid my handbag on the floor. It contained only my purse, my keys and the letter Rab had sent me.

Written in a near illegible scrawl it recorded the ramblings of a lunatic.

The silence grew between us.

He was exerting control, waiting for me to speak first. My eyes were fixed on a scar on the surface of the table, but eventually I looked up and into his eyes.

'Why, Rab?' I hissed.

'What have you done to your hair?' he replied.

It was the letter that had at last given me the courage to confront Rab. The dreadful missive had dropped onto the mat behind the front door, where it lay among the banal communications of everyday life, sandwiched between a gas bill and a letter from a bank I had never heard of, offering me a credit card.

I stood in the hall, transfixed, looking at my name and address which were rendered in black ballpoint pen. I recognised Rab's handwriting immediately. I moved slowly from the hall to the kitchen, carrying the letter as if it were a dead rat. I laid it on the table.

My first instinct was to tear open the envelope, but I was suddenly afraid. I couldn't touch it. What could he possibly have to say to me? What could I want to hear from him? It lay there for a long time, violating my home, as I sipped my morning coffee.

Then I realised that this might be what I had been yearning for. It could reveal the reason why my children had to die.

That was it.

Rab had finally come to his senses. He had at last been stricken by guilt and remorse, and had decided to explain the reasons for what he had done. I opened the envelope, extracting the thin sheet of prison writing paper which bore the logo of the Scottish Prison Service and Rab's prisoner number.

I read his first words and I felt sick to the pit of my stomach.

I would give anything to share his exact words with you because they are the only ones which he has ever offered to explain his actions. In my opinion, they give a truly chilling insight into his twisted thinking about the dreadful events of Saturday 3 May, 2008. It may, however, surprise and outrage many of you to know that even monsters who slaughter their own children have rights.

I understand that if I reveal the contents of the letter, word for word, Rab can claim that I have breached his 'copyright'. So I can only describe the effect of his bizarre missive.

I ignored the appalling grammar and strained to read the scrawl, a mixture of the cursive and block capitals. The room swam around me. I reached for the table to steady myself. It was as if I had been doused by a bucket of ice-cold water as I read how Rab found it very hard to forgive them … and me.

The letter fell from my hand onto the table. My body temperature exploded from cold to hot in a micro-second. I was drained of strength. *Forgive me? Forgive them?* The worst moment of my life had been finding my murdered children. On my deathbed, when I am recalling all that was good and bad in my life, those horrible words will be remembered as the second-worst thing that ever happened to me.

But the torture wasn't over as he dismissed his murderous actions as 'piss' and went on to boast about his sex life and how many orgasms he'd had since his teens.

I read on, my rage increasing as each sentence revealed the bizarre mind of this monster who had calculated his sexual pleasures down to the last second. With each word, I believed madness had been unleashed and brought into my world. There could be no peace anymore. I cried. The tears falling onto the letter could never wash away the cruelty of those words.

I sat for hours, immobile, a rock, the letter discarded on the floor. In the course of the day the front door was knocked several times, briefly bringing me out of my trance. I ignored the knocks, slipping back into the reverie. Slowly, as the time passed, I came to a decision.

Tomorrow, come what may, I would get in my car, drive to the prison and face down this demon. My demon.

The long walk from the reception area had not calmed me. I shook uncontrollably, dreading what was to come.

Minutes before, I had stood at the desk in front of a bewildered prison officer, pleading with him to be allowed to see Rab.

'It's outwith visiting hours, Ma'am,' he told me.

'I have to see him, I have to see him,' I begged.

His face showed the resignation of one confronted by a madwoman whom he knew would not be dissuaded. He looked at me for a moment and said, 'Wait here, please.'

He disappeared.

I waited.

I hadn't slept since I received the letter the day before. Rab's poison had filled the night with ghosts that terrified me in the darkness. I had lain on my bed, the words stabbing at me until dawn came. I rose, showered and dressed. I stepped out of the house into a dreary grey day that matched my mood. I saw nothing on the journey to Perth until the prison loomed before me. Somewhere in this stark and imposing building that housed the mad and the bad, Rab was waiting.

He had the answers.

I needed to know why my children had died.

From this distance in time, I know now that on that day I was unhinged. I realise that Rab's letter had been constructed to harm me, to elevate my pain to another level. But I was so driven by my madness that I believed if I came here, if I looked into his eyes, if I asked him why, he would tell me what I yearned to know. I was not offering him more control. I had none left to give. He had already won the war and there were no more battles to lose. All I could hope for was that I might sneak under his guard. That he might reveal his secrets.

The warder returned. He knew who I was now. I was the child murderer's wife. His face had softened from that of the bureaucrat to that of a man, possibly a father.

'Please follow this gentleman,' he said in a kind voice, indicating another prison officer who had appeared from nowhere.

I followed the second officer through a labyrinth of corridors, to the door of the visitors' room.

'I don't like your hair like that!' Rab said.

My hand flew to the side of my head, flicking strands away from my face. It was involuntary. I was self-conscious.

'Why, Rab?' I said again.

'You're wearing jeans again,' he said.

'Why, Rab?'

Sadness, remorse and anger combined to strengthen me.

'Why, Rab?'

A mantra.

'Don't like them, the jeans. We'll have to change that, and the hair,' he said.

Still controlling. And I was still being controlled. For a fleeting second I thought I shouldn't be wearing these jeans or have my hair this way – because Rab didn't like it! It's impossible to convey the level of control one human being can have over another.

'Why?' I demanded again.

His face was cruel. There would be no mercy for me here. I was distraught. I grabbed up my bag, pushed the chair away from the table and stood up.

'Sit down!' he said. 'I'm not finished.'

I obeyed, as I had always obeyed.

I looked into his eyes. He was enjoying this. Another victory. When he wrote the letter he knew I would come. I was still the puppet, still dancing on his strings. God forgive me, but a part of me still needed Rab. Just saying those words horrifies me now, but I was so ground down, so needful of support, so anxious for someone to take charge, that I still saw him as the representative of some kind of order. This murderer, this maniac, still held my life in his hands. And now he was treating me as if we were sorting out our problems after a silly domestic tiff.

I steeled myself.

'Tell me, Rab,' I said. 'Tell me.'

I was blinded by tears.

When he didn't answer I made to stand up.

'Sit down!' he said.

I made a third attempt to leave – and for the third time he ordered me to sit. He was sitting upright in the chair now, glorying in the silence. I looked at his face. The smirk was permanent.

'Why, Rab? Please! Just tell me!' I whispered.

I was distraught, no longer sustained by my anger, and I felt weary to my bones.

He shrugged his shoulders, as if I had asked him why he was late home from the pub. I knew then that he was playing a game he had played so many times before. He was feeding on my pain.

He must have squirmed with delight when the prison officer had entered his cell and told him he had a visit from his wife. Another exquisite opportunity to torture me. This was not a man. This was a devil that had escaped from the darkest pit in hell and assumed human form.

I stood up. This time I was leaving. It was over. I would never know the answer to my 'Why?' Only he knew. I felt instinctively that he would never tell me. If he did, it might offer me some comfort – and he could never allow that. He was about to tell me to sit, but a warning look from one of the guards froze the words on his lips. I looked at him and tried to sum up the energy to ask him, one last time, why he had killed our children. I couldn't.

The words wouldn't come. I turned, dragging my feet towards the door.

I followed a silent warder back through the corridors. I passed the reception desk, and the first officer I had spoken to nodded a farewell to me.

Into the light. Deep breaths. The slow walk to my car.

I eased into the driver's seat and began to cry as I had not done since the night my children died. I sat there for hours until it was dark. When I had no more tears, I placed the key in the ignition and started the engine. I drove out of the shadow of the big building.

I do not remember the journey home. All I remember are the last words Rab had spoken as I left the visitor's room.

'I hope you're stoppin' all this divorce shite now?'

———————

27

Revenge

'Ash – like Rab – was thoroughly evil, although he would not perceive himself as being so.'

Ian Stephen

Giselle: And we were so alike, you and I, yet so different. You wanted answers. I wanted Ash dead.

I went to the hospital to kill him.

I did not want answers. What would they mean? There was nothing in the world that Ash could have said to me – no excuse, no reason, no rationale. He could not blame a disturbed mental state. He could not talk to me of stress or anger or frustration. Nothing mattered to me. How could I, or any normal person, fathom the mind of a monster that was capable of brutally killing his own children? Even if such a creature were to break his silence and offer a warped explanation for his actions, how could any of us make any sense of it? Why would we want to?

His death would be answer enough.

This was a beast I had never known, not the man who had once brought me flowers, showered me with gifts – the charmer who had won the affection of a naïve young woman.

I knew only that when he arrived at my home on that dreadful day – when he had filled his sons with such a sense of excitement at the prospect of going to play football – that he was planning to kill them. He had smiled at me. He had asked for an extra nappy for Jay-Jay and bottles of diluted Ribena for the two of them to drink on the car journey to the place where he would end their lives.

Had he always been the monster? If he had, I had been unable to see behind the mask. I saw only a weakling, a dreamer. My greatest regret – June's greatest regret – is that we could not foretell the future. We suffer every day because we believe that, somehow, in some way, we should have seen some sign.

Don't believe there wasn't a small part of me that wanted to know the reasons why. But my hatred was so great that I was prepared to live with not knowing why, if only I could avenge my babies.

I had seen what Ash had done to them, how he had defiled them. That's what made me determined to kill him. The anger had not ensnared me immediately. It would arrive later. In the aftermath of the death of my sons I was too numbed to feel anything. I was in the dark place. In the world, but not of it. My loved ones and friends encircled me, protecting me, offering words of comfort that had no hope of reaching me.

And then one day a tiny part of me emerged from the crippling grief. The anger came. It was such a fierce thing, the awesome power of which I had not realised could exist within me. It began as a slow-burning flame, then, as the days and weeks passed following the loss of my Paul and my Jay-Jay, it

*became an inferno, consuming every fibre of my being. I couldn't
eat. I couldn't sleep. At last I knew what I wanted to do.*

I would kill him.

*The old man's eyes flickered but he didn't wake up. I had never
seen him before in my life, but I held his hand, stroked his hair
and soothed him with words that might have been spoken by a
dutiful and much-loved grand-daughter.*

*That was clearly how I was being perceived by the other visi-
tors to Ward 6 of Glasgow Royal Infirmary on the day I went to
kill Ash. The visitors' eyes found mine and they smiled at me. I
returned the smiles. My devotion to the old man who lay comatose on the hospital bed was obvious to them.*

But he was only my 'cover'.

*Monitors bleeped constantly and reassuringly above his
bedside cabinet but they couldn't distract me. My eyes rarely left
the bed at the end of the ward. The one hidden by the green
curtains and guarded by a police officer.*

*I willed the policeman to take a comfort break or to think
what a nice idea a cup of coffee would be. Anything that would
take him away from the bed where Ash lay, recovering from the
injuries he had inflicted on himself after killing our sons.*

*I fingered the gold medallion that hung around my neck on
a chain long enough to allow the medal to touch my heart. It
was my talisman, inscribed with the names of my dead sons. I
held it and prayed the policeman would leave, if only for the few
moments I needed.*

Just long enough for me to take Ash's life.

* * *

'I can't tell you, Giselle.'

'You have to,' I told the woman. She was a friend of the family who had once been a nurse at the Royal Infirmary. I could see my question made her uncomfortable. I had passed through the grief that had overwhelmed me and I was now driven by something infinitely darker and more sinister.

'I shouldn't say,' she repeated.

The newspapers had recorded that Ash was in the Royal, but the Royal was a huge building and one of the largest teaching hospitals in Europe.

'He's in there, somewhere,' I said.

'Why do you want to know?'

'I just have to …'

She looked at me long and hard. 'It's no great secret,' she said. 'People with burns go to the Burns Unit. Ward 8.'

Ward 8, I repeated in my mind.

I left a warm summer's day at the gates of the hospital and made my way to the door of the imposing Victorian building. As I entered, the reception area was alive with people. I imagined everyone must know why I was here and what I intended to do, but I soon realised I was invisible. A patient? A visitor? How could anyone tell what I was?

The strangest thing was that I could sense Ash was here, somewhere in this building. Don't ask me how or why, but my senses seemed to be heightened. I was operating at some hitherto unknown level.

Ward 8. Find Ward 8.

I couldn't ask anyone. It might provoke questions I could not answer, not if I didn't want to be carried off in a police van. I was dressed smartly. I had taken particular care of my appear-

ance. I didn't want to stand out. A nurse passed me, smiling.
Did she know? How could she?

I looked for any indication of the location of Ward 8.

Two doctors passed, deep in conversation, and I almost asked
them for directions. Even with murder in your heart, it is hard
sometimes to suppress the real you. I found a sign with direc-
tions. I walked along the brightly lit corridors with their high
ceilings, slowly at first, but my steps quickened with each over-
head sign that pointed the way to the Burns Unit.

Stay calm. More people, civilians as well as medical staff. I
didn't stand out. Then I saw the sign – Ward 8.

What was going through my mind? Bloody murder!

I paused. Think about this, I told myself. I had brought no
weapon. I would have to use whatever means were at my
disposal. I could strangle him? Smother him? Drag the tubes,
with their life-saving medication, from his body? I didn't know
yet how I would do it. I would know when the time came.

My heart beat like a piston in my chest. Into Ward 8.

He wasn't there! I almost cried out. The newspapers had got
it wrong. I thought at first that they had been lied to, that in fact
Ash was in another hospital.

'Giselle,' a voice said. My heart stopped. I turned slowly, fear-
fully, towards the direction of the voice, to find an old friend.

'What are you doing here?' the person asked, eyes looking
over my shoulder.

'Ash?' I said.

'What?' he replied.

'Where's Ash?' I repeated. 'He's supposed to be in Ward 8.'

There was a long moment of silence.

'He's in Ward 6,' he said.

'Thanks,' I said, walking away.

I followed the signs back along the corridors until I found the ward – and Ash. Green curtains around a bed. An arm hand-cuffed to a bracket on its side. A foot lying outside the coverlet. I would have recognised the arm, even if the handcuff had not indicated he was a prisoner.

A police officer was by the side of the bed, sitting on a visitor's chair. Watchful. I hadn't expected this. I was gripped by a sudden fear but my feet had taken me into the ward, dragged there by an unconscious desire to get closer to Ash. The policeman looked in my direction. There was no hint of recognition in his eyes. I was just another visitor. He didn't know me. Why should he?

I was just another face in a gathering crowd. It was apparently visiting time and, standing barely 5ft tall, I did not make an impression. I caught the policeman's eye. Something in my demeanour seemed to alert him. He raised his leg, propping his foot on another chair, barring my way.

I cast my eyes downwards and kept walking, joining the crowd that was filling the ward. Individuals were breaking off to go to the bedsides of those they had come to visit. I kept going. How was I to get out of this? There was no throughway, no 'back door' to take me out of the ward.

I was trapped, with no clear intent. Don't stop, I told myself. Don't attract attention. What was I to do?

The crowd had started to dissipate. Patients and visitors were exchanging greetings. I was alone.

Then I saw the old man.

I looked around frantically.

No one else had entered the ward.

The old man lay alone. He obviously did not have any visitors. Heaven knows what instinct carried me to the side of his bed. If a late visitor did arrive to see him, the game would be up.

I took his hand.

'Hello,' I said softly.

I did not dare use a name. I looked back at the police officer. He was no longer looking at me and he had replaced his foot on the floor. I stroked the old man's hair. Five minutes passed ... then ten ... then twenty. I never took my eyes off the green curtains. I watched a nurse disappear behind them, then a doctor. They both emerged minutes later after doing whatever it was they had come to do to sustain a life not worth saving. Thirty minutes passed. The policeman was immobile. Forty-five minutes.

The old man in the bed had not stirred. The visitors in the beds adjacent to him smiled at me. If only they had known my true motive. It would have wiped the smiles from their faces.

My eyes on the green curtain. Any second now I would be discovered, denounced and dragged away. It didn't happen. But I could not sit here forever. Visiting hour was drawing to a close. All these individuals surrounding me would merge back into a crowd and make for the door.

I decided I would go for the direct route – walk back up the ward and lunge suddenly at Ash, in the hope I could damage him before they dragged me off. I replaced the old man's hand on the coverlet. He was still asleep, still oblivious to me. I stood up and walked slowly towards the green curtains. Something stirred in the police officer. His foot came back up onto the chair. It was impossible. I knew it was impossible. I knew that I could never barge my way past him. He would be too strong for me.

I almost wept.

I came level with the green curtains. The handcuffed arm and the exposed foot mocked me. I was overwhelmed again by what Ash had done, how he had killed our children and how he was too cowardly to make a serious attempt to take his own life. I looked at the curtains that hid this useless creature who had no place in any decent world. He would not even know I had been here, would never realise how close he had come to dying.

I turned my back and retraced my steps through the corridors into the reception hall, where people still did not recognise me or know my pain. I emerged into a day that was still summer and that still managed to be normal. The world went about its business and I returned to the dark place on the silent hill where my babies had been laid to rest.

I would have to rely on the justice of others.

28

Brutal and Merciless

'To kill two children – each vulnerable in different ways – is almost unimaginable.'

Lord Menzies to Rab Thomson,
Edinburgh High Court, 3 October 2008

June: Both of us had waited so long for the reckoning. Today, it was my turn.

Rab stood in the dock, stony-faced, cold, remorseless, defiant – for the moment. It had been five months to the day since he had murdered our children.

In the same court, three weeks earlier, he had admitted his guilt. There would be no trial. Now, he was appearing for sentence before Lord Menzies. He would know within minutes how many years he would spend behind bars. For a man like Rab, who had spent his life outdoors, any period of incarceration would be torture. I prayed to God that every second of every minute would hang like a rock around his neck, pulling him down into the abyss.

I knew now what he had done.

The awful truth had at last been revealed to me in the prosaic surroundings of a wood-panelled waiting room, where I had been taken by a woman from the Procurator Fiscal Service.

'June,' she said, 'I want you to prepare yourself.'

I think I have already said that it was bizarre that I remained unaware of precisely how my children had died, even though I had been the one to find them. On that dreadful evening the shock of it had blinded me.

'You may hear things in there,' she went on, referring to the court. She then told me what had happened to my children. Her quiet, measured tone belied the horror of her words. I learned that Rab had stabbed Ryan 14 times and Michelle 12 times. The revelations had sent me running from the room, into a toilet, where I screamed in pain.

Now I was looking at Rab, this monster.

Dr David Saddler, a forensic pathologist from the University of Dundee, had concluded that Rab had used three knives. The first had broken during the frenzy. He had gone to the kitchen and armed himself with a second. With a third – the largest – he had slashed his wrists and left the blade at his bedside for me to find.

I was composed now, waiting to see justice be done. I was flanked by Linda and my brother Jim. I felt a pressure on my shoulder from behind. I turned. It was one of the detectives. He did not have to say anything.

And then the judge spoke, telling Kevin McCallum, the Crown Prosecutor, that it was unnecessary to describe in graphic detail how my children had died. It was a kindness but it was too late. There was a pause as Lord Menzies adjusted his heavy red robe and turned slowly towards Rab.

'Stand up!' he ordered.

Rab stood. His hands hung by his side.

When Lord Menzies spoke again, his voice was flat and stern.

'What you have done is indescribably awful. Your daughter Michelle was 25 but she had significant learning difficulties. Your son Ryan was aged only seven.

'Neither of them had done any harm to you and you were in a position of trust towards each of them.

'Both were entitled to look to you for care, support and protection, yet on 3 May of this year you brutally murdered them.

'For a man to kill his child is a ghastly, horrific crime. To kill two children – each vulnerable in different ways – is almost unimaginable.

'I have read the various psychiatric and social enquiry reports to see if there is any explanation for your actions. They make bleak reading but they provide no explanation, far less any excuse for what you did.'

Rab showed no emotion until Lord Menzies sentenced him to a minimum of 17 years and warned, 'It is possible you may never be released from prison.'

And then Rab cried, slumping forward, sobbing like a whimpering child.

Linda and Jim held me in an iron-grip.

'Say nothing!' Jim hissed.

I was torn between two emotions – the savage delight at seeing Rab brought to heel and my disappointment at the sentence.

I heard a sharp intake of breath from behind me. I looked at the detective who had sought to comfort me and his expression was furious. Several of his colleagues were staring in disbelief. Detective Superintendent Alistair McKeen, the head of Fife Constabulary CID, leapt to his feet and left the court. Later, he would tell the waiting reporters, 'This was the action of a deeply embittered and twisted individual who could not face losing control of the family he had dominated for so long.'

The police had supported me so faithfully throughout my ordeal. I felt dreadful on their behalf, as well as my own.

Richard Baker, then the Shadow Justice Secretary to the Scottish Parliament, was also shocked by the apparent leniency of the sentence.

He said, 'These were horrific murders. This wasn't just a domestic tragedy. This was wanton evil.'

His colleague Tricia Marwick, the Member of the Scottish Parliament for Central Fife, added, 'It was a particularly heinous crime and it deserved a bigger sentence.'

Within days, the Crown announced their intention to appeal the sentence.

At the hearing, Alex Prentice QC, on behalf of the Lord Advocate, told Lords Osborne, Eassie and Malcolm, 'The Crown position is that the judge erred. He did not take into account the merciless nature of the attack. Child murder might well attract a punishment of 20 years and, in this case, we have a double murder in particularly brutal circumstances.'

To my utter disbelief, the Appeal Court judges ruled the sentence was not 'unduly lenient', in spite of the 'heinous nature of the offences'. The detectives who had worked on the case regarded the judges' decision as almost a betrayal.

'He never for a second showed remorse,' one detective told me privately. 'He would hardly speak to us and he kept saying, "No comment, no comment".'

The officer told me that Rab also refused to explain the strange 'suicide note' he had left behind. It read, 'Too much pain, lies and hurt. Don't blame yourself. I will look after them. Just like your mother. Move on alone. Love Rab xxx.'

The detectives were mystified by the reference to my mother. I wasn't. It was a final barb, a message for me alone. Even after he had robbed me of my children, he had to play the puppet-master. Rab could not resist goading me over my strained relationship with my mother. If the suicide note provided an insight into his warped mind, two psychiatrists would offer me the opportunity to lay aside at least a little of my burden.

When the courts were trying to establish if Rab was sane and fit to plead, he was sent for assessment to Scotland's State Hospital for psychiatric patients. As part of the process I was visited by two doctors who wanted to know about our life together. I told them that I was tortured by the belief that I was somehow to blame for what had happened – if only I'd had the strength to stay, to do what Rab wanted, perhaps he would not have gone over the edge.

As they left my home, after hours of conversation and note-taking, one of them paused at my front door and told me, 'You do realise, June, the truth is that he has been like this since he was a child ...'

When I closed the door, I wept. No matter what they said, I would always believe that the price of my freedom was my children.

29

Cold and Evil

'The victims were defenceless and in your care.
No doubt they loved you and assumed you would
care for them as a father should.'

Lord Brailsford to Ashok Kalyanjee,
High Court sitting in Paisley, 20 September 2009

*Giselle: And this was my day when the justice of others would
be done. There was as little comfort for me as there was for
you.*

*It would not be my justice. My justice would have been to send
Ash to a grave rather than to a prison cell. Had I been granted
the opportunity in the hospital when he lay helpless in a bed, he
would not be here.*

*He would not be standing in the dock, posturing in his smart
grey suit. He would not be looking with defiant eyes at the judge
who, today, would decide his fate, almost a year and a half after
he killed Paul and Jay-Jay.*

*This justice of others had been such a long time coming. It had
been ten months since he appeared in court to confess what he*

had done. He had offered his guilt but not his remorse. The judge had wanted background reports prior to sending him to jail. The sentencing had been repeatedly delayed and it had been nearly a year, rather than a matter of weeks, between his guilty plea and justice being served.

That was all over now. The system had been played and Ash had lost. I looked at this coward and I hated him. I hated him with a fierceness that terrified me.

I heard a voice – deep, sonorous and authoritative. Lord Brailsford was speaking to me and my family. He wore a kindly expression. He said he appreciated how heart-rending this was for us.

His face darkened as he turned to Ash and said, 'You have pleaded guilty to the murder of your sons. This crime was premeditated, planned and organised.

'You used deceit and lies to persuade the children's mother and the children to go out with you. You purchased the murder weapon in advance and acquired petrol in a can, apparently to incinerate yourself and the victims.

'The victims were defenceless and in your care. No doubt they loved you and assumed you would care for them as a father should.

'One of the victims witnessed what happened to his brother. I cannot imagine the suffering that child must have endured before his own murder.

'This is as grave a crime as can be imagined. I do not know what caused you to commit it. You were clearly under some form of psychological stress – but you have been found sane and fit to plead.

'There is no mitigation for a crime of this enormity. The sentence of the court is one of life imprisonment. I am required *to fix the punishment part of that sentence – the minimum period you will remain in custody. That period will be 21 years.'*

It was over. He would be nearly 70 before he was released. This justice of others demanded two decades of his life. It was a shorter sentence than I had received. I would be imprisoned by my loss for the rest of my days.

Throughout the judge's deliberation, I had watched Ash closely, searching his face for something, anything, that indicated sorrow or remorse. There was nothing. Any normal person, who had just been told he would spend the next 21 years behind bars, would have at least betrayed a sense of shock, some hint of emotion.

One of the two gaolers who were flanking him placed his hand on Ash's shoulder and tried to turn him towards the door that led from the court and down to the cells. Ash was reluctant to go. Then it struck me. He was enjoying himself. Knowing him as I did, everything about him screamed that he loved being the centre of attention. It was as if he were playing the role of the lawyer rather than the convicted killer. In his warped mind he had at last 'made it'. Ash was finally important. I watched him disappear through the door.

I felt hands on me. My father, my brothers and my sisters grasped me firmly but gently.

'Stand up, darlin',' my father said softly, taking my arm.

'I'm fine, Da,' I told him. And I was.

In the beginning I had tortured myself.

Would Paul and Jay-Jay still be with me if I had acquiesced to Ash, had given in to his demand that we live with his mother? I had gone beyond that now. My eyes had been opened by the revelation that Ash had been leading a secret life of drinking and gambling away thousands of pounds.

He had, it seemed, been living in a house of cards that had tumbled down, driving him over the edge. That was what caused the 'psychological stress' the judge had referred to. I had caught a glimpse of the drinking because of the rambling phone calls in the night. I had not, however, realised the extent of the problem until police interviews with Ash revealed he had been drinking a bottle of spirits a day.

He also confessed to them that he was addicted to gambling. With each revelation, it was as if I had been handed the missing pieces of a jigsaw. I remembered that on one occasion he told me he had won a 'fortune' at the casino but that the money was gone because he owed a lot of cash to 'bad men'. I hadn't believed him.

Such behaviour seemed so out of character for a man who professed to be clean-living. I was wrong. His world had been crashing around his ears and, knowing him, he would have been horrified at the thought of his mother learning the terrible truth. That was why he had been at such pains to leave behind the message on the dictaphone that had been thrown from the car before he set it on fire. It was an exercise in justification by a self-indulgent weakling.

In the months and years that have followed his conviction and imprisonment, such narcissism has become Ash's hallmark.

He once paid dearly for his arrogance. Reports indicated that he had been scalded with hot water thrown in his face by another prisoner. Ash had apparently told him, 'They were my kids. I can do what I like with them.'

Even the most hardened of criminals do not suffer child killers.

But perhaps the most telling example of who and what Ash was came when he contacted the Driver and Vehicle Licensing Agency and requested form Number V33, which is an application for a refund of the unexpired portion of a car's road tax. Ash informed the DVLA that his Mercedes had been off the road ... since 3 May 2008.

He got a refund of £50.

He bought chocolate with the money.

30

Reaching for
the Light

'Human beings find inner resources of strength
to survive the most dreadful loss. The love that
surrounds these mothers is a living thing – it
gives them the will to go on.'

Ian Stephen

**June: We couldn't let them defeat us, could we? These vile
creatures. I take comfort from striking a blow for abused
women everywhere.**

'You've made legal history,' Cameron Fyfe said.

The voice of Scotland's top civil litigator was quiet and
professional, but what he truly wanted to do was punch the
air. He is, however, too reserved a man to indulge in theatrics.
Thanks to him, I now had the right to sue Rab over the
murders of my children and the abuse I had endured for 27
years. A pinprick of light in the darkness! Who would have
believed it?

Until February 2010, any woman in Scotland suffering at
the hands of an abusive husband or partner had two choices.

She could flee or she could divorce – the same rights as a woman who had not been abused. Now she had a third choice. She could sue on the basis of the abuse alone.

A Sheriff had granted me a Warrant of Arrestment, the wherewithal to pursue Rab for compensation. Such a concept had never before been tested in law. I had gone to Cameron Fyfe because he had a reputation for breaking new legal ground on behalf of victims of all kinds. He had argued to the court that a battered woman had the right to be recompensed for what she had suffered. The money, he said, would allow her to rebuild her life – and financially censure the abuser.

It is a tragic fact in the lives of victims like us that we too often end up living a hand-to-mouth existence in women's shelters, without the financial capability to move on.

In truth, I had no desire to sue Rab for blood money.

I did, however, want the house where we had lived, the house where he had killed my children. I wanted to own it and raze it to the ground. Under the existing matrimonial rights laws I owned only half of the marital home at Muiredge. Rab's 'half' of the house was his only major asset. If I could sue him and win, he would only have the proceeds from his share of the house with which to settle. The Sheriff had agreed with Cameron that I could pursue compensation against Rab for my years of abuse and, in another legal first, for the murder of my children.

Cameron told me, 'No matter what you decide to do, June, you've set a precedent for abused women everywhere. It hammers home the message that zero tolerance means just that, by hitting them where it hurts, in the pocket. This will send a message to abusive husbands that they may not only end up in the divorce court; they may end up penniless.'

It was a massive victory for me. I had felt cheated by the criminal justice system over Rab's sentence, but at least I had given abused women another weapon with which to fight back – in the civil courts. In the end, I got my way and Fife Council offered to demolish Muiredge.

It was a blessed relief because not only had I come to regard the house as a place of evil – I had been inexorably drawn back there as I struggled with my grief. It was as if I was tethered to it by an invisible cord.

A kindly stranger with a special gift would cut the cord and set me free.

Giselle: We've both made a difference. No other mother will have to suffer as I did.

Paul Martin had read the report. His words were tight with anger. 'Strathclyde Police should be utterly ashamed of the way they treated a distraught mother, frantically begging them for help!'

My Member of the Scottish Parliament would not be placated. 'I can't make up my mind if this was incompetence or a total lack of understanding of this type of crime.'

He was not going to let this rest. Mr Martin had no qualms about challenging the system that had failed me.

'The Scottish Government must look at this whole issue,' he went on.

The report in my hand, the contents of which had so incensed the MSP, outlined the findings of an inquiry by Central Scotland Police into how Strathclyde Police had responded to me on the

*day my babies were murdered. The findings presented a cata-
logue of failures on every level. It told me nothing I did not
know already. Instead of searching for my boys, Strathclyde
Police had logged the 'case' as 'non-urgent' and the inexperi-
enced civilian worker had filed the report in the wrong place.
Police failed to check Ash's flat despite it being only yards from
the station. When they did know the awful truth they had felt
too 'uncomfortable' to tell me. The civilian officer became so
distraught and 'embarrassed' that she had asked to go home.
Not exactly what one would expect from a frontline
professional.*

*In their report, Detective Superintendent David Wilson and
Detective Inspector Gordon Dawson concluded, 'Giselle Ross
was not treated with empathy. Her report appears to have been
minimised. Her treatment – after the bodies of her children
were found – lacked any respect and fell well below the standard
expected by a victim of any crime, let alone the murder of her
only children.'*

The memory of how I was treated still wounds me.

*In a newspaper report, George Hamilton, Strathclyde Police
Assistant Chief Constable, was quoted as saying, 'We're sorry.
This will be of little comfort to Giselle Ross but, God forbid, if
anyone else finds themselves in this scenario, they will be treated
differently. Strathclyde Police made mistakes. Giselle should not
have been treated the way she was and we will learn from those
mistakes. Sadly, even if we had handled things differently, the
outcome would not have changed. The tragedy is that her boys
were brutally and horribly murdered before Giselle came to the
police office. But the trauma she suffered was exacerbated by the
less than acceptable treatment she received. It will not be
allowed to happen again.'*

*Mr Hamilton would deliver the same apology to me in person.
He was right. His words were of little comfort but at least I found
solace in the knowledge that no other worried mother would ever
be treated as I was. I had at least made that difference.*

**June: Sometimes we find the light comes from unexpected
sources.**

I'd heard that Frank Pilkington had helped so many people
who were struggling with emotional pain. Could he help me?
A mutual friend approached the renowned psychic on my
behalf. When he heard of my plight, he came immediately.
We were now standing in the living room of Muiredge,
surrounded by the debris of my previous life. Long-forgotten
toys and DVDs that we had once watched as a family lay
beneath thick layers of dust.

Once the court case was over, Muiredge was no longer a
crime scene and, in spite of myself, I'd been inexorably drawn
back there. I couldn't help myself.

I would sit in the ruined shell of the house. I would tend
to the overgrown flowers in the garden, all the time deluding
myself that at any moment the children might return. The
familiarity of the surroundings comforted me. I touched the
boles of the trees, below which Ryan's imaginary witch's cat
had once played. I looked up at the canopy where the cheeky
monkeys lived. I would sit in Michelle's room. I could see the
glitter dust from the sparkly things she had once loved. The
spirit of my children still inhabited this place. I reasoned that
I could find them here.

'Why did Michelle have a pain in her leg?' Frank asked me suddenly.

I was taken aback. I had just received the pathologist's report. It indicated that Michelle's thigh was injured, probably in the struggle with Rab. No one could know that.

'It was her left leg,' Frank went on.

I nodded.

He moved quickly, disappearing from the living room. I followed and found him in Michelle's bedroom.

He was looking at where Michelle's bed had once been.

'Here?' he said.

I nodded again.

I had looked so many times at the same spot. It was where my Michelle had died.

'What keeps bringing you back here, June?' he asked me.

'What?' I said.

'You sit in the garden, don't you? Waiting for them?'

I nodded for a third time.

'Your children aren't here,' Frank said. 'They're with you wherever *you* are. Don't come back here! There's nothing for you here.'

Giselle had to meet this man.

Giselle: We've both learned to take comfort from where we can.

'I can't get it out of my head that the last thing they saw was him,' I told Frank.

'It wasn't,' he replied.

'Jay-Jay was so small,' I told him. 'He probably didn't understand what was happening, but he saw.'

'That wasn't the last thing he saw,' Frank repeated.

'But my Paul,' I said. 'He was so tortured-looking. He saw Jay-Jay die and the last thing he saw in life was his own death.'

'I promise you, it wasn't,' Frank said.

'It's all they will remember.'

'It won't be.'

Frank reached across the coffee table that sat between us and placed his hands over mine.

'They saw your mum,' he said.

'Are you certain?' I asked.

'Yes! She was there, waiting for them. They are together now, playing together in a special garden, and your mother watches over them.'

I rose from the chair. Frank knew not to expect me to speak. I walked to the door. He stepped in front of me and he opened it.

As I passed him he said, 'And another thing ... it's time to stop hating God.'

31

The Kindness of Strangers

'No one who has not endured such a loss can understand what the mothers have gone through. By telling their stories they will touch many lives. And that is a comfort.'

Ian Stephen

June: We can always find our children, if we look for them. I saw Ryan in another boy's eyes; I saw Michelle in the love of others.

Nathan didn't see me. He was too intent on patrolling the aisle of the supermarket, no doubt making a mental inventory of the sweets he would try in vain to persuade his mother to buy.

'Not a chance,' I said to the back of his head.

He turned. An instant smile. I felt a sense of well-being. I had not realised the comfort I would find in the company of children. The realisation had crept up on me. You might think that a mother who has lost her own babies would be pained by the proximity of other children. The opposite was true. I grew to love the unaffected nature of the young. They are so resilient, unburdened by the weight of adult misgivings. Nathan's smile was warm, gentle and free from the reticence that constrains grown-ups.

'Mrs Thomson!' he said.

He was happy to see me.

If Nathan had been an adult there would have been hesitation, a sense of not knowing quite what to say to this mother of two murdered children. I was just as happy to see Nathan. His life was inextricably linked to Ryan's. They had been special friends since nursery. They started school together, sat side-by-side in the same classroom. They had been inseparable.

'You're getting so big,' I told him.

I hadn't see him for a while and, looking at him now, I saw the boy my son might have become – bright-faced, tall and strong. Logic suggests that in looking at Nathan I should have experienced an even greater sense of loss. I didn't. I was relieved to see him blossoming. I had been worried about Nathan. In the beginning he had been deeply affected by the loss of his best friend, but here he was – a survivor. There was a lesson in this for me. I realised that the closeness Ryan and Nathan shared ensured that this child would always carry within him a small part of my son. I found that knowledge unbelievably comforting. I was about to ask where his mum was when Dot appeared, pushing a trolley.

'Hi, June, haven't seen you for a while. How have you been?' Dot said.

'Fine,' I replied. 'I can't believe how Nathan's grown.'

'He's getting big, isn't he?'

'Where are you off to now?' I asked Nathan.

'The swimming pool,' the boy said.

Nathan and Ryan were seldom away from the swimming pool. Apart from football, swimming was their favourite pastime. Nathan looked up at his mum, his eyes asking a silent question.

'Go and pick something,' she said ruefully, indicating the seemingly endless rows of sweets.

'See you, Mrs Thomson,' he said, dashing off.

'See you, Nathan,' I said.

I turned back to his mum. She was one of the few adults able to speak to me without a tear in their voice. I was grateful for that.

'Scooby passed away,' she said.

Scooby had been Ryan's pet rabbit. After my son died, I gave the animal to Nathan.

'Was Nathan terribly upset?' I asked.

'That's the strange thing,' his mum said. 'He was happy!'

'Happy?'

'Yeah. I went out to the hutch to feed Scooby and he was gone. We thought Nathan would be distraught, but when we told him he said, "That's okay! Now Ryan will be able to play with him in Heaven."'

Out of the mouths of babes ...

———————

Giselle: I'm glad we are not alone, just you and me. In the beginning I didn't want to go on. Now I know I must. The letter proved it.

It lay on the kitchen table.

It was unsigned. I touched it with a sense of wonder. How kind, how very kind, I thought. The letter informed me that the sender had dedicated two stars in memory of my babies.

It read, 'I wanted to do something to comfort you. I can't imagine how you must be feeling but I hope this will let you know that other people are thinking of you.'

I didn't recognise the writing. It was not from anyone I knew. I checked the package again. I couldn't make out the postmark. I knew only that it was not local. A stranger had offered me proof of the world's kindness.

In my mind I heard the voices of the boys. They were singing 'Twinkle, twinkle, little star' to their 'Granny in Heaven'. When Ma died, I had told the boys that Granny was a star in the night sky.

When Paul sang the rhyme little Jay-Jay would point to the sky and say, 'Jay-Jay go up-a-sky!'

I'd tell him he was too little to go 'up-a-sky', but he was insistent.

'No! Jay-Jay go up-a-sky with Granny!'

The memory of it made me shiver.

I looked at the package from the woman – I presume it was a woman who had sent it. It contained two scrolls, certificates decorated with ornate copperplate text, recording that two stars had been named after Paul and Jay-Jay. They were in the constellation of Canis Major in the northern hemisphere. They were described as 'very large, bright stars' sitting close to Sirius, the brightest star in the night sky. I looked towards the window.

Morning light shone on me. I would have to wait until darkness before I could see them for myself.

I rose from the kitchen table and retrieved my 'treasure chest' from the living room. I had created a box of memories containing things special to my sons: toys, photos and clothing, including Paul's school uniform and Jay-Jay's Bob the Builder hat. It was something to hold, something to keep my boys alive – my route though the long days and nights without them. I took it to the kitchen, rested it on the table and carefully placed my newest treasure inside. I was overwhelmed by the goodness of the woman who had sent it to me. I did not know her. I probably never would, but my babies had reached out to her, touching something good and true deep within her.

If she only knew the light she had shone into my heart.

June: We know that our children will never be forgotten. They don't just live in our hearts and memories. They live on in others.

White violas merged into the sunny faces of yellow pansies, a profusion of flowers surrounding a circular bird bath, decorated with stone sparrows that would forever drink from an endless flow of clear water. A love-heart-shaped rock bearing Michelle's name lay beneath this cascade of blooms. The staff of Rosslyn School and the children who had known Michelle encircled me, watching me expectantly, waiting for my approval.

'It's beautiful,' I said, indicating the memorial to my daughter.

'Everyone helped,' said Marion Robertson, Michelle's former teacher. 'We wanted it to be special.'

It *was* special. I tried to speak but I couldn't. If they had only known what they had done for me with this patch of flowers. They had made me *feel*. I had believed I would never feel anything again, that I would be forever dead inside. The world had come to an end, hadn't it?

I looked down and I saw the possibility of healing in those colourful, fragile flowers.

I looked up into the faces of the children who had all loved Michelle, these blessed youngsters who shared the same innocence as my beautiful daughter.

'Would Michelle like it?' one of them asked.

'More than you'll ever know,' I told her.

———————

Giselle: You're right. We have helped each other understand, survive, go forward. And we are not alone. I knew it when I saw him standing on my hill.

It was mid-morning.

I was late today. I was walking quickly along a lane between the headstones when I saw him. The man was standing at my special place on the hill, looking down on the graves of my sons. He held a posy of flowers in his right hand. He was somehow familiar to me but I couldn't place where I had seen him before. It was as if he sensed my approach and turned towards me.

Alastair Douglas.

It was the humanist minister who had conducted the funeral service for Paul and Jay-Jay.

'Hello, Giselle,' he said.

'Alastair?' I replied.

He had heard my unspoken question. He bent over and placed the posy on the grave. When he straightened up he said, 'I've been a couple times to … you know?'

He said something more but the wind smothered his words.

'Thank you,' I said.

'I hope you don't mind?' he went on.

'No, no. Come any time.'

'I think about them often.'

I realised that I had regarded him as being out of place here. This hill was where my family and I came. Why would anyone else want to come? Alastair lived his life in a world that I expected to go about its own business without regard to me.

This man, who had known my sons only in death, surely must have other places to be, other things to demand his attention? But here he was.

In that moment I knew that evil cannot triumph, that our children are still a force for good in the world and that healing can begin with the kindness of strangers.

32

The Love They Left Behind

'The memories these mothers have of their children keep them alive.'

Ian Stephen

June: This is their legacy, their story as much as ours, isn't it?

As time passes and the light draws nearer, the legacy our children left behind is bathed in a pale glow that is becoming stronger by the day.

For a long time we thought we would not escape the dark and that our children would only be the sweetest of memories, smiling at us from the photographs on the mantelpiece. I realise now that they are so much more than that. They are living beings, released from the prison of their bodies. They surround us, wherever we may be, for every second of every minute of every day, still in our hearts and in the lives of those who held them dear.

I see it in the kindness of my friend Doreen, who, like Giselle, helped me through the darkest part of the night. Doreen gave of herself completely, dried my tears and made me smile when I thought such a thing was impossible. She spoke quietly of my children, bringing them to life, returning them to me time after time.

I see it in my niece Abbi – so grown up now, a female version of what Ryan would have been. He is not gone while she is alive. She witnessed the depths of my despair. She held me. She, too, spoke to me of Ryan and Michelle with a simple wisdom that, sadly, is lost to the young when they grow up.

I see Michelle in my sister Linda. I see Ryan in my father's eyes. When I look at my brothers, Jim, Roger and Gordon, I see my children in them, a hint of what they might have become had they been spared.

I see them in the letters from children, classmates of Ryan and Michelle, that were sent to me when I was at my lowest ebb. Then they were merely a comfort; now they are beacons of hope.

'*We will never forget you because we know you will always be with us forever,*' wrote Chloe.

'*We will miss your smile, your laugh, your cute face,*' wrote Heather.

When I pass the playground of Buckhaven Primary School, where Ryan chased Heather and Chloe, I see the train that was built in his memory, a lasting reminder of a little boy who loved fun. Children who never knew him play on it now, and while it bears his name he will live on in their innocent games.

I see my Michelle and Ryan in Shaun and Ross, the sons who are even more precious to me because I still have them to love and cherish.

Michelle and Ryan are not gone. They are here now with me.

They are beyond harm, beyond suffering, shining brightly in all of us.

———————————

Giselle: They'll be alive forever and ever, long after both of us are gone.

It is never relinquished, never out of his sight, this valueless piece of plastic, fashioned into a child's toy hammer. It bears a fading image of Bob the Builder and it belonged to my Jay-Jay. It is more precious to my father than any of the possessions he has gathered over the course of his long life. I will find him with it in his hand, turning it over, allowing it to provoke the memories. It is, to him, a treasure. He will hold it in one hand and clutch his favourite picture of Paul in the other. For as long as he has these mementoes, my sons are alive.

'Remember how Jay-Jay used to climb on my knee and hit me on the arm?' he will ask.

He will be asking me the same question until the day he dies. I smile and nod, as I have done so often. Da will then be drawn to his wardrobe where Paul's favourite Spiderman outfit hangs.

'The wee man really thought he was Spiderman, didn't he?' Da asks.

I nod again.

In another part of my home little Giselle has gone off to be by herself, taking with her my treasure box, the precious physical reminders of my sons. She has trawled through them so many times – Jay-Jay's tiny clothes, Paul's pristine school uniform. She touches each one tenderly and goes to a place beyond tears.

Katie comes with me every day, accompanying me to my sons' resting place. We do not speak much. There is no need for words. I stand vigil. She is my guardian.

Uncle Tam, so big, so brusque, so vulnerable, still talks about his boys, his little angels. His eyes have a sadness in them that was not there before, because he sees them wherever he looks.

I still hear snatches of my children's voices, captured from recordings, which now live in the mobile phones of my family. When I hear their voices now, I can see that for every minute they were with us my babies were happy and loved.

Whenever they need to be found they always come, reaching out to us from my dad's hands, Tam's eyes, Giselle's memories and Katie's silence.

They are not gone.

33

This Sisterhood of Ours

Our story has been told.

And now there is silence.

It is companionable and without tension.

We embrace.

There is no distance between us. It is a proximity that goes beyond the physical.

It is a long time since we two have been strangers. Now there is affinity, empathy and comfort. In this unique place of ours, we are sisters. We hold the mirror to each other's face and see the same reflection. We are grateful to have found each other; grateful to have discovered the one person in the world who can finish our sentences; grateful to have someone who can truly say, 'I know how you feel!' We have been to each other rocks in a storm-lashed sea, safe havens in a bleak landscape.

We have told our story to one another so many times.

Now we have shared it with you.

You are no longer a stranger.

You know now.

Step onto the rock with us. Be part of our friendship. We need you as much as we need each other. With you by our side, we are no longer alone. Our burden is shared.

We are not afraid you will lack understanding. We do not fear you will judge. We know that you, like us, will not have the answers. Heaven knows, we have tried for so long to find them.

The one thing that we are certain of is that we had to tell this story. For us. For our children. For every person who is suffering.

Don't look away.

Afterword
by Ian Stephen

This is a story for our times, a taboo that few wish to address because it attacks everything in which we believe and hold dear.

We demand that a parent should be loving and nurturing, and not the perpetrator of evil. To kill your own child sets you apart from everything acceptable to a caring society. But we must realise that society is changing and recognise that the family annihilator is responsible for more than one-third of child murders. The 'bogeyman' is no longer just lurking in the darkness. The unpalatable truth is that children may be safer on the street with strangers than they are in their own homes.

It is a dilemma that the legal establishment is already beginning to recognise. Paul McBride, one of the UK's leading QCs, says, 'I have grave concerns that this crime is on the increase. As a society, we need to take notice.'

Mr McBride, who was appointed to defend Ashok Kalyanjee, goes on:

It was obvious to everyone who dealt with Kalyanjee that he was suffering a mental disorder, but not one that could reduce the charge. No rational person could have done what he did, killing one child in front of the other, inflicting burns upon himself and the children's bodies.

As a society we want people to show emotion, remorse. This type of killer shows none. Their victims are seen as possessions, the latest accessory, and not as children to be loved and nurtured.

This is extremely dangerous, because when it comes to family breakdown those children become pawns.

We are living in a particularly brutal society and the venom of one partner towards the other can leave the children in terrible danger. The attitude of these emotionless individuals is, 'If I can't have them, nobody will.'

We have become self-absorbed. The people who commit these crimes may be just plain old fashioned evil, and when evil people commit evil deeds, often the best we can do as a society is lock them away for as long as possible.

It is the bitterest of ironies that we are seeing an alarming increase in this terrible crime because there are more support systems available nowadays to help women break away from bad relationships. In generations past, as June's granny would have said, you made your bed and you lay on it – that's what abuse victims did in earlier, tougher times. Women were often seen as subservient 'chattels'. Now more women will, quite rightly, leave.

That is often the trigger. To an insecure, self-absorbed individual, the loss of status, the threat to self-esteem, the loss of control, of no longer being seen as the head of a family, combine in a constellation of symptoms with often catastrophic results. These are people, usually men, whose lives are about control and 'ownership' – and in a society that is increasingly possession-orientated children can be perceived as possessions rather than as individuals. When that lack of emotional attachment exists, it turns some parents into killers. They are made more dangerous because you are never certain what the trigger has been – or what they plan to do.

June and Giselle would not have had an inkling of the terrible events that would be visited upon them.

Rab and Ash may have emerged from this story as two very different men. Rab was the brute who controlled through fear and violence. Ash was the smooth talker who manipulated with smiles and words. But they are both sides of the same coin. In fact, if anything, Ash is the more sinister – a controlled, superficial, detached, emotionally devoid individual who believed himself superior and used charm to mask his dark side. He enjoyed the image of being a husband and father but he didn't want the hard work or the responsibility that went with it. His main stressor was the fear of being exposed as a gambler. He would do anything to keep intact the image of the world he had constructed. When that world began tumbling down, he went berserk.

Rab and Ash chose women who were respectively needy and naïve. June's childhood-abandonment issues created someone Rab could dominate. Giselle's loving upbringing created a trusting innocent who perfectly suited Ash's brand of manipulation. Ash chose Giselle because he would have immediately recognised that naïvety and inexperience. Someone with more sophistication would have been too headstrong.

They were the perfect prey for the perfect predators.

Once in thrall to these men they found it impossible to break free. Such women have only a very narrow window of opportunity in which to escape – and that is early in the relationship. If they do not escape, the longer they stay the more difficult it becomes to break away.

Even when abuse rears it ugly head, they can be convinced that it will not happen again. The more often it does, and the more often they leave and go back, the more compulsive the relationship becomes. They are stripped of personality. They reach a point where the only view they can express is the one their husband allows. They are separated from family and other relationships. They become isolated and cannot get independent feedback to contradict anything their husband says or does.

These men have an almost hypnotic effect on the women they dominate. Ironically, the victimiser may often be insecure to an almost paranoid extent. They may often be men who have been dominated or deserted by their mothers. They go on to invest that insecurity in their partners and the need to dominate them is paramount, which is why they cannot bear to let them get away. They believe the family cannot exist without them at its heart.

When their worst fears are realised by perceived rejection or the threat to their carefully constructed worlds, they become highly dangerous. They may be likened to a person contemplating suicide. They struggle to reach a decision – a 'solution' – but, once having decided on what they perceive to be a 'logical' course of action, they enter the planning phase. Everything is meticulously worked out. The difference is that the victim is not them but their family. Throughout it all they will appear normal to those around them.

Rab and Ash would have believed they were doing the 'right thing'. Such a thought process may appear irrational to you and me, but it would have been 'acceptable' to them because it allowed them to stay in control. Some family annihilators may even see themselves as 'protecting' their children and, in the end, when the terrible deed is done, it is invariably never their fault. Rab's suicide note and Ash's taped message were exercises in self-justification and an effort not to allow their wives to have the last word. They wanted to control to the bitter end, make their women experience guilt as well as terrible loss. The attempt to kill themselves was no more than a pseudo-gesture made in order to engender sympathy.

One of the burning questions is why these men choose to end their children's lives in such a brutal fashion. The answer is simple. If, for example, they gave them sleeping pills, they would have to watch them die. However, with that first stab wound the control is released, and they stab and stab until they become calm and controlling again. They are, in many respects, like serial killers.

In Rab's case, he posed his dead children. In doing that, he saw himself as the 'loving father'. He wanted them to look 'nice' and not grotesque. In Ash's case, he saw his children only as possessions.

Both of these men are thoroughly evil, although neither would perceive themselves to be so.

Could they ever experience remorse? In a sense, they could feel 'sorry' that they had to do 'that' to the children, but the blame is laid on the wife. *They* made me do it, they would say. In all likelihood, they will emerge from prison after their long sentences and still be the same men, still with that sense of being aggrieved, still deflecting the blame for their actions onto others, still without remorse. Rab will expect June to be waiting; Ash will have no inkling of the horror of what he has done.

Can we recognise them? Identify them as monsters in our midst? In most cases they are very socially adept. They are often charming, popular and they only show the world the face they want it to see.

They are the nice guys … and they live next door.

Ian Stephen is a chartered clinical and forensic psychologist. A former Director of Psychological Services at Scotland's State Hospital for psychiatric patients at Carstairs, he has spent his career working with serial killers and the most dangerous and violent offenders in Britain. Ian worked closely with the actor Robbie Coltrane in the development of the television series *Cracker*.

Help and Support for Victims

Rape Crisis England and Wales
www.rapecrisis.org.uk
0808 802 9999

Rape Crisis Scotland
www.rapecrisisscotland.org.uk
0808 801 0302

Women's Aid
www.womensaid.org.uk
0808 200 0247

Scottish Women's Aid
www.scottishwomensaid.org.uk
0800 027 1234

Welsh Women's Aid
www.welshwomensaid.org

Wales Domestic Abuse Helpline
0808 801 0800

Northern Ireland Women's Aid
www.womensaidni.org
0800 917 1414

Eire Women's Aid
www.womensaid.ie
00353 1 800 341900

Victim Support
www.victimsupport.com
0845 303 0900

Marion Scott and Jim McBeth are husband and wife. Marion is an award-winning journalist with the *Sunday Mail*, who has won praise for campaigning on behalf of abused children and victims of injustice. Jim writes for the *Daily Mail*. He is a former feature writer with the *Daily Record*, chief writer with the *Scotsman* and focus writer of the *Sunday Times*. They are regular contributors to national radio and television, and co-authors of *No More Silence*, published by HarperCollins.